IMAGES
of America

LYONS

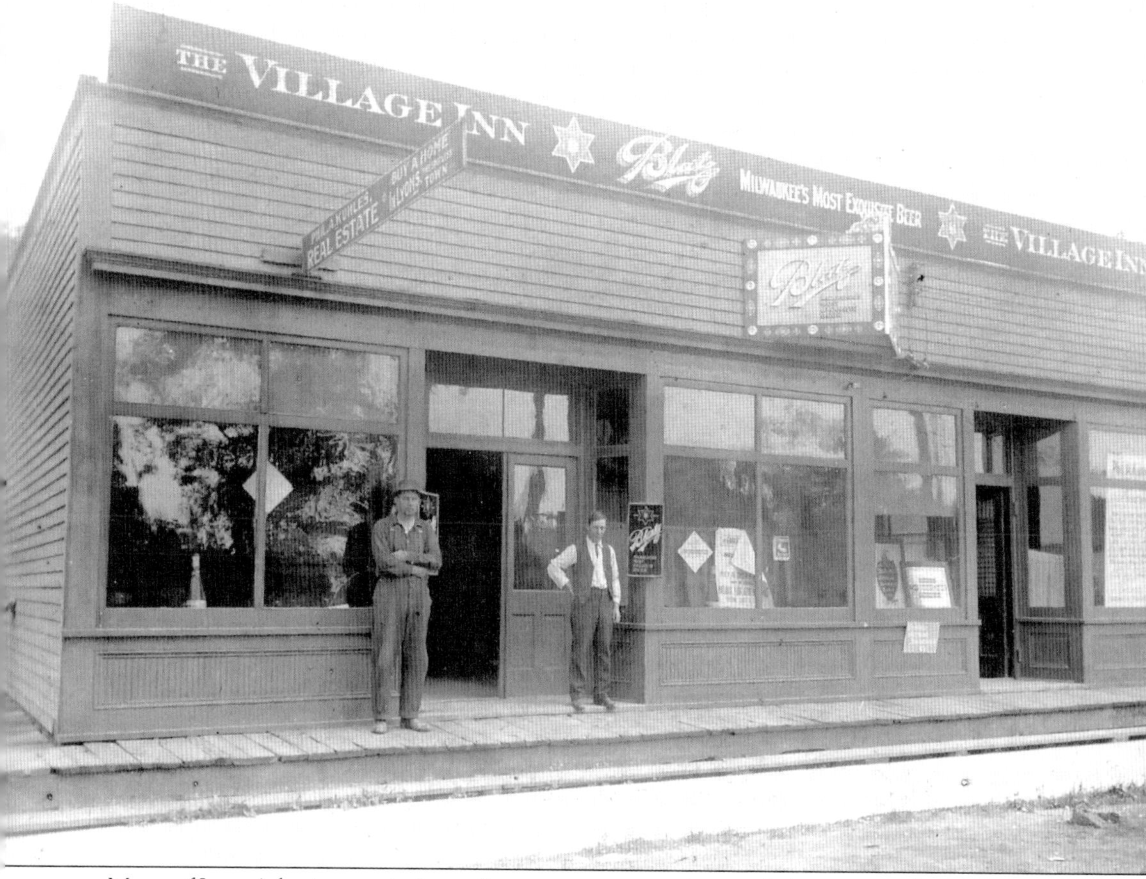

Many of Lyons's businesses in its earliest years gravitated around the corner of Ogden and Joliet Avenues. The Village Inn, a Lyons pub, located just east of the corner during the late 1800s and early 1900s, also housed the office of a real estate and insurance agent, Phil A. Kuhles. The sign hanging in front encourages visitors to "buy a home in Lyons, the spotless town."

On the cover: Starting in the 1890s, many Lyons taverns held gatherings called "skillies" at their picnic groves. George Mitch, one of Lyons's first police officers, stirs a pot of stew at this one, believed to be at Neher's Grove around 1900. (Courtesy Lyons Historical Commission.)

IMAGES
of America

LYONS

Mark Athitakis

ARCADIA
PUBLISHING

ISBN 978-0-7385-4040-5

Published by Arcadia Publishing
Charleston, South Carolina

Printed in the United States of America

Library of Congress Catalog Card Number: 2006921003

For all general information contact Arcadia Publishing at:
Telephone 843-853-2070
Fax 843-853-0044
E-mail sales@arcadiapublishing.com
For customer service and orders:
Toll-Free 1-888-313-2665

Visit us on the Internet at www.arcadiapublishing.com

This book is dedicated to my parents, two immigrants who settled in Lyons.

Contents

Acknowledgments 6

Introduction 7

1. Le Portage and the Birth of Lyons 9

2. The Hofmann Tower and Other Diversions 31

3. Work and Play in Lyons 55

4. Crises, Controversy, and Change 95

Bibliography 127

ACKNOWLEDGMENTS

Anybody who chooses to research the history of his or her hometown should be lucky enough to have somebody like Nadine Pankow for a guide. Pankow, head of the Lyons Historical Commission, helped me navigate the commission's marvelous archives at Zion Lutheran Church, scored me access to the roof of the Hofmann Tower, and indulged my countless questions on Lyons's history. Simply put, I could not have written this book without her. Former mayor Kenneth Getty, whose three issues of the *Village News* in 1985 strongly influenced this book, was similarly generous with both his time and his tremendous archive of photographs.

For information on Lyons's earliest history, thanks to Gary Mechanic and the rest of the volunteers at Friends of the Chicago Portage (http://chicagoportage.org), which offers regular (and highly recommended) walking tours of the Chicago Portage National Historical Site during the summer and fall, and also does crucial research and preservation work throughout the year. Mechanic patiently and engagingly helped me understand just how important the site is to Lyons's history as well as Chicago's; his knowledge and enthusiasm inform the early portions of this book.

Elaine Serafino, Margaret M. Hayes, Marion Keeber, Rita Dow, and John Pantos made crucial photographic contributions and answered questions; Lyn Anderson Raines at the *Lyons Suburban Life* helped to get the word out; and the patient staff of the Lyons Public Library and the Chicago Public Library pointed me in the right direction numerous times. I am grateful for Jeff Reutsche at Arcadia, who expressed an early confidence in this project and helped shepherd it to completion.

Finally, thanks to my wife, Shawn Neidorf, whose suggestions, encouragement, and unflagging support throughout my research immeasurably improved this book.

INTRODUCTION

In September 1673, explorers Louis Joliet and Fr. Jacques Marquette were returning north from their travels up the Mississippi River when Native American guides directed them to a faster route connecting the Mississippi to Lake Michigan. Instead of proceeding up the Fox and Wisconsin Rivers (which is how they made their way south), they could take advantage of a route connecting the Illinois River, the Des Plaines River, and the south branch of the Chicago River. That passage, which soon became a crucial route for the booming fur trade in the region, began in what was called "Le Portage"—located in what is now Lyons. Using the portage, travelers could connect with a waterway called Mud Lake, and from there reach what would become one of the world's largest cities.

Mud Lake, as the name suggests, was swampy territory, running from what is now Harlem Avenue to Thirty-first Street and Kedzie Street in Chicago, and the canoe passage was arduous. Fur trader Gurdon Hubbard described it in 1818 as often lacking enough water to float a boat, and filled with leeches and mosquitoes. "Those who had waded the lake suffered great agony, their limbs becoming swollen and inflamed," Hubbard wrote. "It took us three consecutive days of such toil to pass all our boats through this miserable lake."

If there is a common thread in Lyons's history, it might be reflected in that quote—it speaks to a place that is benefited from its location, but which has also had its share of struggles. About two square miles in size, Lyons is neatly tucked 11 miles away from Chicago's Loop and has always been near a major transport route; in the 18th century it was Le Portage, in the 19th century the Illinois and Michigan Canal, and in the 20th century the Sanitary and Ship Canal and Interstate 55. Lyons's residents have benefited from the strong industrial base within and surrounding the city, from its limestone quarries—including the 61-acre location of the Materials Service Corporation—and the nearby plants for Western Electric, Reynolds Aluminum, and Electro-Motive.

Those large businesses supported Lyons families through the Great Depression and beyond, but for much of its history Lyons was more famous for its smaller businesses; namely, taverns. Harley Bradford Mitchell, in his 1928 book, *Historical Fragments of Early Chicagoland*, described the town in the early 20th century as "Lyons the bibulous, the unregenerate, the chosen abode of Bacchus and Terpsichore." In 1908, a LaGrange newspaper, agitating against Lyons's 24 taverns in advance of a prohibition vote, used more down-to-earth language: Lyons, it said, was "desecrating all the virtues that decent men hold sacred."

Lyons gained a reputation as the Chicago area's "Sin City" throughout the 1960s, 1970s, and 1980s. Strip clubs such as Michael's Magic Touch, Club Algiers, French 75, My Uncle's

Place, and others began to become known as dens of prostitution and drug dealing, and the federal Operation Safebet investigation through the 1980s resulted in 76 indictments and 57 convictions. Lyons's mayor during that time, William G. Smith, inevitably became attached to Lyons's negative reputation, though he was never charged with any involvement in corruption—he resigned as mayor in February 1989, shortly after a heart attack, and died two months later.

Lyons has settled down in the years since, for better and, perhaps, for worse—though the fact that a fast-food restaurant now occupies the site of Michael's Magic Touch certainly qualifies as an improvement, the fact that a fast-food restaurant occupies the site of the colorful Mangam's Chateau is harder to be enthusiastic about. The Hofmann Tower still stands as a symbol of Lyons's remarkable past, though it is in disrepair and requiring (according to a conservative estimate) $500,000 in infrastructure improvements. Hopefully this book will offer a glimpse into what made Lyons such a fascinating town that played a crucial role in Chicago's history and why the things that made it interesting are worth preserving.

One

LE PORTAGE AND THE BIRTH OF LYONS

In the early 1800s, Lyons became a prime location for settlers west of Chicago, as Native Americans in the region—mainly Potawatomis—left either by treaty or by force. David and Bernardus Laughton, two fur traders, opened their trading post near the banks of the Des Plaines River near the portage in the 1820s, as well as a tavern farther upriver—thought to be the first such buildings outside of Chicago.

The fur trade fell away with the Native Americans' departure, and new settlers began pondering ways to encourage growing industry in the region. Louis Joliet arguably had the first inkling of the idea that would reshape the region: in 1673, he wrote in his journal that "it would only be necessary to cut a canal through half a league of prairie to go in a bark by easy navigation from Lake Erie to the Gulf of Mexico." A century and a half later, that notion would become reality in the form of the Illinois and Michigan Canal, which opened in 1848.

The construction of the Illinois and Michigan Canal brought waves of settlers and immigrants from Germany, Poland, Ireland, and elsewhere to work, many of them settling in what soon became Lyons. (The genesis of the town's name is uncertain, though many believe it is a tribute to Lyon, France, named by one of the many French fur traders in the area during the 18th century.) The first business owners in town appeared to be tavern owners, providing rest stops for travelers around Chicago. Joshua Sackett is believed to have opened the first such establishment in 1832, in what is now known as the Hofmann "triangle property." In 1856, the three Mueller brothers—Henry, Adolph, and Phillip—built their brewery near the Des Plaines River in an area called Cooksville (a region bridging Lyons and Riverside, named after developer Isaac Cook). In 1871, residents caught the Great Chicago Fire from its roof; the brewery itself succumbed to fire in 1873.

By the late 1800s, Lyons had become a town of taverns, rest stops, and quarries whose limestone and granite fed into the construction of many buildings in the area. Lyons was officially incorporated on August 16, 1888.

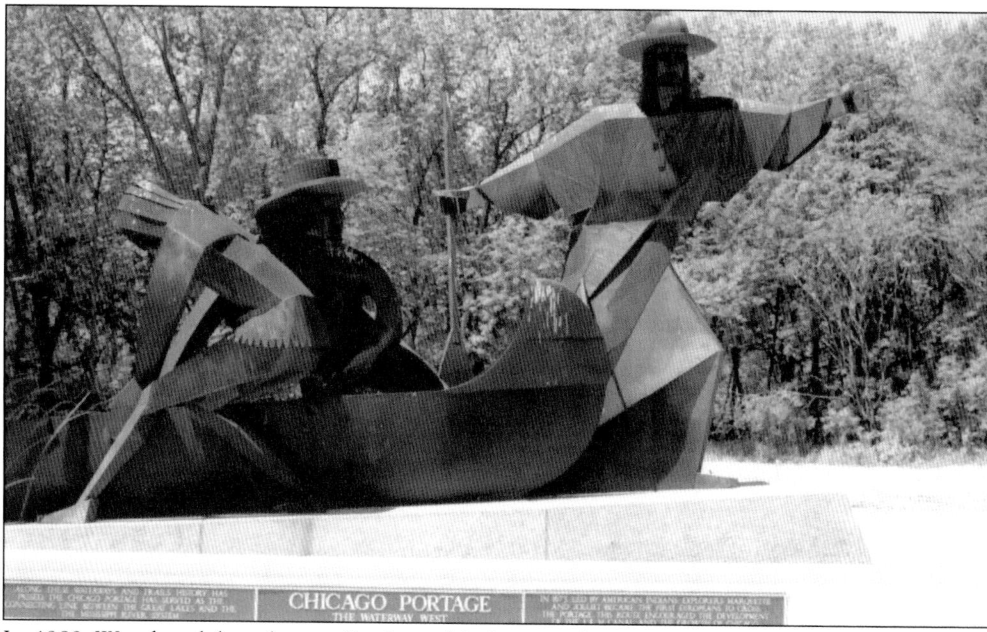

In 1989, Woodstock-based artist Ferdinand Rebeccini designed his statue *The Waterway West*, which depicts Fr. Jacques Marquette, Louis Joliet, and a Potawatomi guide portaging their canoe. The text of the statue reads: "Along these waterways and trails history has passed. The Chicago Portage has served as the connecting link between the Great Lakes and the Mississippi river system. In 1673, led by American Indians, explorers Marquette and Joliet became the first Europeans to cross the portage. This route encouraged the development of the I&M Canal and the growth of Chicago."

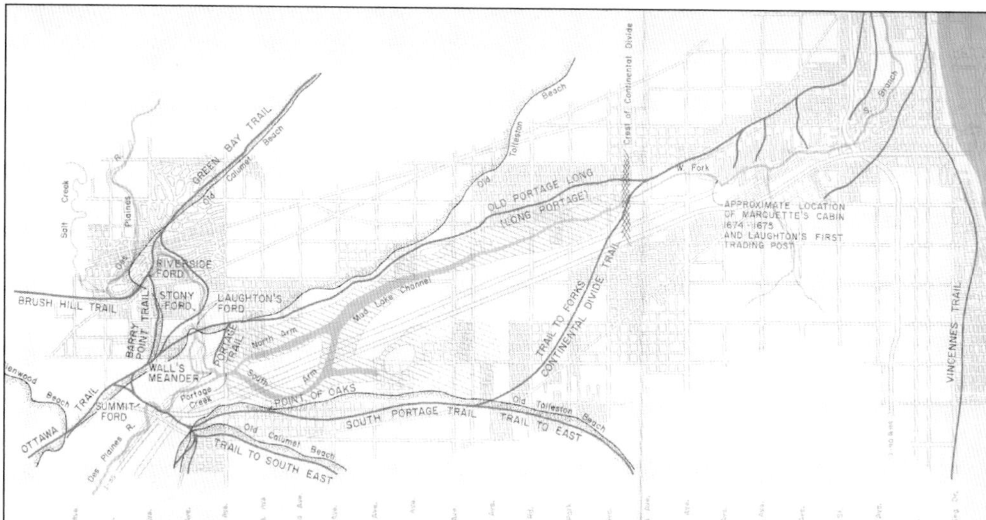

This map, designed by the Friends of the Chicago Portage, shows the location of various portage trails that connected what is now Lyons to the city, as well as the first location of the Laughtons' trading post, in an area by the south branch of the Chicago River then called Hardscrabble (near what is now Damen Avenue). The shaded area marks the boundaries of Mud Lake.

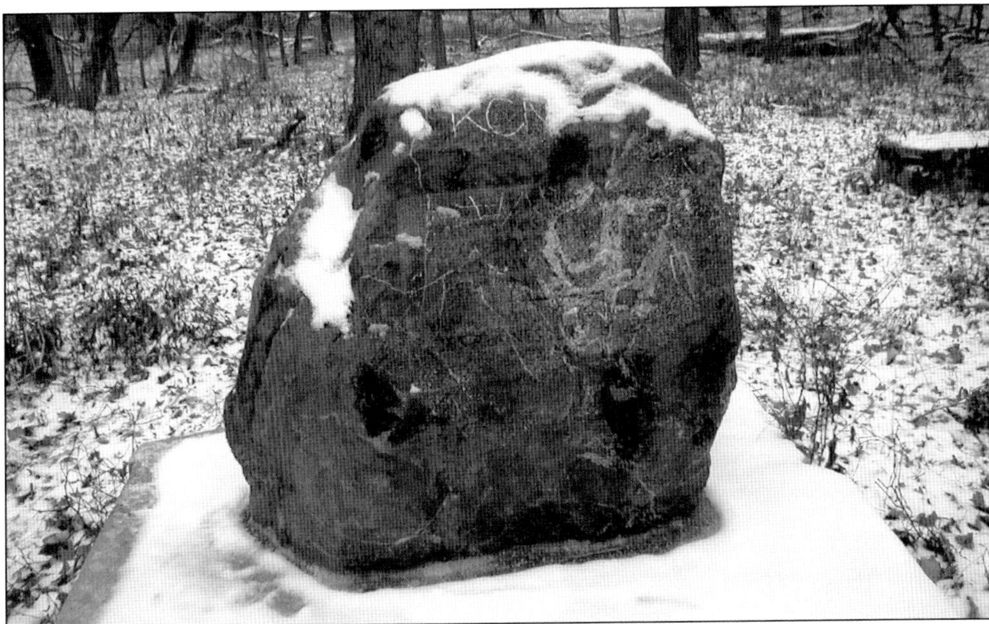

This site in the Ottawa Trail Woods marks off the location of the Laughtons' trading post. The stone marker has become unreadable due to weathering and vandalism. When installed in the late 1950s it read: "This is the site of the trading post established and operated by Bernardus and David Laughton, fur traders, in 1833. Laughton's ford on the Des Plaines lies directly west." The tavern is believed by many historians to be farther upstream in neighboring Riverside. Both the trading post and tavern, built in 1927, were the first such structures west of Chicago. The Laughtons died within a week of each other in 1834. The causes of their deaths are unknown.

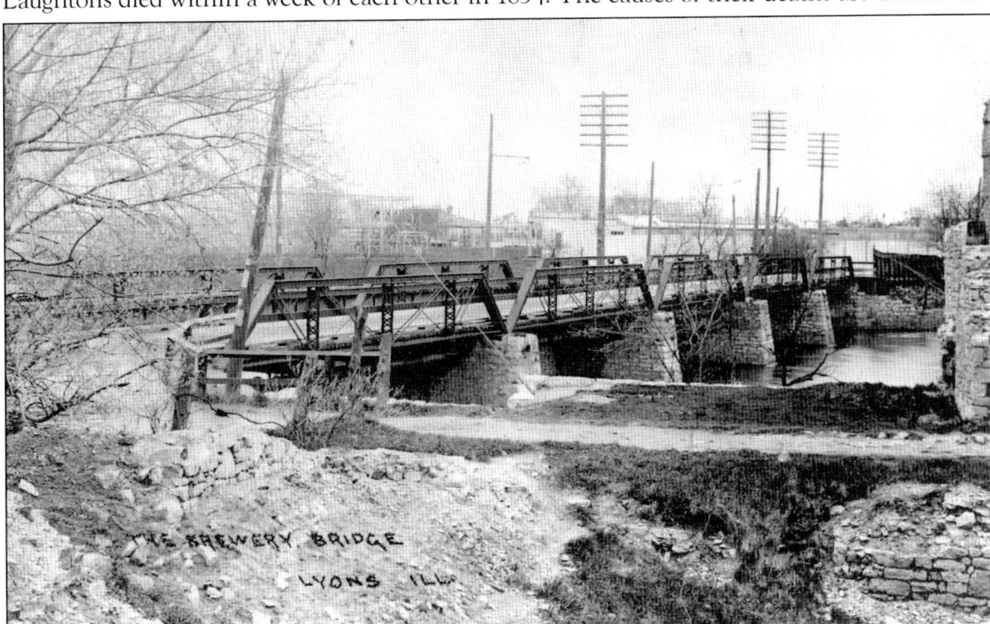

The Mueller Brothers Brewery was built on the east bank of the Des Plaines River, Just north of this bridge on the Plank Road (later Ogden Avenue). A limestone quarry, from which materials for the brewery and other buildings came, was located across the bridge in what is now Cermak Park.

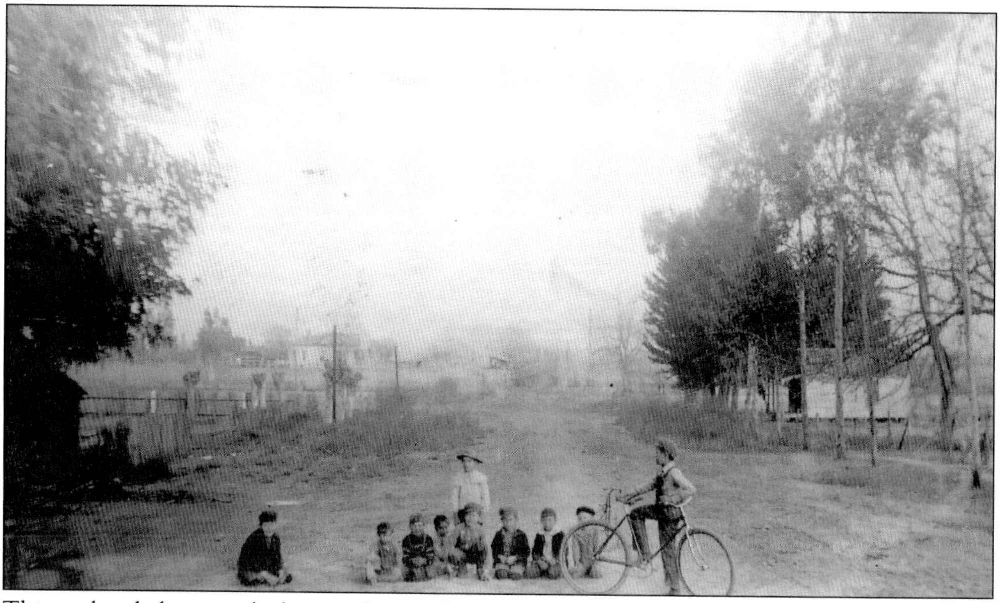

This undated photograph shows a dirt road in Lyons. Like most of the Chicago area streets that do not follow the city's familiar grid system, what is now Ogden Avenue once functioned as a Native American trail and a stagecoach line running from Chicago stopped at Lyons, Naperville, Aurora, and Ottawa. As the construction of the Illinois and Michigan Canal created a new transportation corridor in the area, roads started to become redeveloped as well, and it became known as the Plank Road.

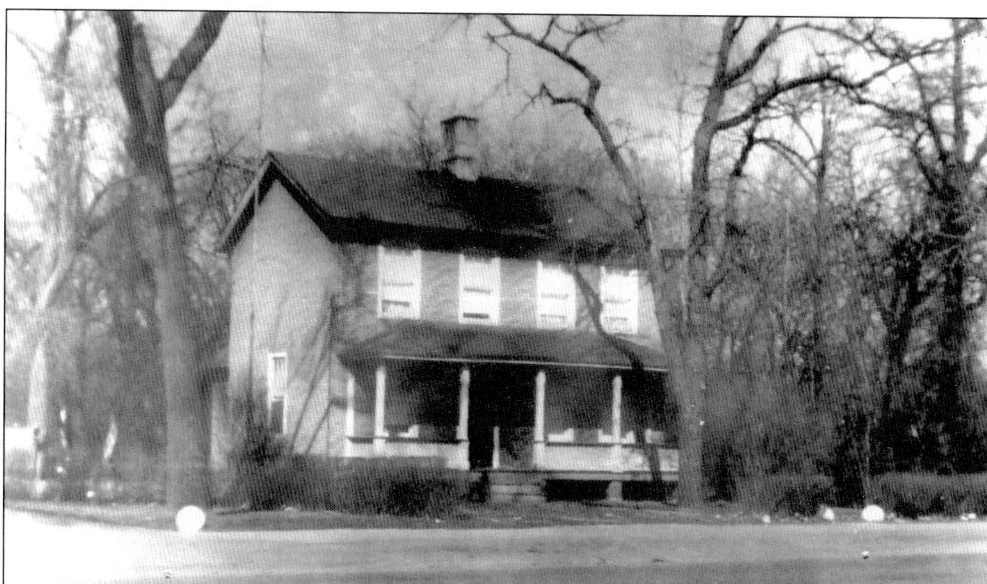

Mail service came early to Lyons thanks to Theodorus Doty, who purchased the right to build a dam on the Des Plaines River from one of the town's earliest residents, Stephen Forbes, in 1843. In 1848, Doty established Lyons's post office, likely out of his tavern on Ogden Avenue. Shown here is mayor Thomas Collins's home on Ogden Avenue, which was located next to the Zion Parsonage and the first Zion Lutheran Church. The home doubled as Lyons's post office in 1854, when postmaster Elias Prescott lived there. The Collins home burned down in the 1960s.

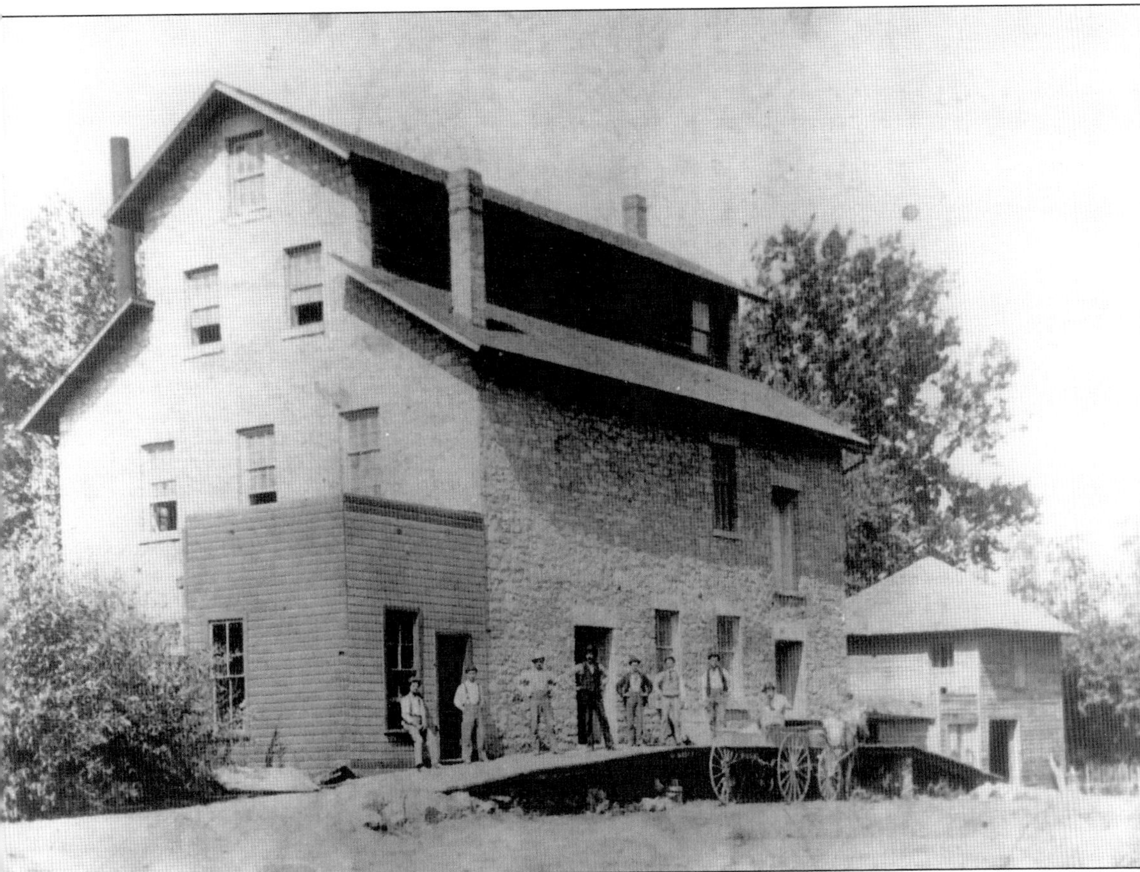

In 1835, Stephen Forbes, the first elected sheriff of Cook County, constructed this building as a sawmill on the south bank of the Des Plaines River, near the current site of the Hofmann Tower. Stephen White, who moved to Lyons from Vermont in 1830, purchased the property in 1854. When Dr. George M. Fox married White's daughter, Harriett, he took over control of the property, converting it to a gristmill. In 1866, Fox constructed a dam on the Des Plaines River to power the mill. The building also served as a tavern, one of the few rest stops between Chicago and Naperville at the time. Mill Bridge Street in Riverside and the Mill Bridge Roller Rink took their names from the mill.

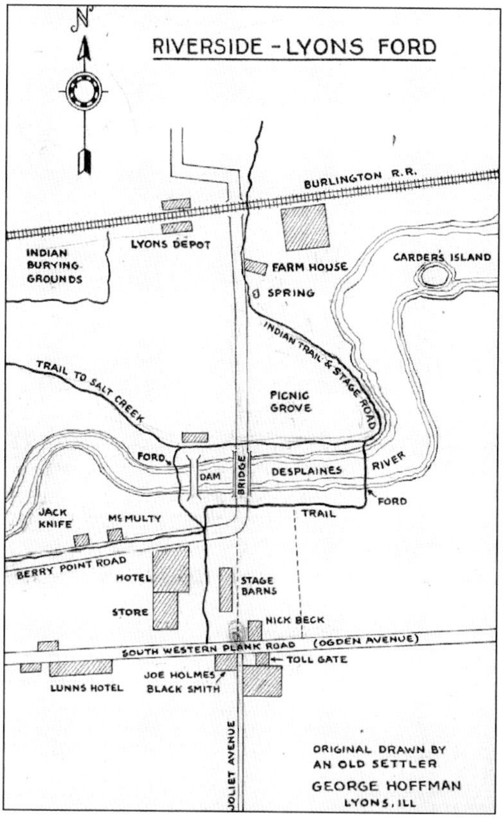

This map of Lyons, based on one originally drawn by George Hofmann Sr., details various sites along the Des Plaines River in Lyons in the 1860s, among other places, it cites a Native American burial ground in what is now Riverside, just south of the Burlington Railroad tracks, and cattle pens near the northeast corner of Ogden and Joliet Avenues.

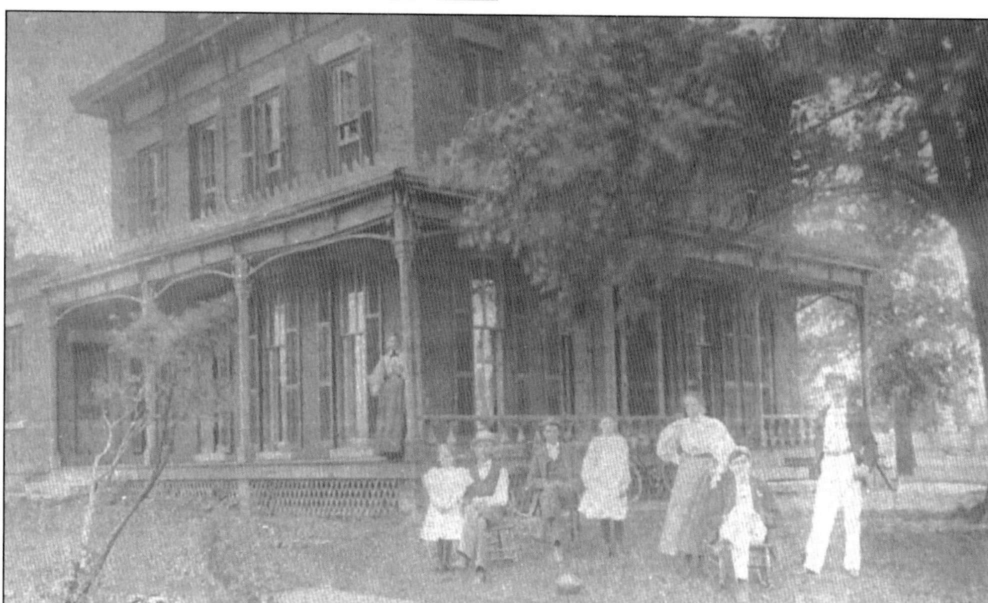

Early settler Stephen White built his homestead in 1850 on the south side of Ogden Avenue between Leland and Lawndale Avenues. This photograph, from 1896, shows various members of the White family. Fred Schultz, a local quarry owner, is believed to be standing at the far right. The home remained standing until the late 1960s.

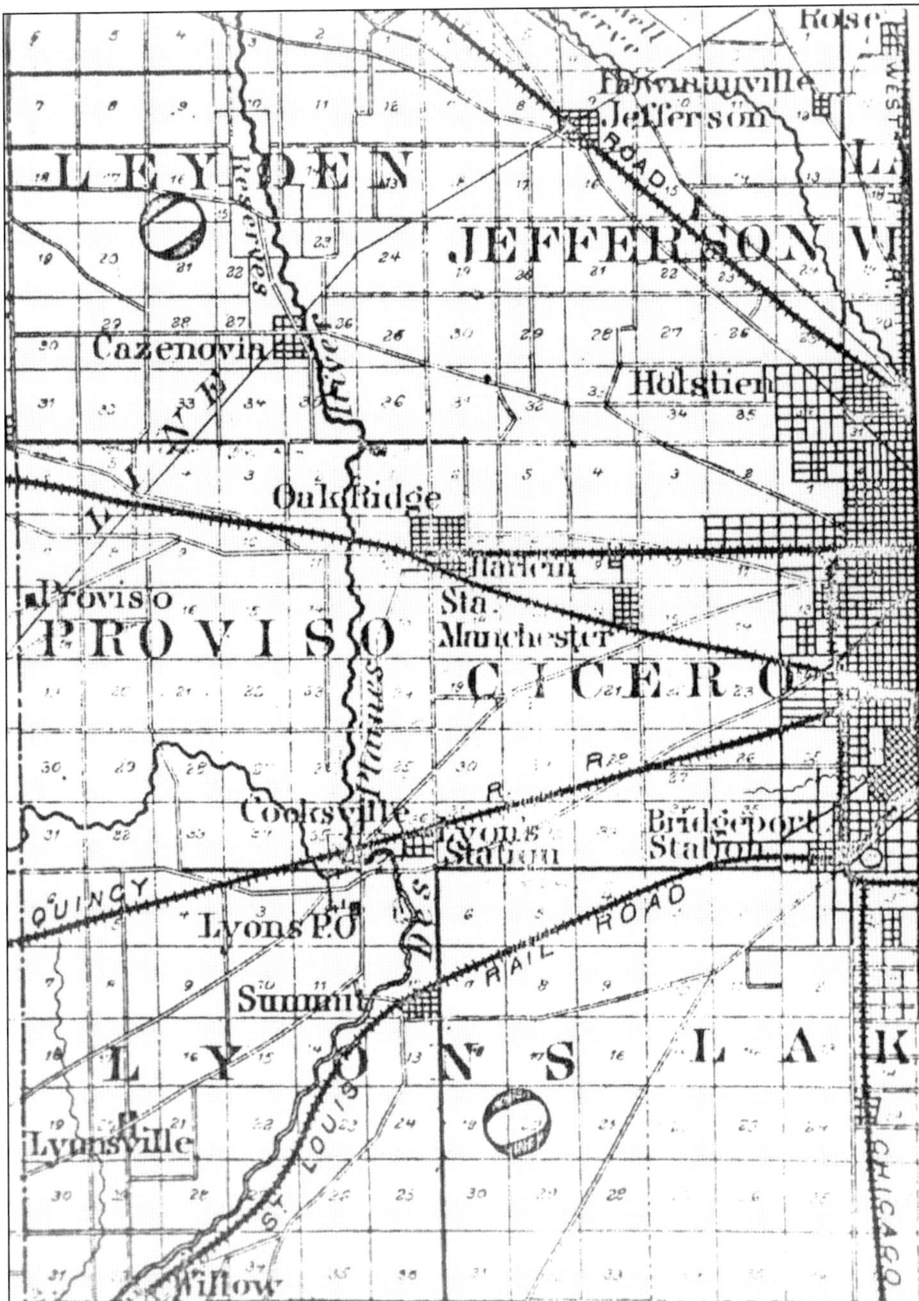

This map from 1869 shows some of the early boundaries of Cook County townships, including Cooksville, which later became part of Riverside, and the Quincy Railroad, which was constructed in 1864. In an 1858 petition written by leaders of numerous communities lobbying for the railroad, Lyons was described this way: "It is estimated that this would be one of the most remunerative stations within 50 miles of the city. There are inexhaustible quarries of stone here of the very best quality for lime and suitable for building purposes. . . . There is an extensive Brewery at this place [likely the Mueller brothers'], which now furnishes freight equal to one car load per day. With railroad facilities, this establishment would more than double its present freight."

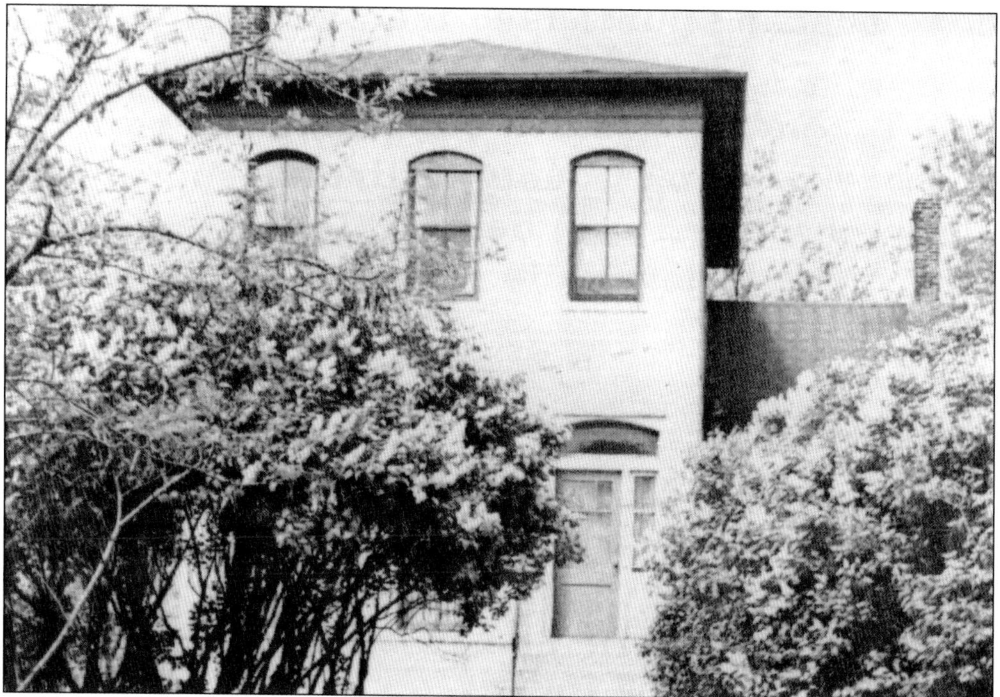

This stone house on Joliet Avenue was one of the first homes in Lyons. The Palmer House was so named for being the home of Sarah J. Palmer, a daughter of local tavern owner William Lunn. The White family owned the house until 1865, when it was deeded to Palmer; it stood until 1963.

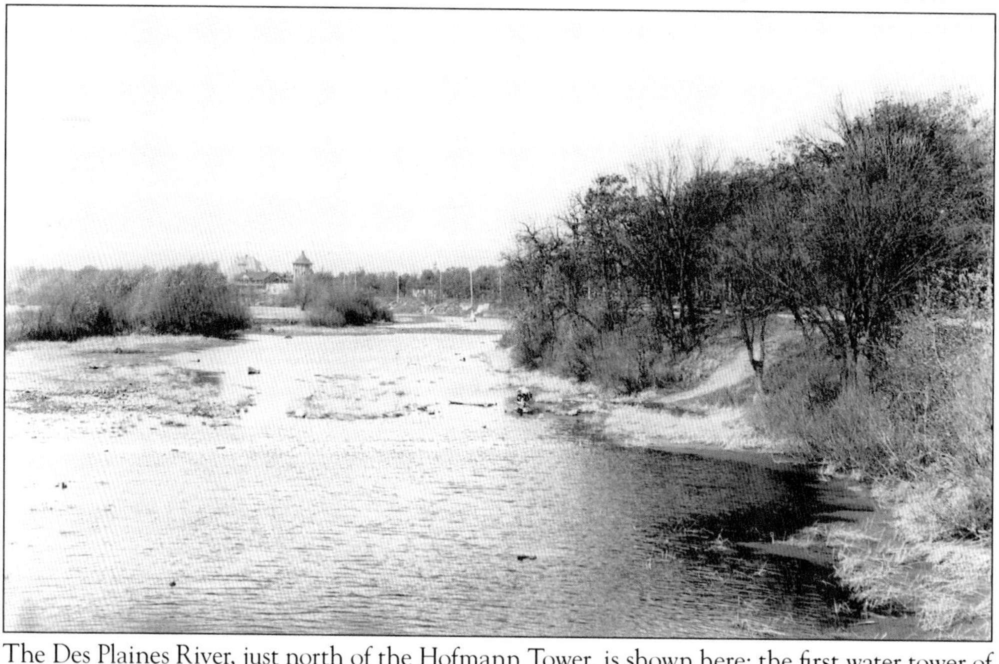

The Des Plaines River, just north of the Hofmann Tower, is shown here; the first water tower of neighboring Riverside, which was built in 1871 and burned down on New Year's Eve 1913, can be seen in the distance. In order to store beer barrels, the Mueller brothers would dig small caves along the banks of the river.

Fred Schultz, who along with Stephen White was a prominent quarry operator and property owner in town, built one of the first homes in Lyons in the 1860s; he would later become one of Lyons's first trustees when the town was incorporated in 1888. In the 1920s, his home, generally called the Schultz Mansion, became Sophie's, a restaurant and cocktail lounge.

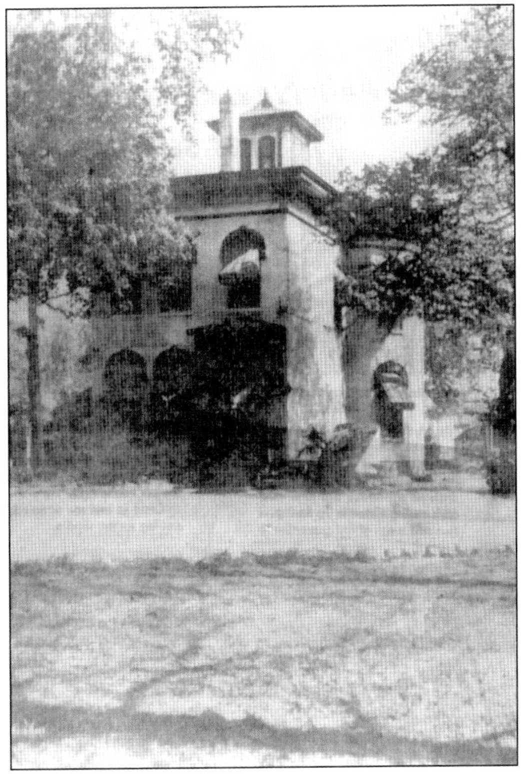

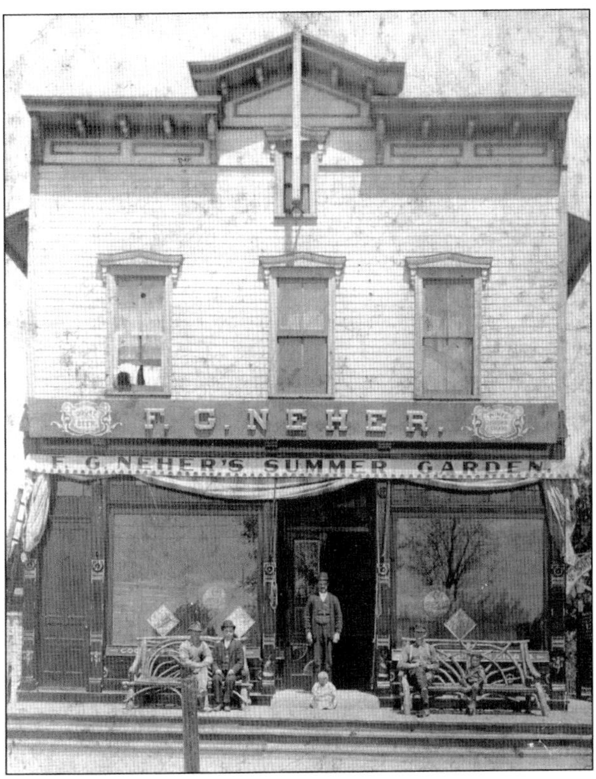

The Neher family arrived in Lyons in 1866, building its homestead in Cooksville, near the site of the Mueller Brothers Brewery. George Neher Sr. served as postmaster in Lyons from 1890 to 1894, and mayor from 1896 to 1898; and the family long played a role in Lyons's business and political life. This photograph shows Neher's Tavern shortly after it opened in 1888.

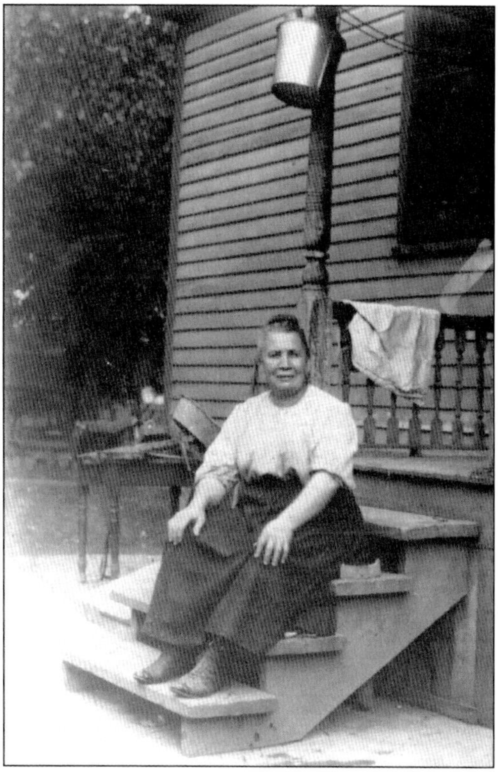

This c. 1920 photograph shows "Grandma" Neher on the steps of Neher's Tavern. Born in 1865, she married Frank Neher in 1888, the same year the tavern opened. She died in 1959 at 91 years old.

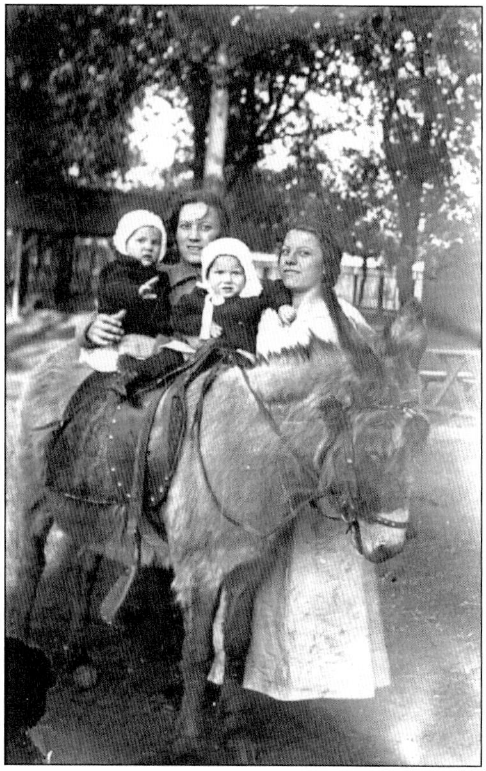

Donkey rides were part of the entertainment at some of Lyons's amusement parks and picnic groves. This photograph shows the infant Darnstadt twins, Ray (left) and Bill Jr., held by sisters Kate (second from left) and Laura Neher, in the 1890s.

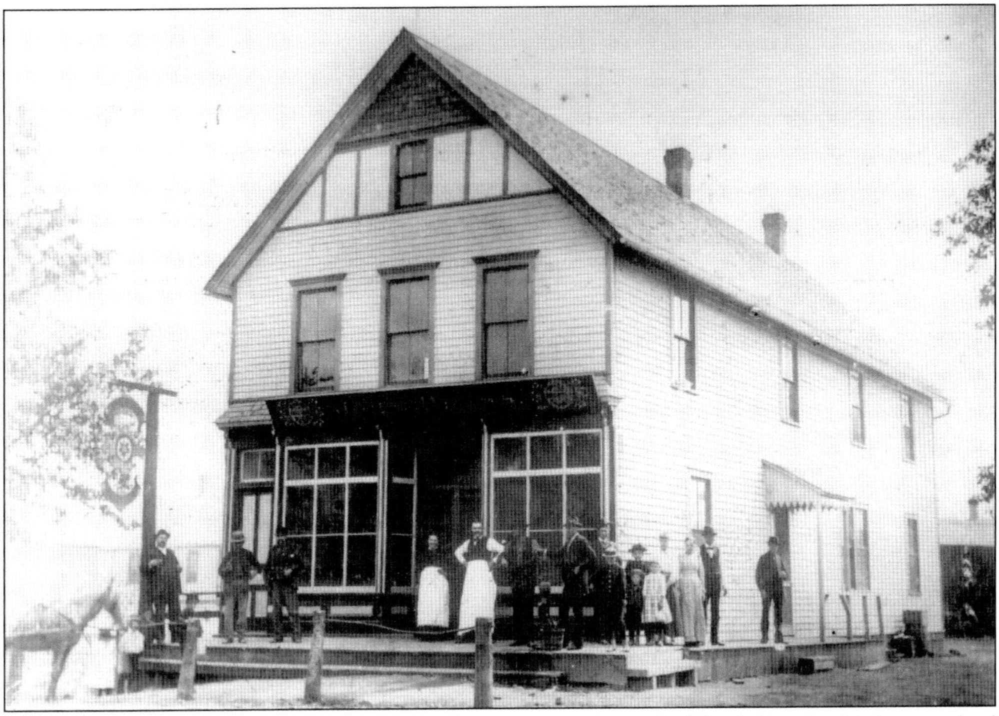

By the late 1800s, many taverns had started to crop up along the Plank Road, which smoothed the way for travelers and shippers to connect from Chicago to Naperville. John Reuss, one of the tavern owners in town, operated his on the corner of Ogden and Prescott Avenues.

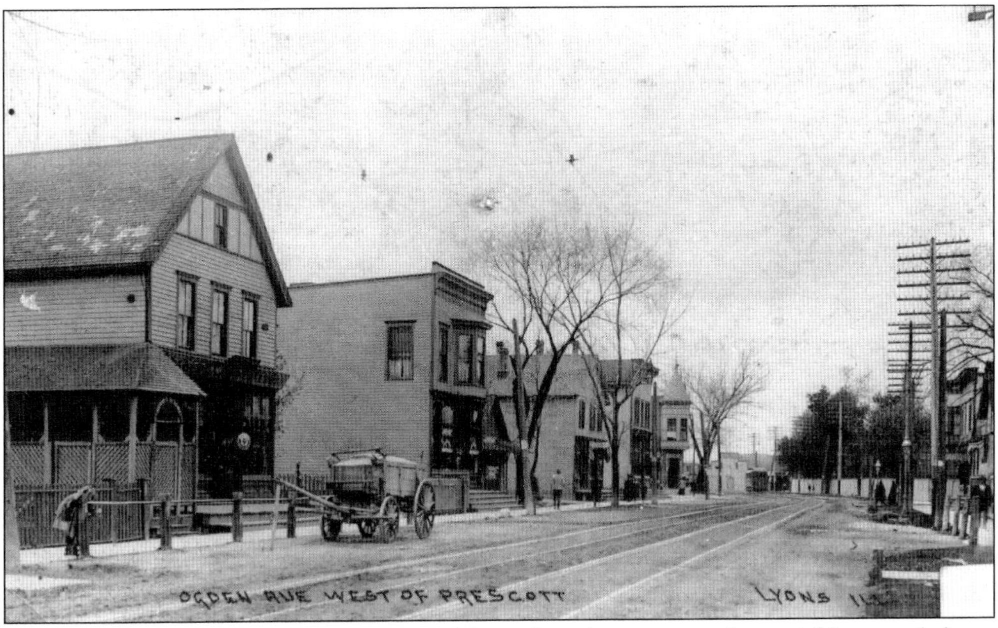

This photograph places Reuss's tavern, at left, within the context of its neighbors, and shows Ogden Avenue looking east; M. Zastera's is just to the west of it, and George Virzine's restaurant is west of that. By the time this photograph was taken, Reuss's tavern had added a summer garden, in keeping with many Lyons taverns.

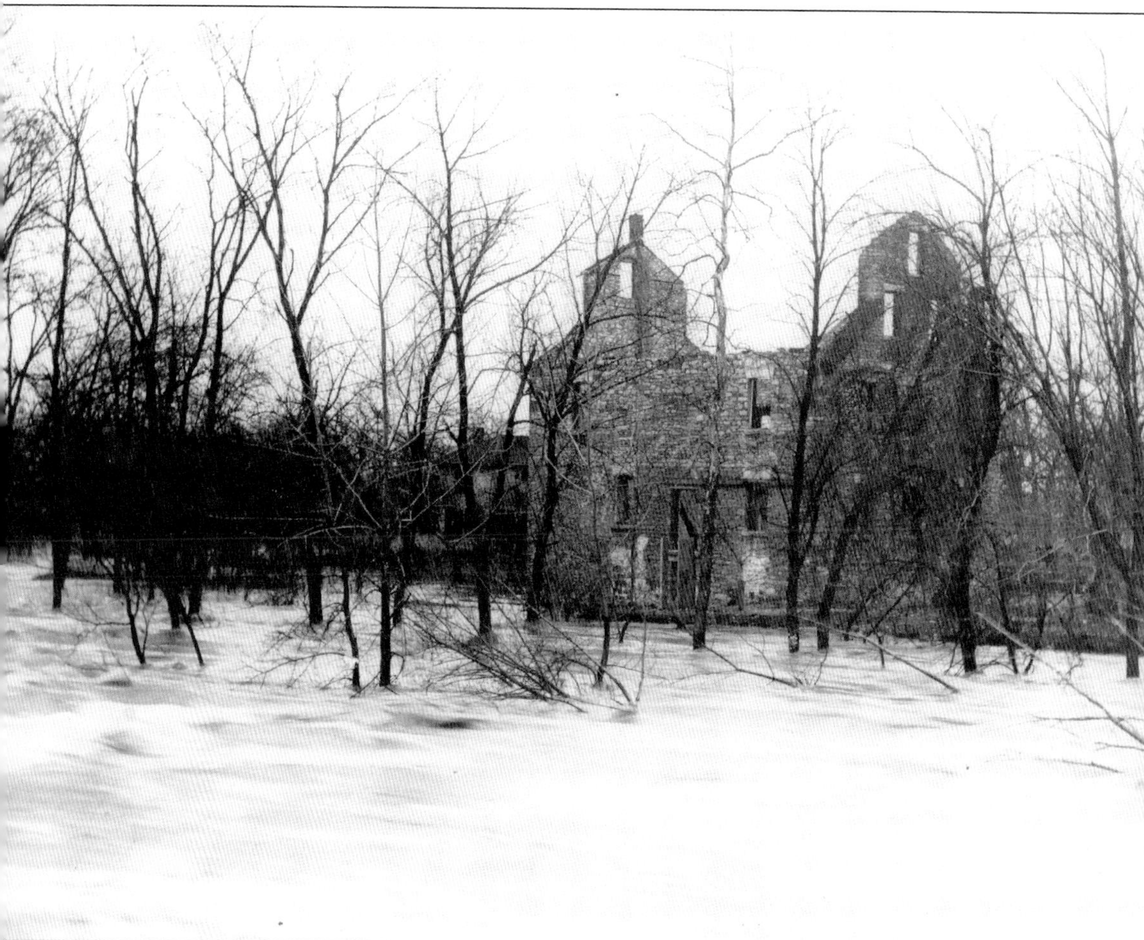

The Fox Mill burned down in 1890. This photograph shows the remnants of the building shortly before the site was leveled in 1893.

Lyons's first mayor, Thomas Collins, presided over the meeting incorporating the village on August 16, 1888. He served until 1891. One of the first tasks accomplished by the first administration was to erect a calaboose—a jail—to handle lawless weekend drinkers. The jail later moved into the village hall once it was built 12 years later.

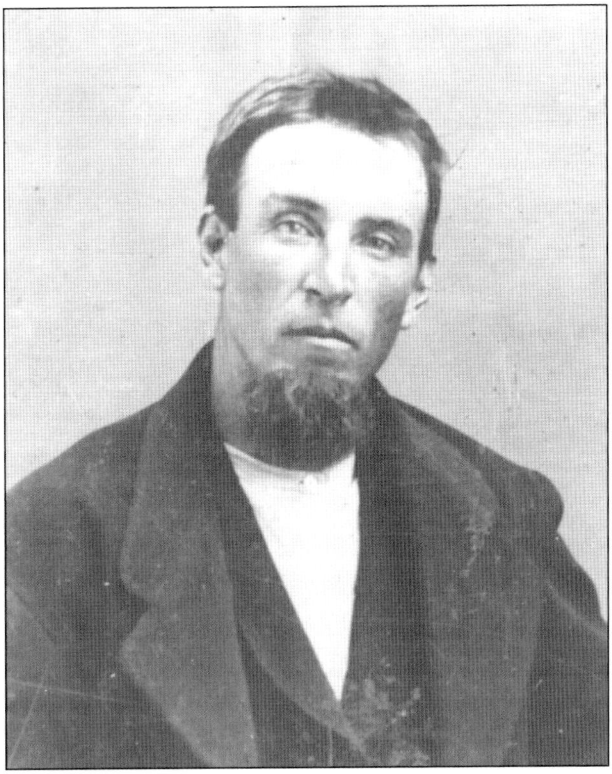

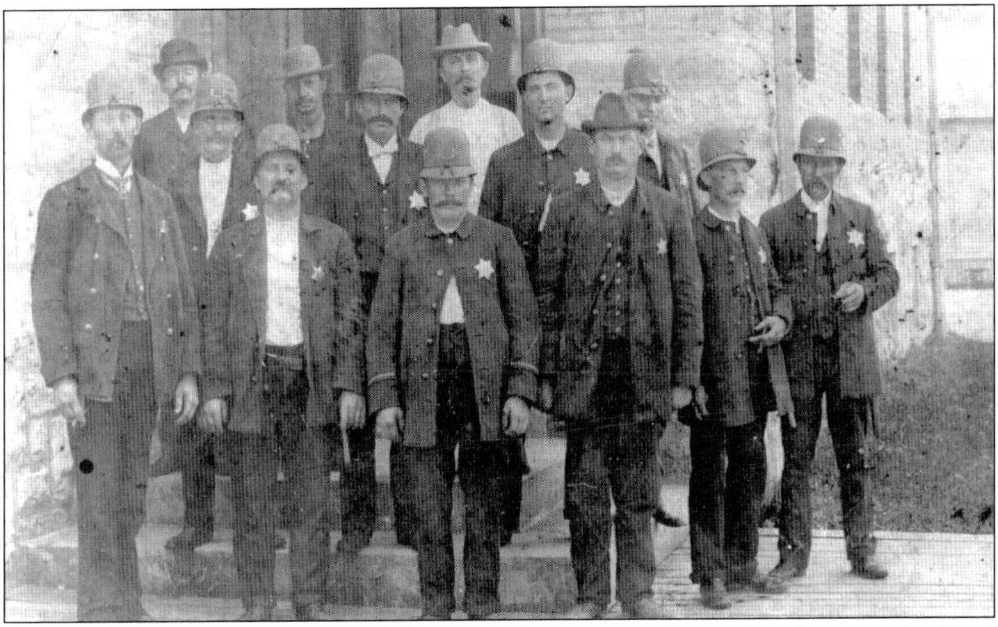

Mayor Collins established the Lyons Police Department not long after the village's official incorporation, on September 6, 1888. This photograph shows one of its earliest staff of officers. From left to right are (first row) August Muser, Herman Darnstadt, unidentified, George Mitch, Frank Bo John, and Henry Maves; (second row) John Keefe, Charles Masters, and Charles Gatz. James Fitzgerald, who was appointed the first village constable, is at the far right of the third row.

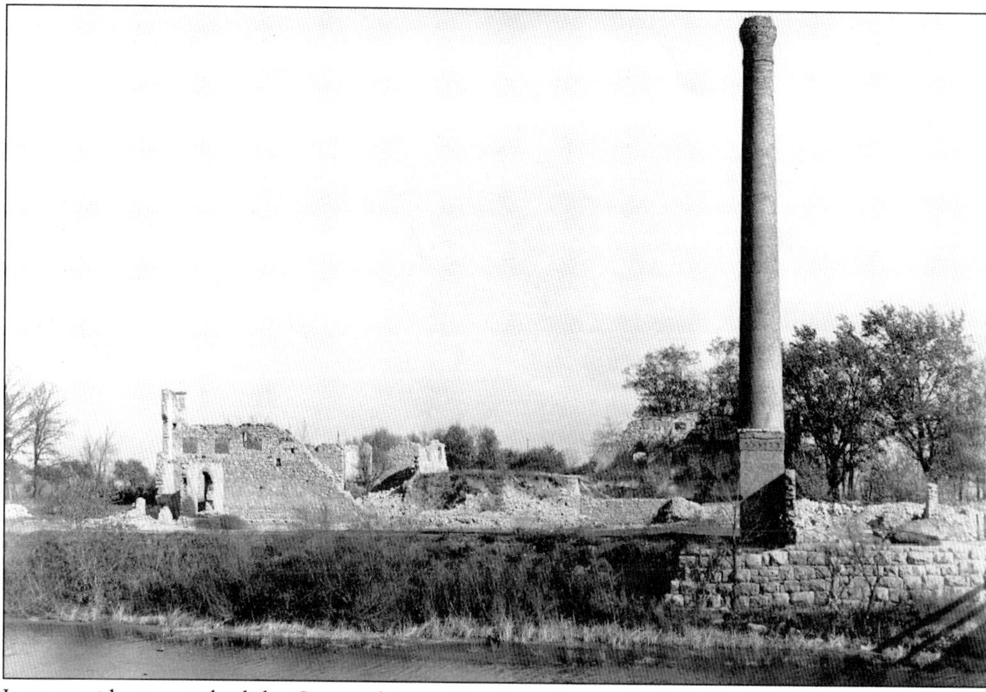

Lyons residents watched the Great Chicago Fire from the roof of Mueller's brewery on October 8, 1871; and Mueller's itself succumbed to fire two years later. The ruins remained standing until the mid-1890s, when a local boy was killed by a collapsing wall. The smokestack remained standing until about 1910, when its bricks were used in the construction of a home in Riverside.

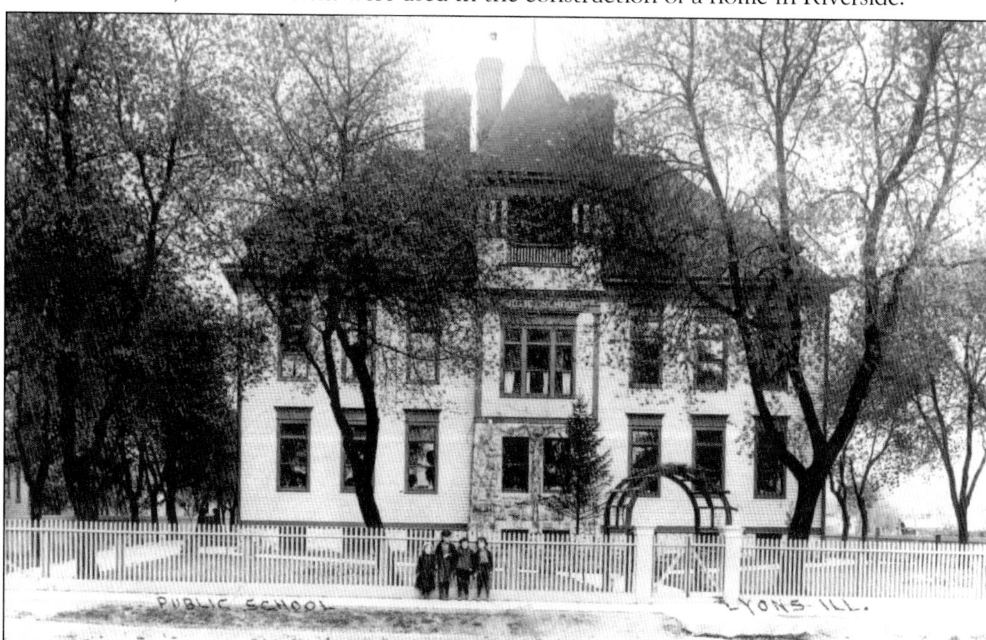

The first school building in Lyons was a log building at the present site of Zion Lutheran Church. The Washington School building on Joliet Avenue, shown here in a postcard from 1915, was built in 1870.

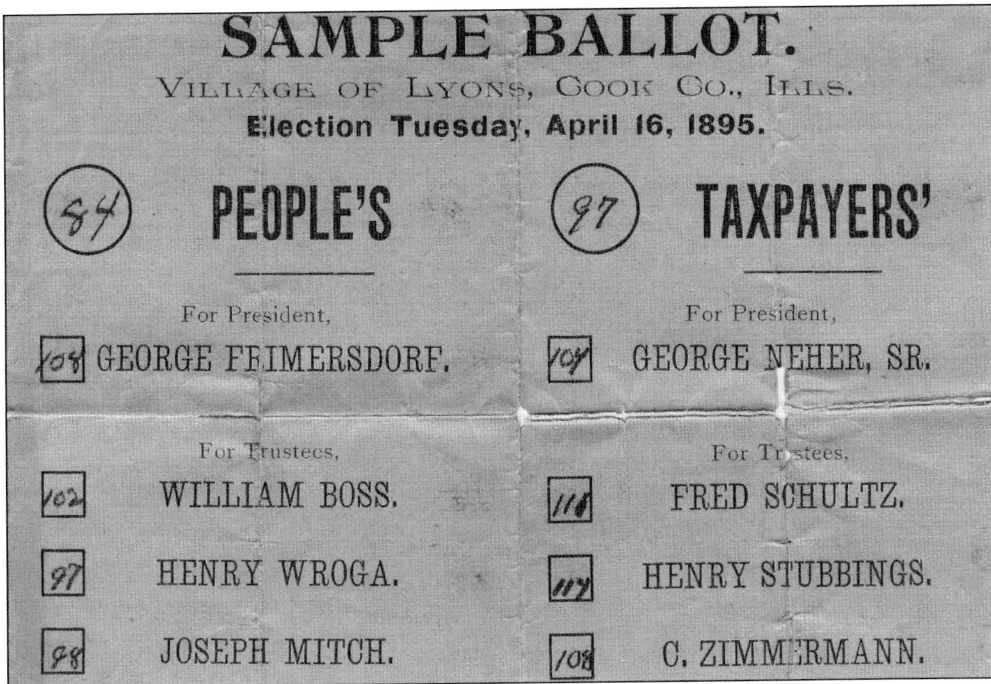

SAMPLE BALLOT.

VILLAGE OF LYONS, COOK CO., ILLS.

Election Tuesday, April 16, 1895.

PEOPLE'S	TAXPAYERS'
For President,	For President,
GEORGE FRIMERSDORF.	GEORGE NEHER, SR.
For Trustees,	For Trustees,
WILLIAM BOSS.	FRED SCHULTZ.
HENRY WROGA.	HENRY STUBBINGS.
JOSEPH MITCH.	C. ZIMMERMANN.

George Neher lost the 1895 mayoral election to George Frimersdorf, a blacksmith who was one of Lyons's first trustees, but he would win the following year, serving from 1896 to 1898. During Frimersdorf's tenure, tracks for the local trolley line were installed on Ogden Avenue.

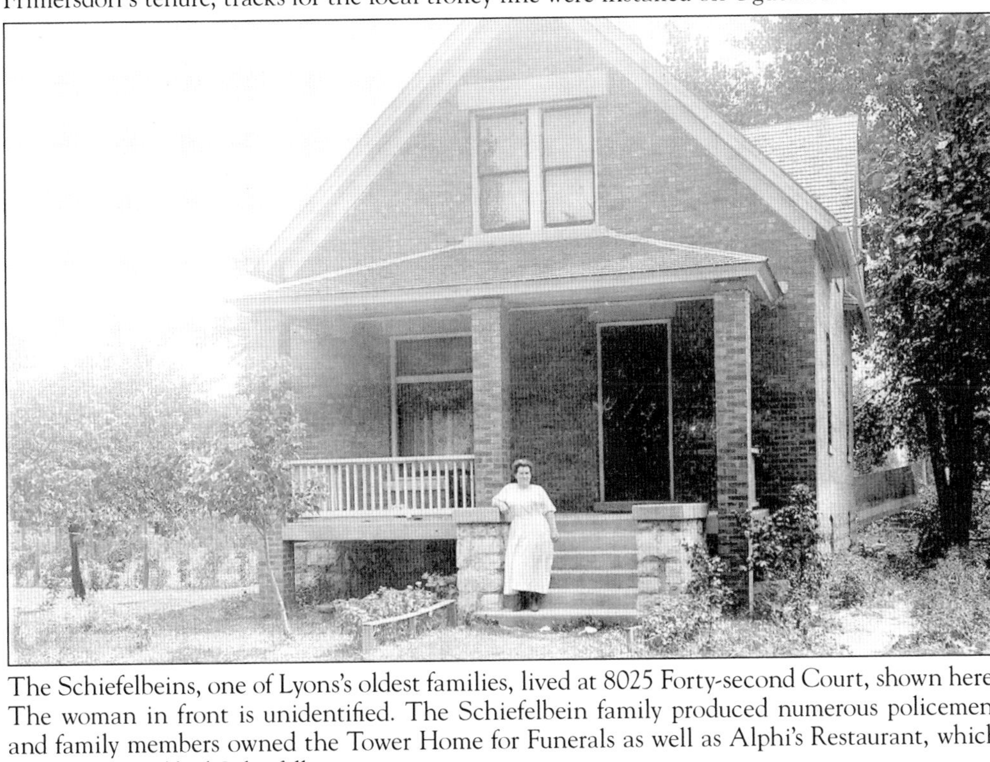

The Schiefelbeins, one of Lyons's oldest families, lived at 8025 Forty-second Court, shown here. The woman in front is unidentified. The Schiefelbein family produced numerous policemen, and family members owned the Tower Home for Funerals as well as Alphi's Restaurant, which is named for Alfred Schiefelbein.

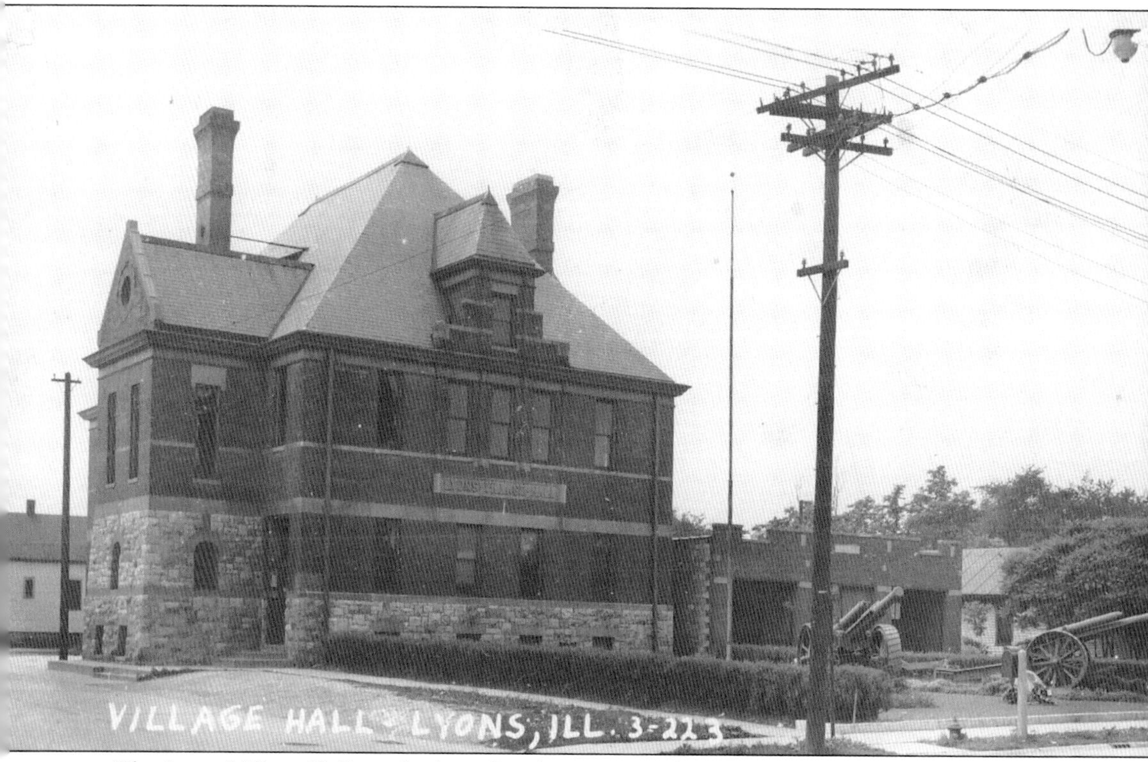

The Lyons Village Hall was built in October 1900 on the corner of Ogden and Center Avenues, on a lot purchased for $1,000. Hofmann and Arden was the main contractor; Nick Metz and Son (which continues to operate today) was contracted for masonry work. This image of the building from the 1930s shows a pair of World War I cannons that were donated to Lyons; they were sold for scrap in support of the war effort during World War II.

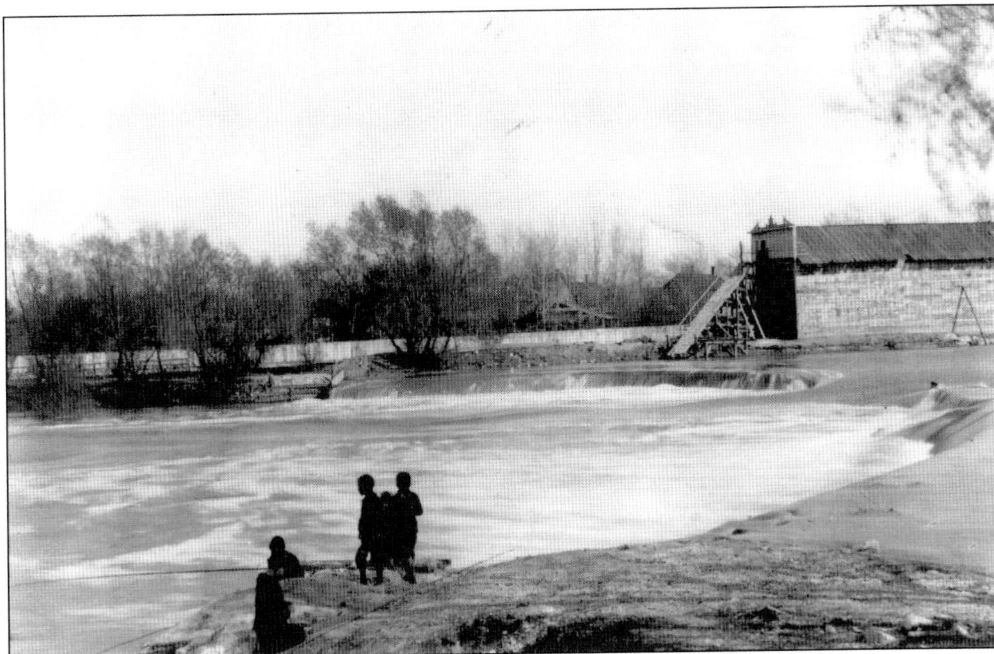

In the late 1800s, Tim Ryan's icehouse occupied the property alongside the Des Plaines River off what is now Lawndale Avenue. Ice from the Des Plaines River was removed and stored during the winter months, and delivered to local homes and businesses. Ryan himself owned a tavern at 8039 Ogden Avenue, near what later became a tavern called the Ranch, and is a senior home today.

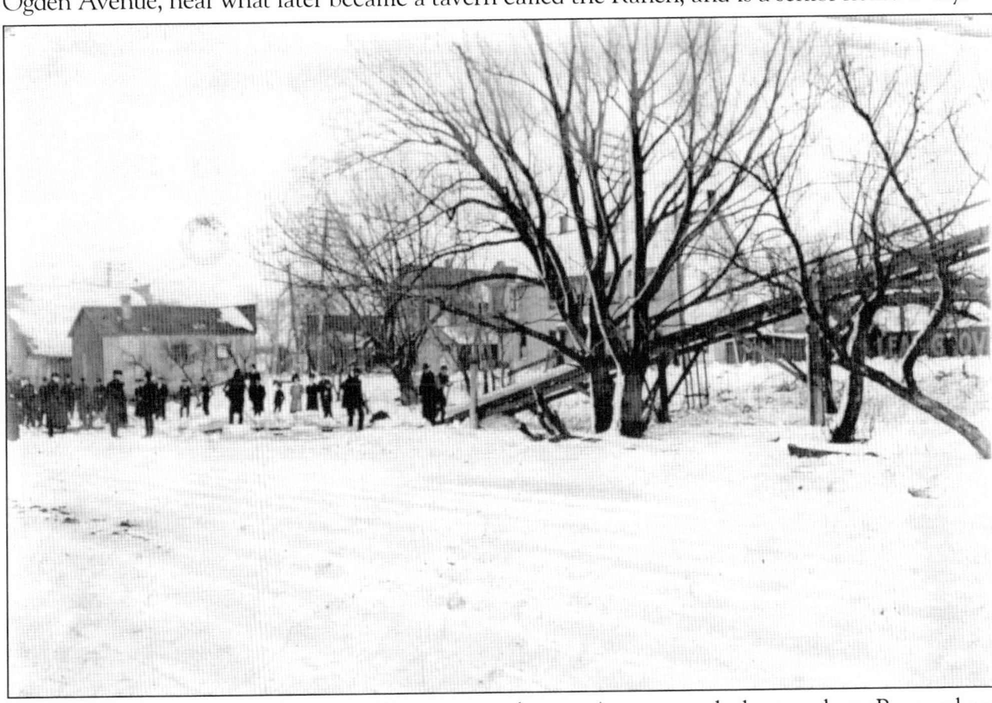

Residents await deliveries from the Tim Ryan icehouse. An apocryphal story about Ryan relates that in 1900, Ryan treated the ice with red dye in an attempt to brand his business, keeping local taverns and restaurants in red ice cubes.

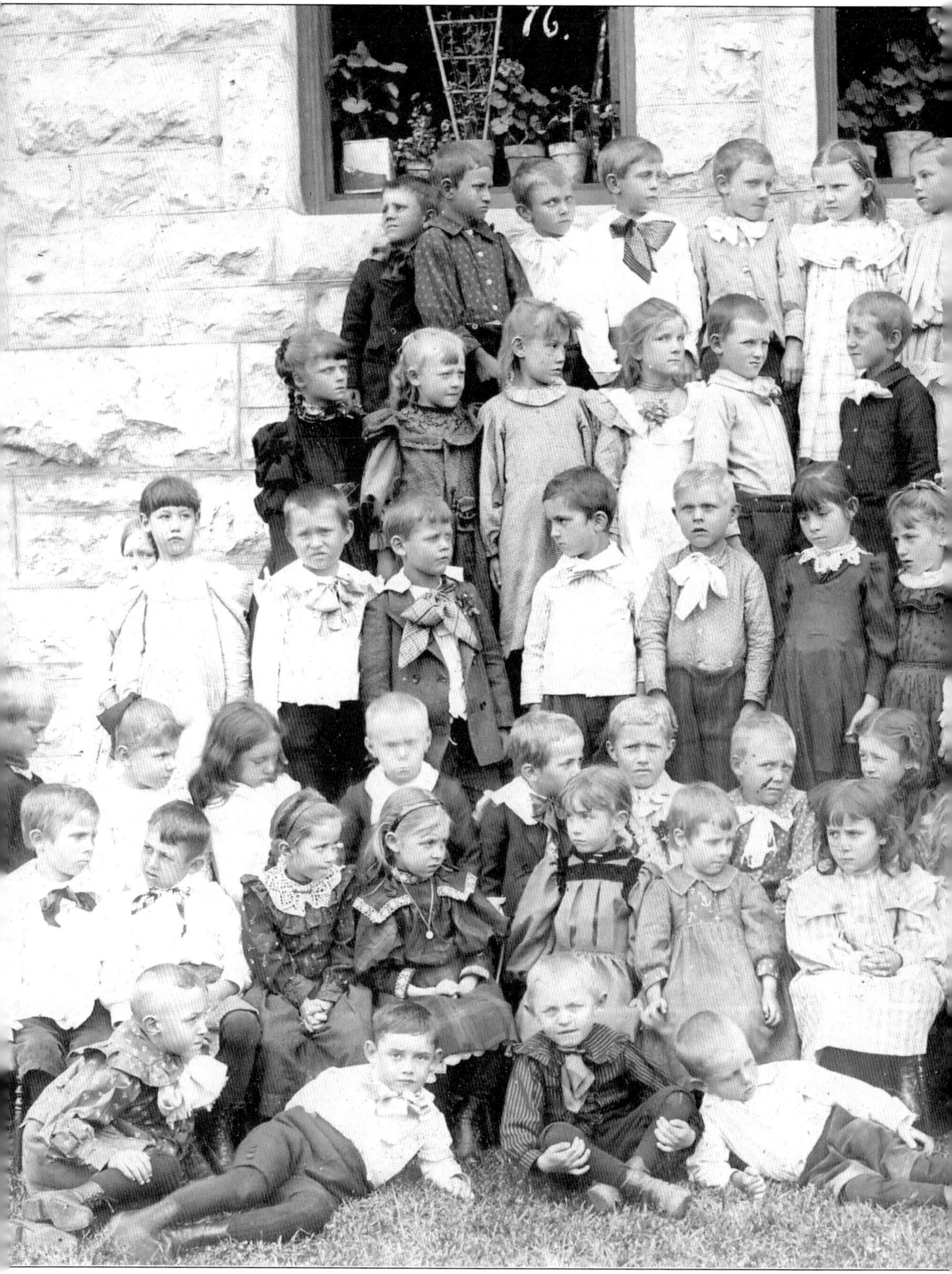
76.

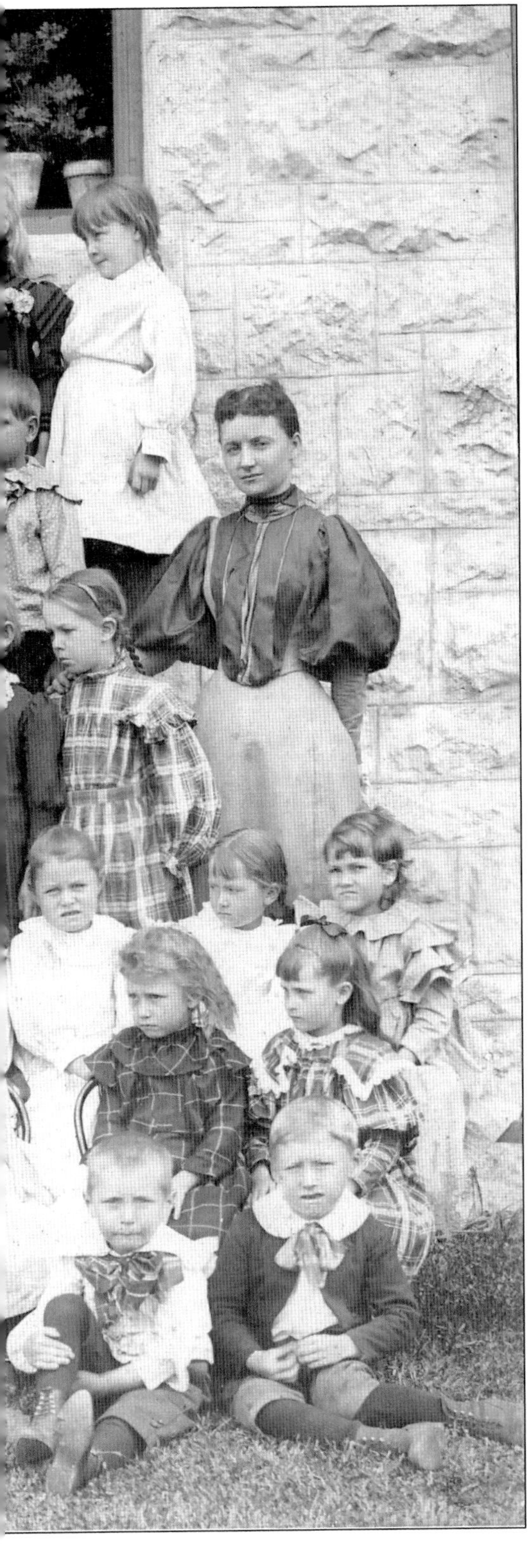

This photograph captures the first-grade class at Washington School in 1896. Pictured from left to right are (first row) John Reuss Jr., George Neher, Louis Lange, Albert Stubbings, Fred Boss, and Eric Lungerhausen; (second row) Frank Schwytzer, Frank Neher, Lizzie Buk, Helen Salisbury, Helen White, Ellen Brown, Jesse Leach, unidentified, unidentified, and Annie Ensinger; (third row) unidentified, Emma Kohls, unidentified, Gust Schiefelbein, unidentified, unidentified, Charlie Stieg, Minnie Gerber, Emma Koeneman, Annie Beyer, Sadie Benke, and Virginia Hofmann; (fourth row) unidentified, Louise Lange, John Schueneman, Carl Gath, Henry Hosman, unidentified, Annie Thode, Tillie Groth, Ida Thode, Irene Garber, and teacher ? Spellman; (fifth row) Lizzie Taschner, Ella Gieseler, Mamie Frank, Annie Schimmelpfennig, ? Stark, William Krueger, William Burdorf, and Paul Stednitz; (sixth row) William Darnstadt, Emil Beyer, Fred Steinhoff, John Schumacher, Ernest Mester, Elizabeth Kirschbaum, Lottie Polivka, Lizzie Panko, and Helen Ryan.

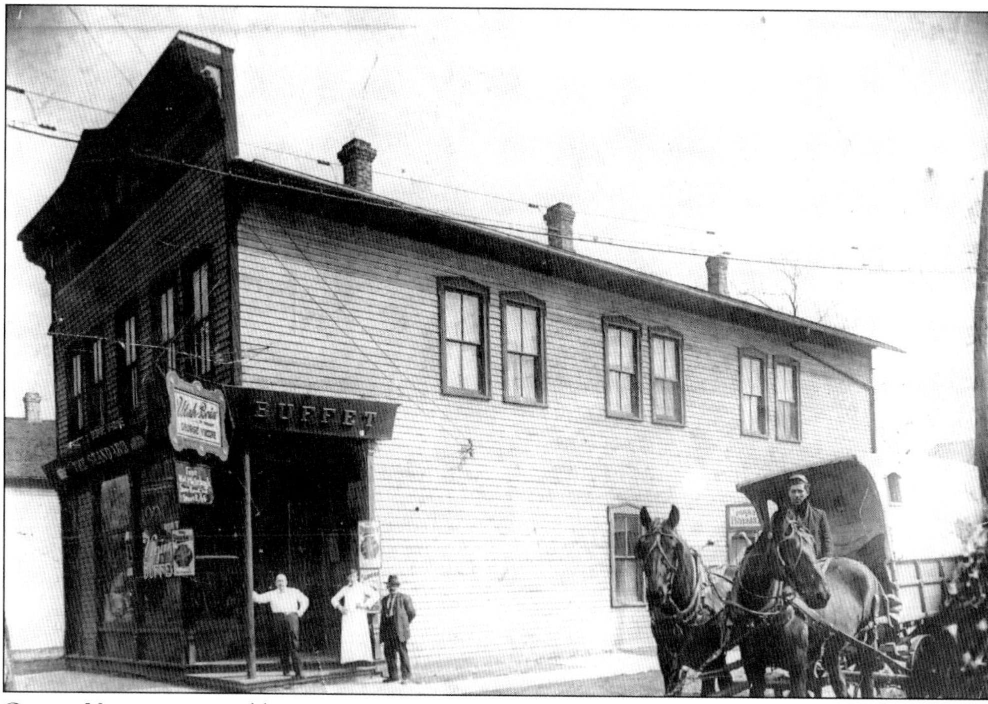

George Virzine operated his tavern and restaurant on the corner of Ogden and Joliet Avenues. His son Tom is standing in front, wearing the apron. The slate sign hanging in front lists sauerkraut and spare ribs on the menu. Frank Savin is driving the ice wagon.

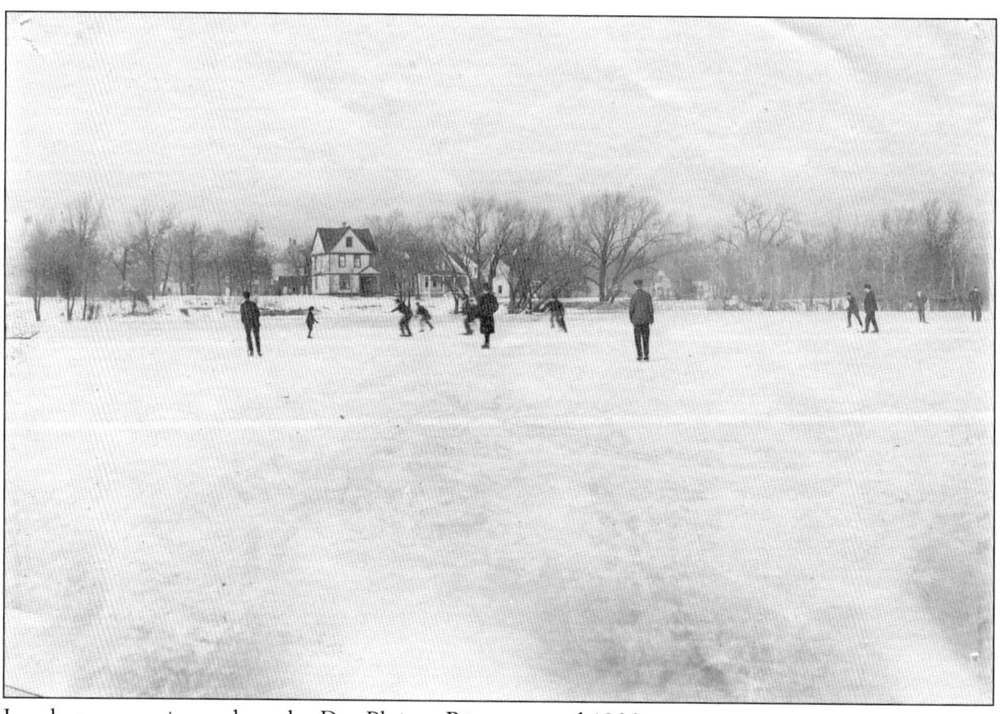

Ice-skaters are pictured on the Des Plaines River around 1900.

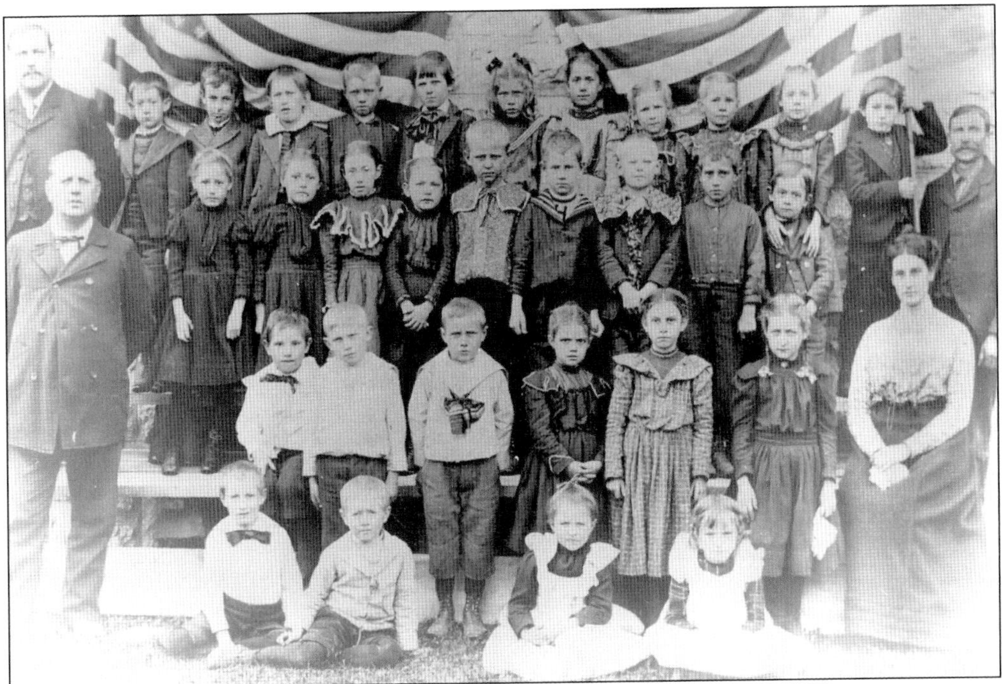

A Washington School class photograph from the late 1800s is seen here. The school building served Lyons students for many decades. After numerous additions to accommodate a growing number of students, a new building was constructed in 1954.

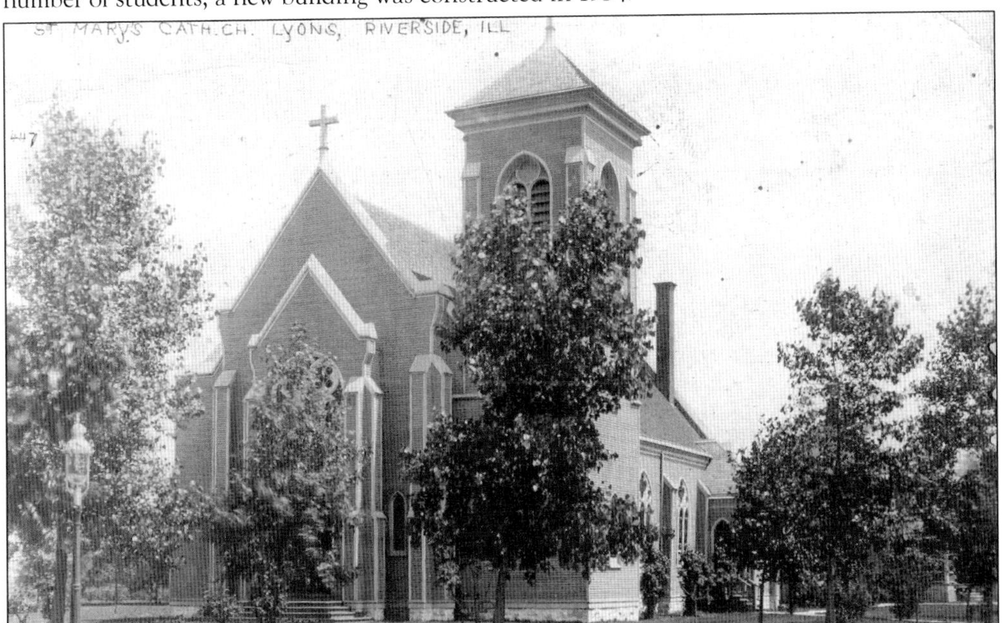

The first Catholic church in Lyons was St. Mary's, located at the corner of Forty-fifth Street and Joliet Road on a site donated by Dr. George Fox. As the congregation grew, a larger church, shown here, was built in 1901, near the Burlington Railroad tracks in Riverside; its first mass was held on December 8, 1901. Lyons would be without its own Catholic church until 1926, when St. Hugh's opened.

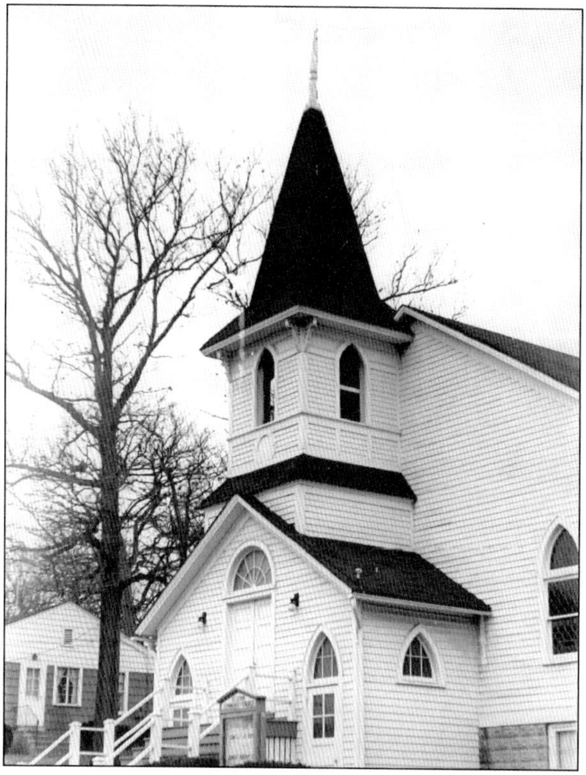

A German Evangelical congregation purchased the building after the congregation moved to Riverside, and moved it in 1903 to its present location at the corner of Prescott and White Avenues. In 1960, it became the Lyons Evangelical Free Church.

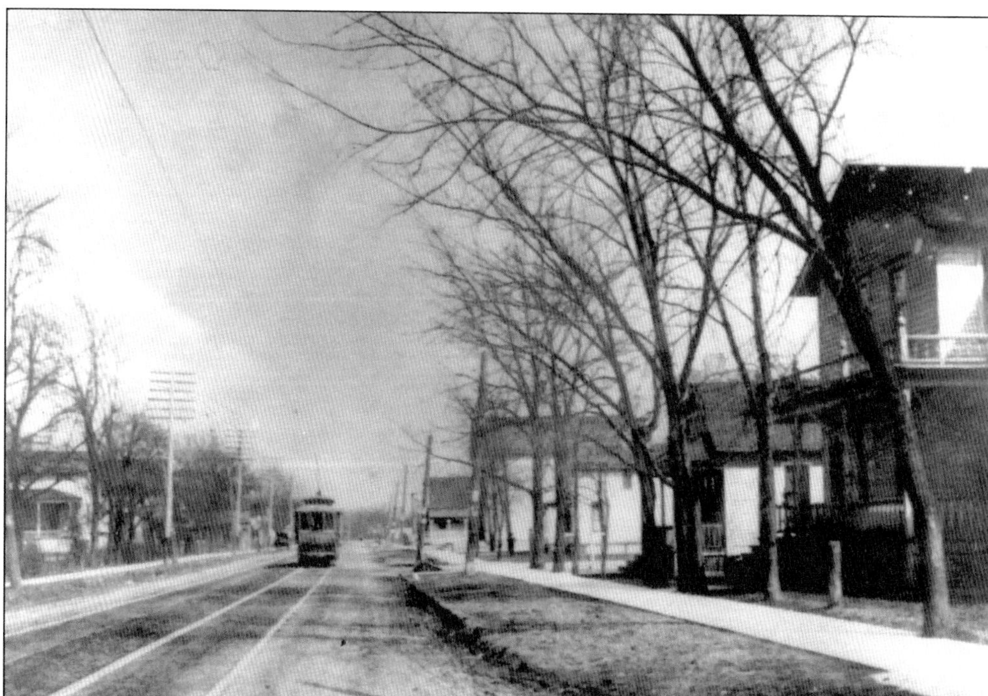

This photograph was taken from the corner of Center and Ogden Avenues, looking east, shortly after streetcar lines were finished in 1896.

Two

The Hofmann Tower and Other Diversions

The Hofmann Tower, built in 1908 by George Hofmann Jr., is Lyons's defining structure—and to this day a key location for civic events. But despite the long shadow it has over the town, surprisingly little is known about the building, or the man who commissioned it. It may or may not have been inspired by the bridge towers of the Hofmann family's native Germany; it may or may not have been able to generate its own electricity; it may or may not have been a tribute to Hofmann's wife, Della Hofmann (née Castle), who died in 1902.

It is clear that Hofmann was an ambitious man who made his mark on Lyons just as it was booming. He was one of three brothers, including Alves and Valentine, who operated the family's Chicago brewery in the late 1800s. George's father owned the "triangle property" and the nearby Chateau Des Plaines property, which he came to own in the late 1890s. By the early 1900s, he had clearly begun envisioning using the acreage to host parties and picnics. By the time the tower and Cream City Amusement Park had been built, Lyons had become well known as a town that was open to large parties and lax about enforcement of liquor laws. Though the larger Lyons Township voted to go dry in March 1908, Lyons's 40-some taverns openly flouted the law; the June 8, 1908, edition of the *Chicago Record-Herald* reported that bars were serving "mead," "near-beer," and a "foamy potion which anybody but a Lyons saloon-keeper would suppose really was beer."

Prohibition, enacted on July 1, 1919, shuttered the taverns in Lyons (at least openly) until its repeal in 1933. In his later years, Hofmann worked as an inventor out of his home on Joliet Avenue, filing patents for a "feed attachment for drill presses," a "liquid fuel burner," a "furnace," and a "liquid fuel vaporizer." George Hofmann Jr. died on March 18, 1942.

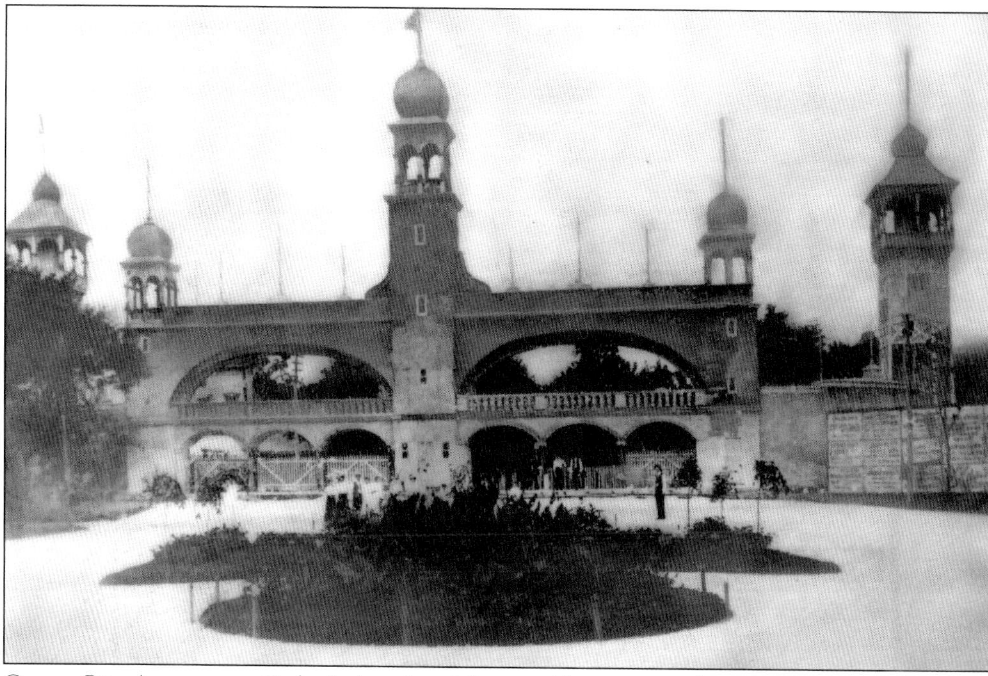

Cream City Amusement Park, designed and financed by a group of investors as a competitor to Chicago's White City, was built in 1905 on property that was previously Fred Schultz's quarry. Its broad entry pavilion was directly across the street from Neher's Tavern, which can been seen through the arch on the left in this photograph.

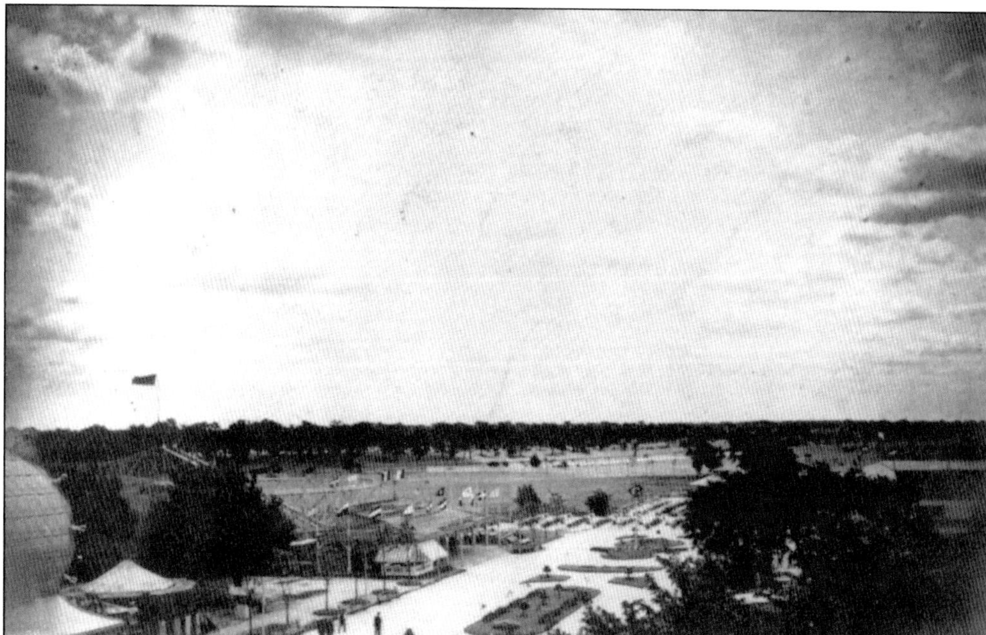

This photograph of Cream City, taken from one of the towers at its entrance on Ogden Avenue, offers a panoramic view of the grounds. Its roller coaster is at left; the park also boasted a lagoon and a dance pavilion where live bands performed on weekends.

Frank Neher Jr. is shown here with his wife Laura Stolbrink, in a photograph taken at Cream City.

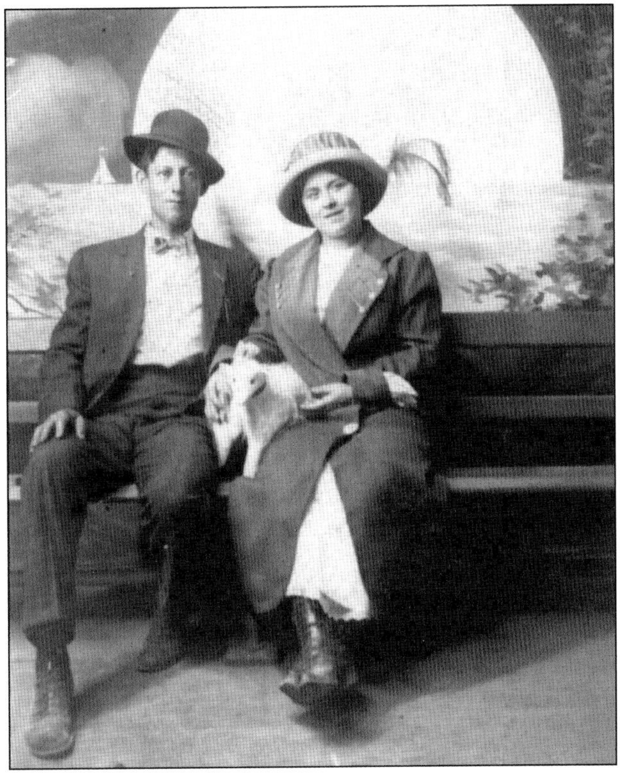

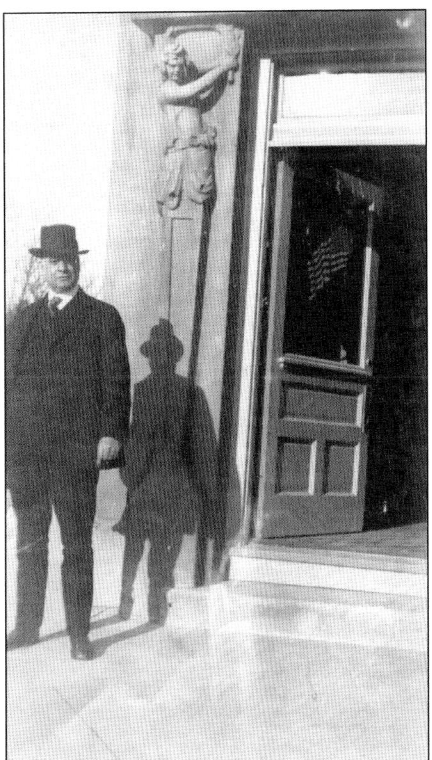

This undated photograph shows George Hofmann Jr. at the site of his property on the banks of the Des Plaines River. By the time the tower was built, his father and two brothers, Alves and Valentine, had passed away, leaving him to run the brewery business on his own. His wife, Della Hofmann (née Castle), died in a carriage accident in 1902. He lived at 3911 Joliet Avenue until his death.

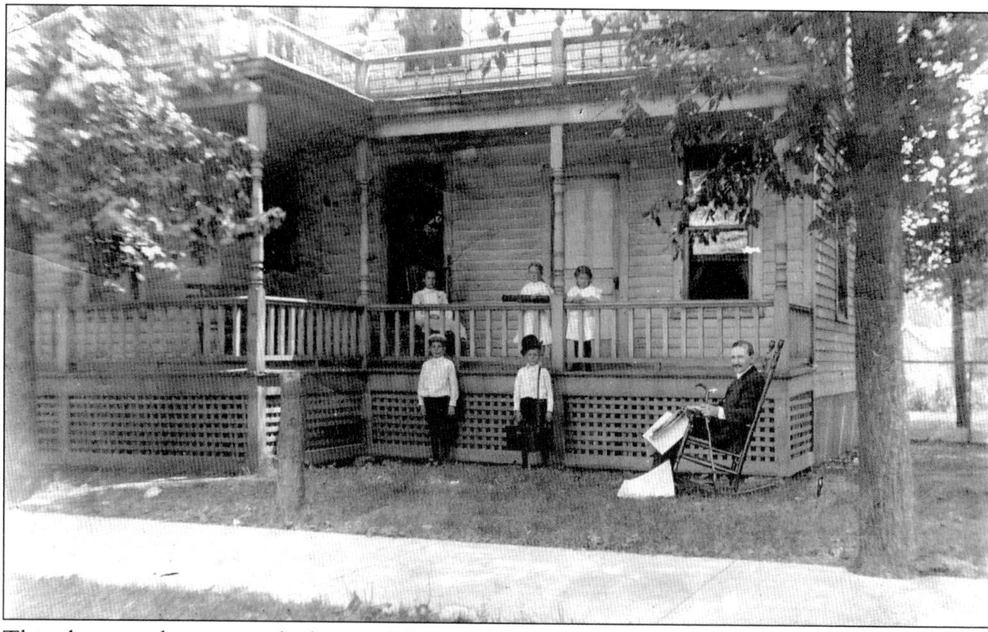

This photograph captures the home of the Smith family, at 7833 Ogden Avenue, in 1901. Charles H. Smith, mayor of Lyons from 1903 to 1911, is sitting in the rocking chair. During his tenure the town would modernize its fire department and sewer system and see the construction of both the Hofmann Tower and Cream City Amusement Park. Smith's nephew William G. Smith would be elected mayor in 1961.

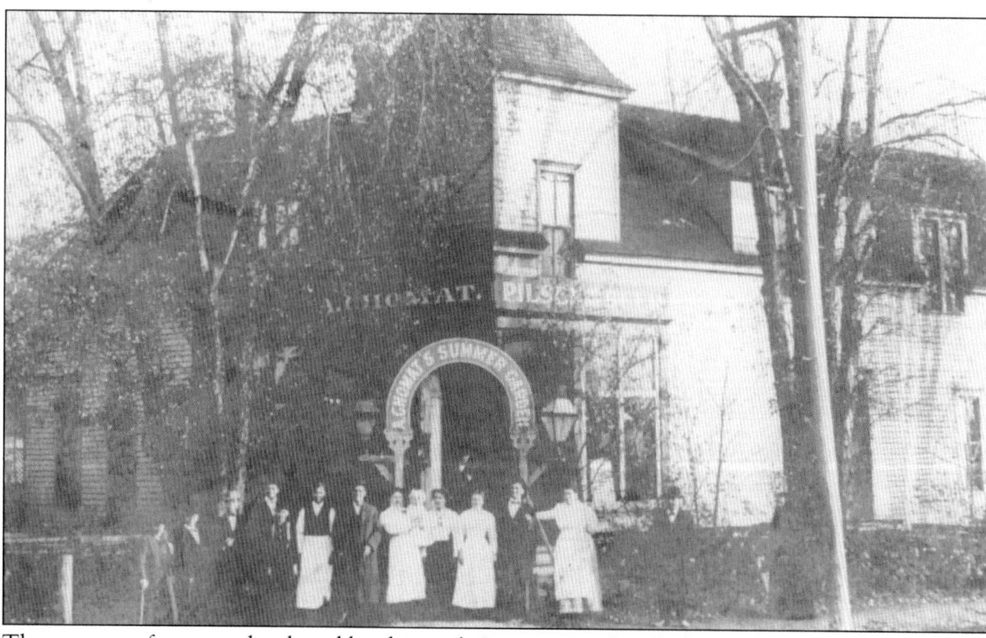

The amount of open undeveloped land in early Lyons, paired with the number of taverns in town, prompted the growth of many picnic groves. Prime spot locations were along the banks of the Des Plaines River, as with the groves owned by the Neher and Hofmann families. But ones that did not boast a river-side location operated as well. A. Chomat's Summer Garden, located at the corner of Ogden and Custer Avenues, opened in the late 1800s, later becoming Zahora's Grove.

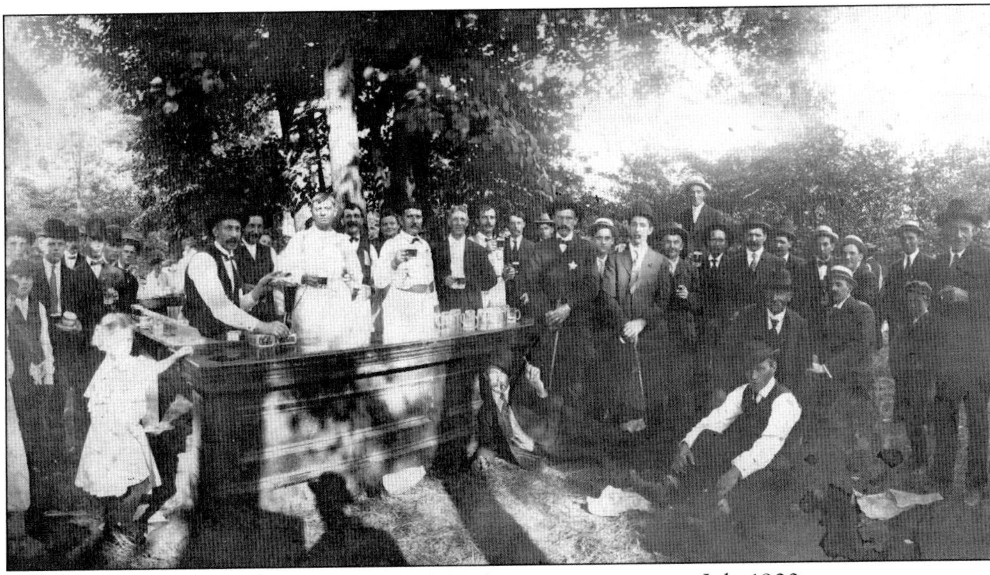

A picnic is held at Neher's Grove, one of the first picnic groves, in July 1900.

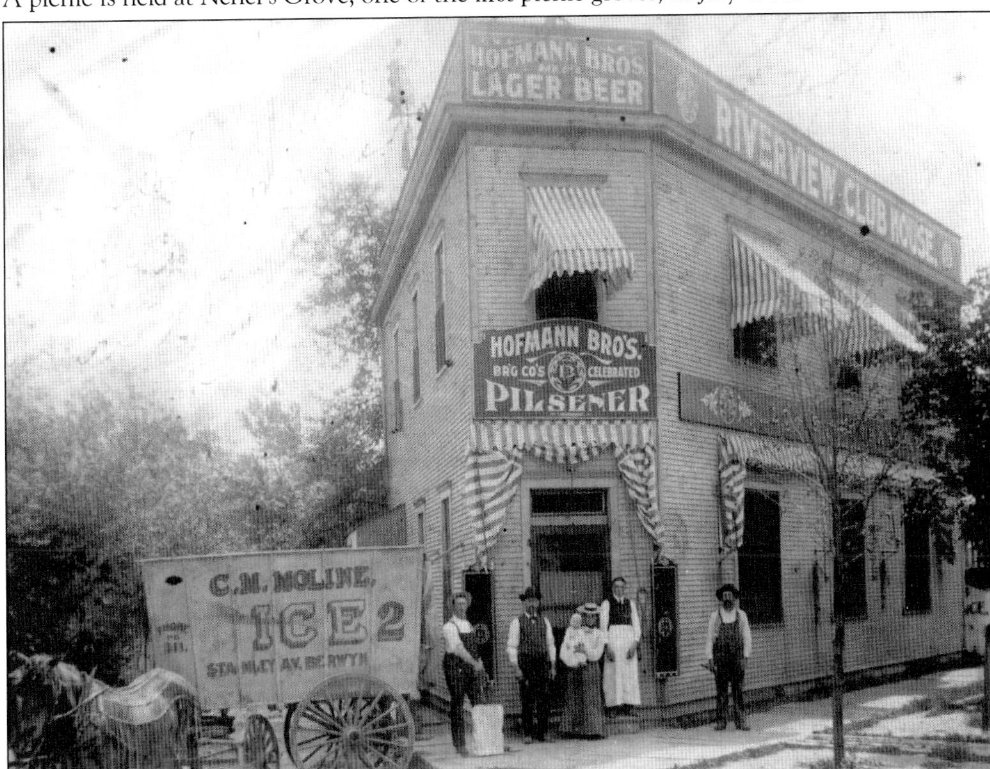

Before it was remodeled to look like the tower, the Riverview Club House was a simple wood-frame affair that housed the offices of the Hofmann Brothers Brewery. The brothers' father, George Hofmann Sr., bought a number of properties in Lyons and Summit during the Civil War, and the corner of Joliet and Ogden Avenues housed a slaughterhouse owned and operated by the Hofmann family. George Jr. sold the brewery business to the Peter Fox Brewing Company in the 1930s, after the repeal of prohibition.

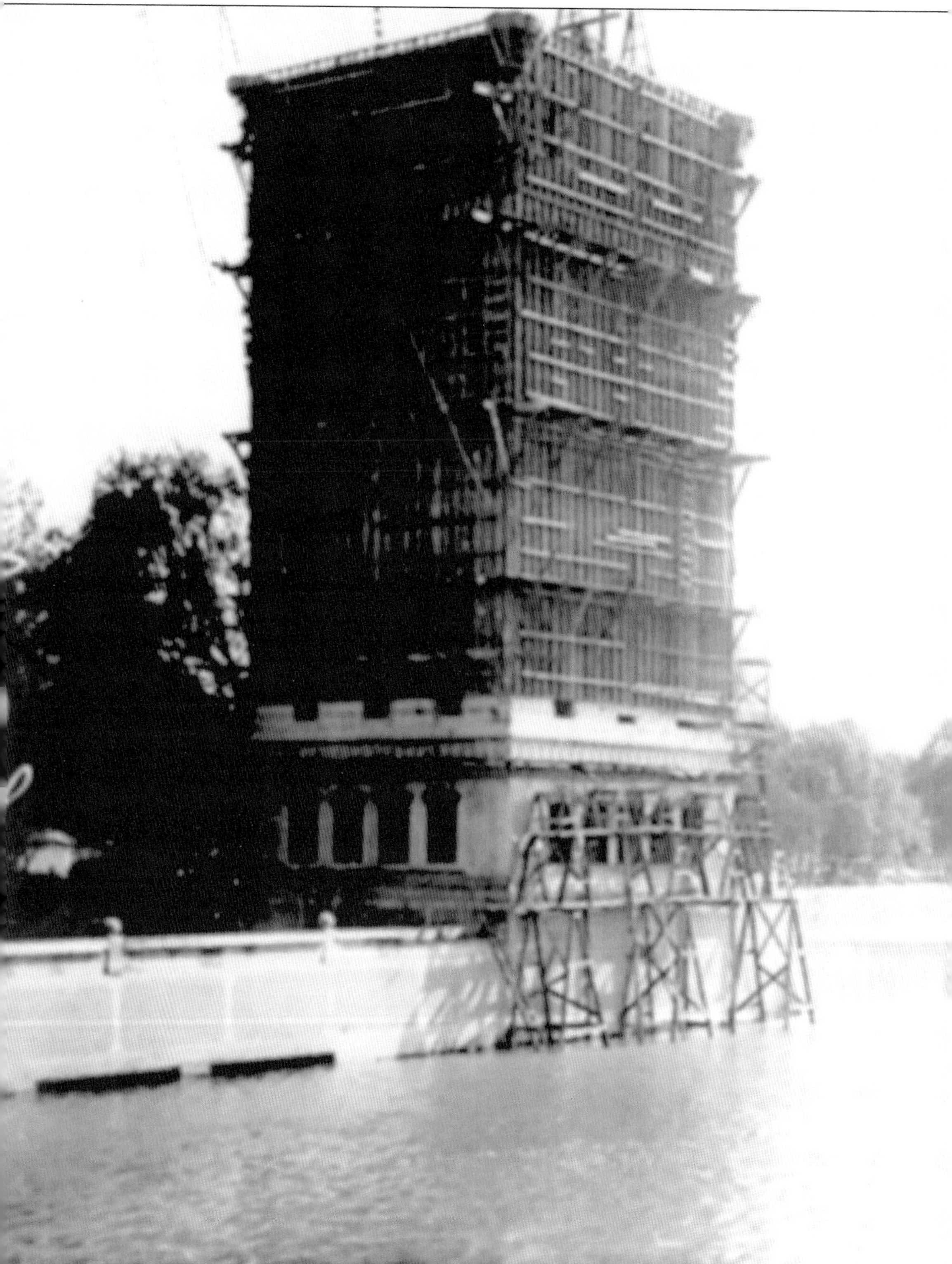

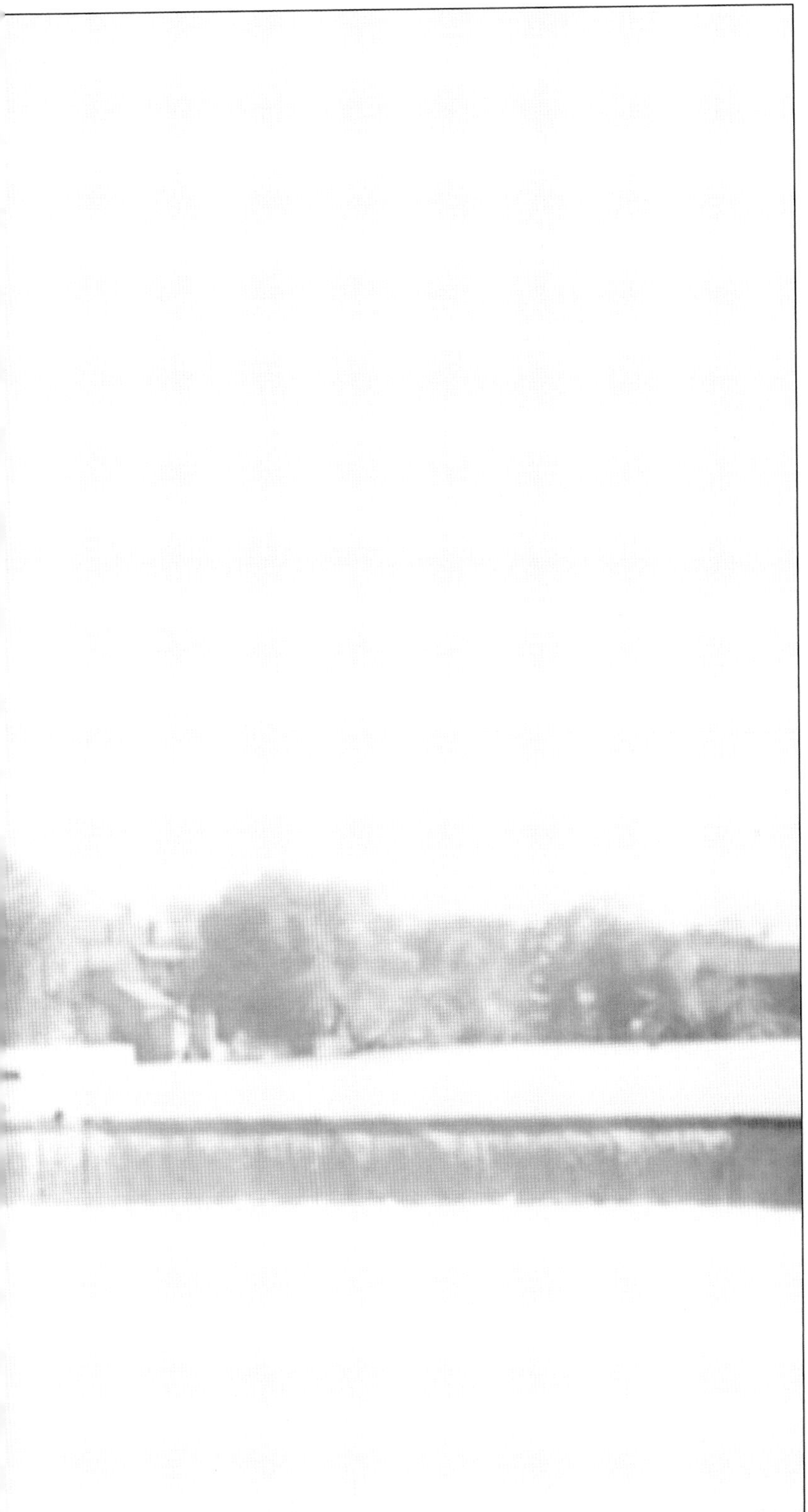

The tower was built in 1908 at a cost of $400,000, using concrete—a more affordable method that Frank Lloyd Wright helped pioneer with Oak Park's Unity Temple, which was finished the same year. The H. W. Sauber Construction Company, based in Lockport, built the tower and also made improvements on the dam. Construction was complete on September 6.

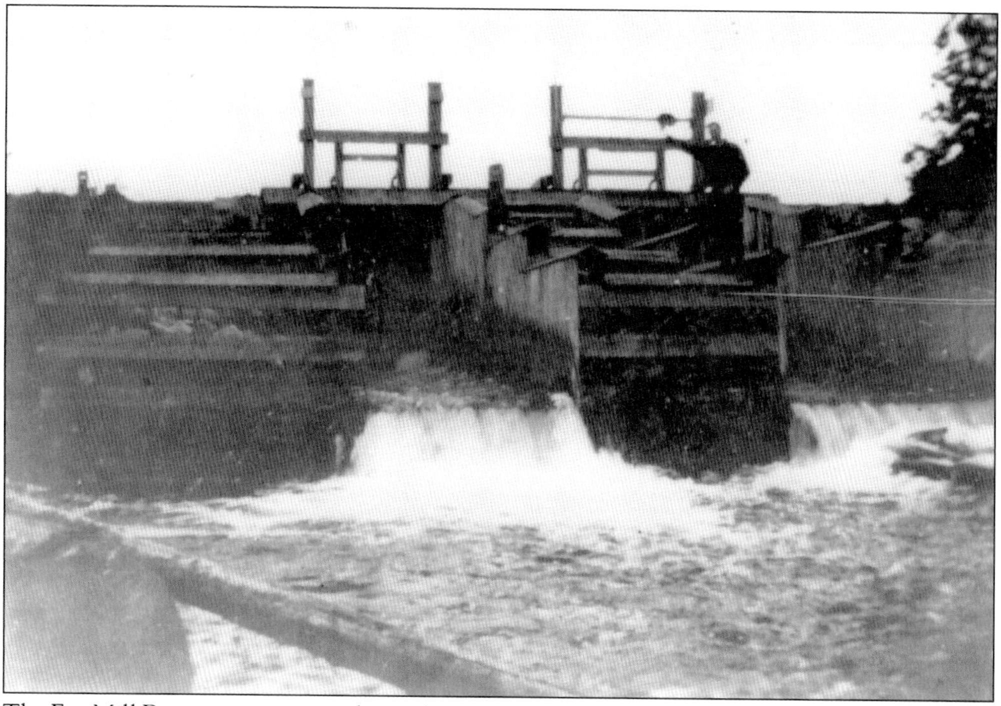

The Fox Mill Dam was constructed out of stone and timber. As the tower was under construction in 1908, Hofmann had the old dam demolished and replaced with a new one built of concrete. This photograph shows the dam under construction.

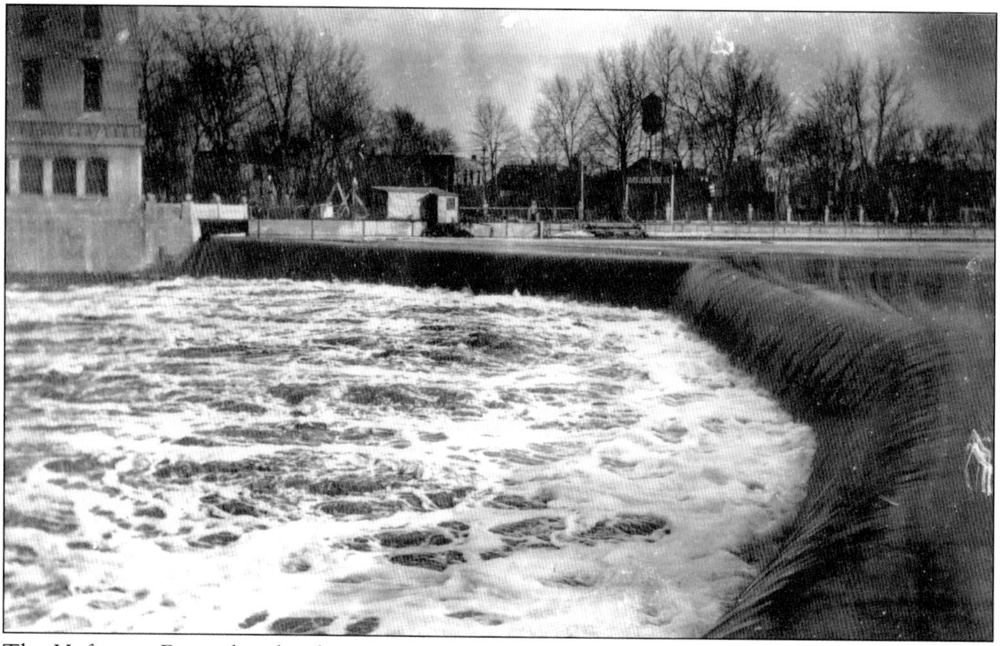

The Hofmann Dam, shortly after its construction, is shown here. It remained there until 1950, when it was replaced with a new concrete wall. Lights around the complex were supposed to be powered by turbines at the base of the tower, but according to Joe Dow, George Hofmann Jr.'s longtime assistant, the dam never generated the necessary amount of electricity.

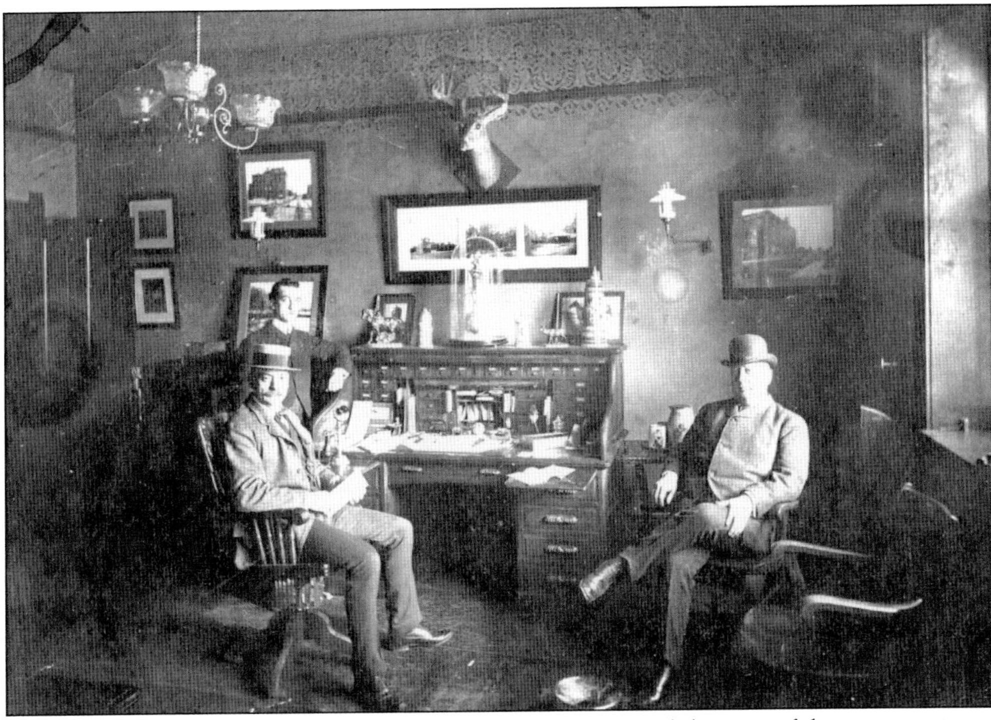

This photograph shows George Hofmann Jr., at far right, around the time of the construction of the tower. The other two men in the photograph are unidentified.

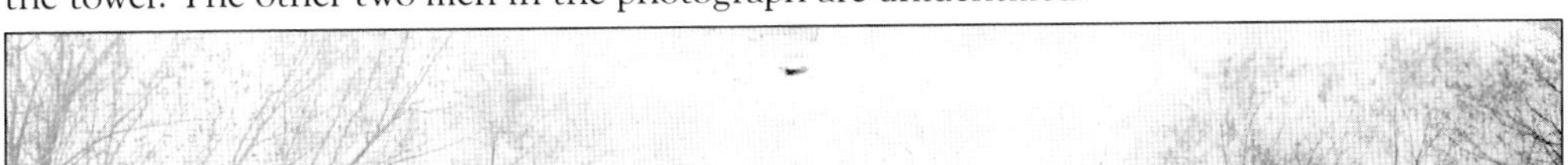

This photograph of the Barrypoint Bridge, then the Old Mill Bridge, going into Riverside, was taken around the time of the construction of the Hofmann Tower; the offices of the H. W. Sauber Construction Company are at the right. The steel-railed bridge was constructed in the late 1800s. Weakened, it was condemned in 1913, and later repaired. It would be replaced with a concrete bridge in 1959.

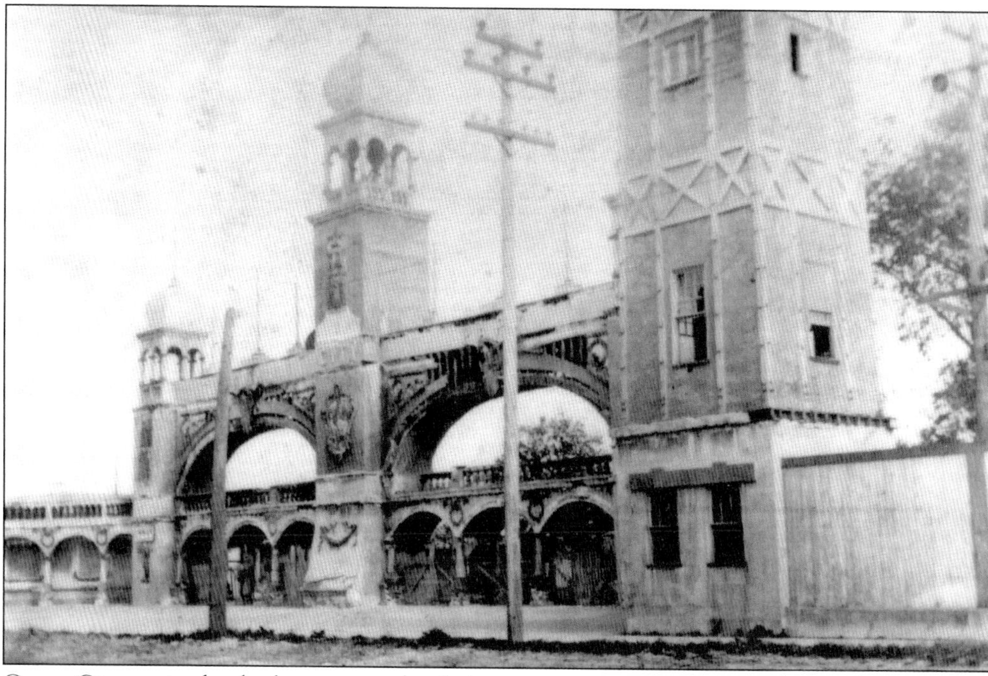

Cream City survived only about a year, thanks in part to intense competition from White City and, it is believed, the beginnings of sewer work on Ogden Avenue that made reaching the park difficult. This photograph shows the front entry gates and towers to the park shortly before demolition.

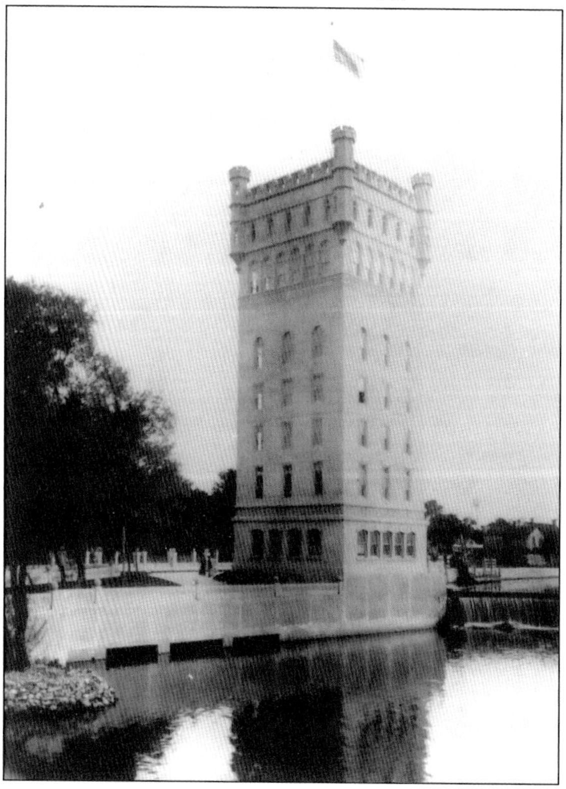

At the time of its construction, the Hofmann Tower was the tallest building west of the Loop. Served by a number of area streetcar lines, the tower offered something of a replacement for the now defunct Cream City, emphasizing its picnic groves, the central Niagra Park on the triangle property, its riverside location, and panoramic views from its roof. This photograph of the tower and Niagra Park shortly after it opened captures the colonnades, with rounded concrete tops, that lined the paths around the area.

George Frimersdorf operated his blacksmith shop in this building, later a garage, on the corner of Ogden and Gage Avenues next to Cream City. The Lyons Villiage Hall was built during his tenure as mayor; it is rumored that he successfully lobbied for the building's location in order to be near his place of business.

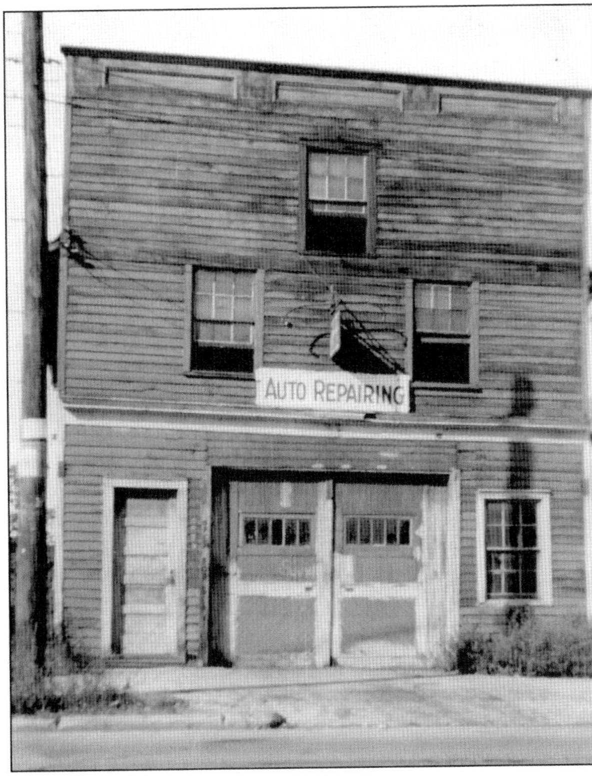

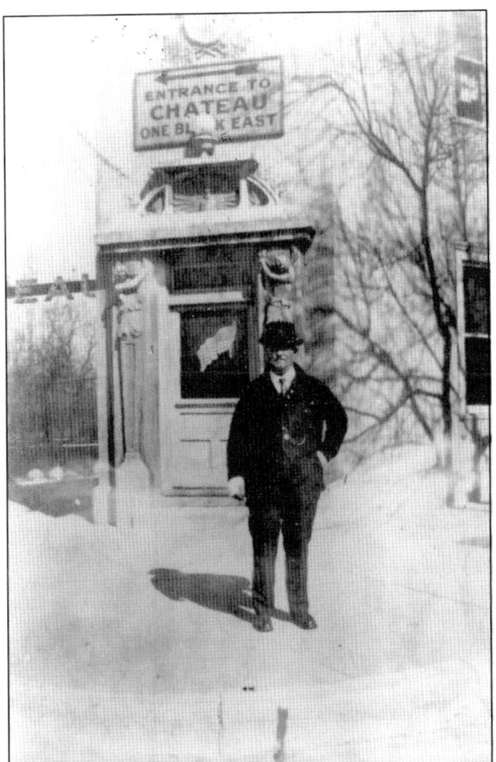

Joe Dow was a foreman for H. W. Sauber Construction Company when he met Hofmann. He stands in front of an entrance to Chateau Des Plaines, a resort built in the 1890s on property owned by Valentine Hofmann, George Hofmann Jr.'s uncle. The property included three connected buildings including a hotel, tavern, and picnic grove, occupying 40 acres of land running alongside the Des Plaines River. George Hofmann Jr. later inherited the property, which eventually became Mangam's Chateau.

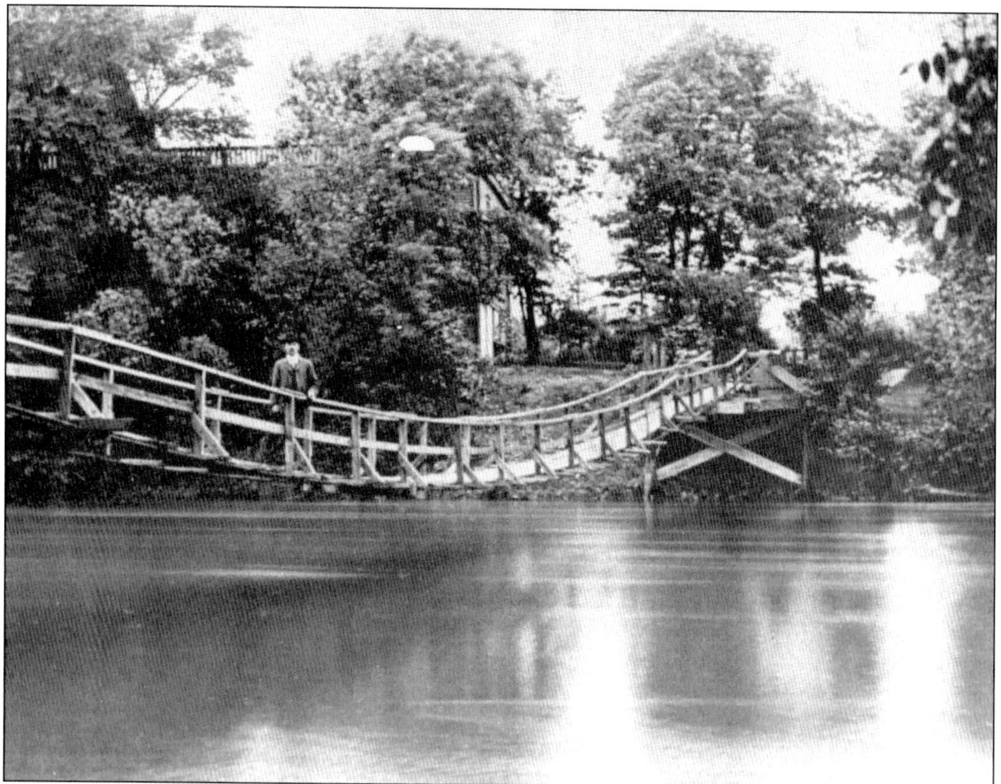

The "swinging bridge" connecting Lyons and Riverside was constructed around 1910 as part of the larger construction of Riverside, the planned community to the north designed by Frederick Law Olmstead; a Riverside hotel can be seen in the background. It was replaced with the current bridge in 1948.

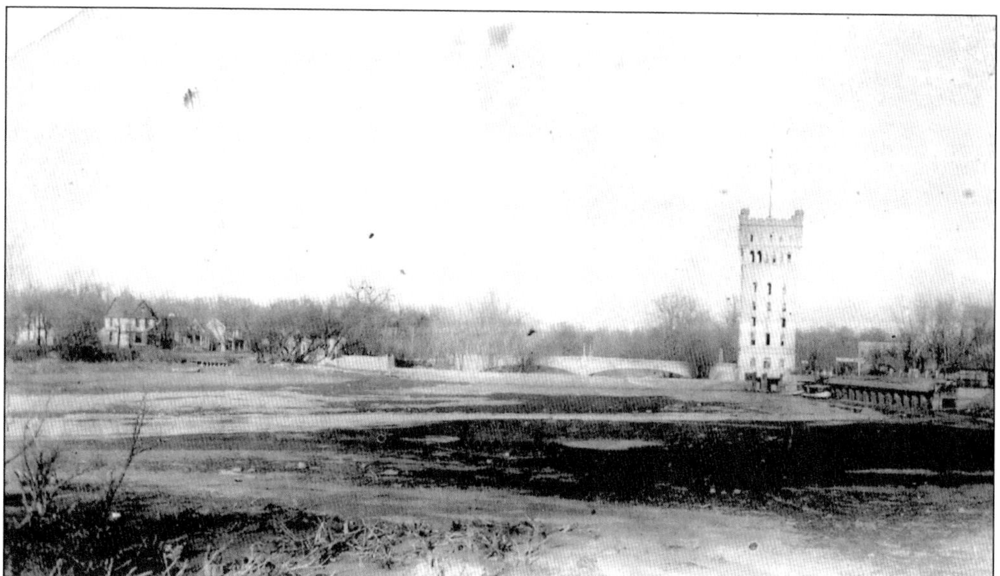

This snapshot looking north up the Des Plaines River captures the breadth of the area Hofmann used for boat rides near the tower. The boat launch is at right.

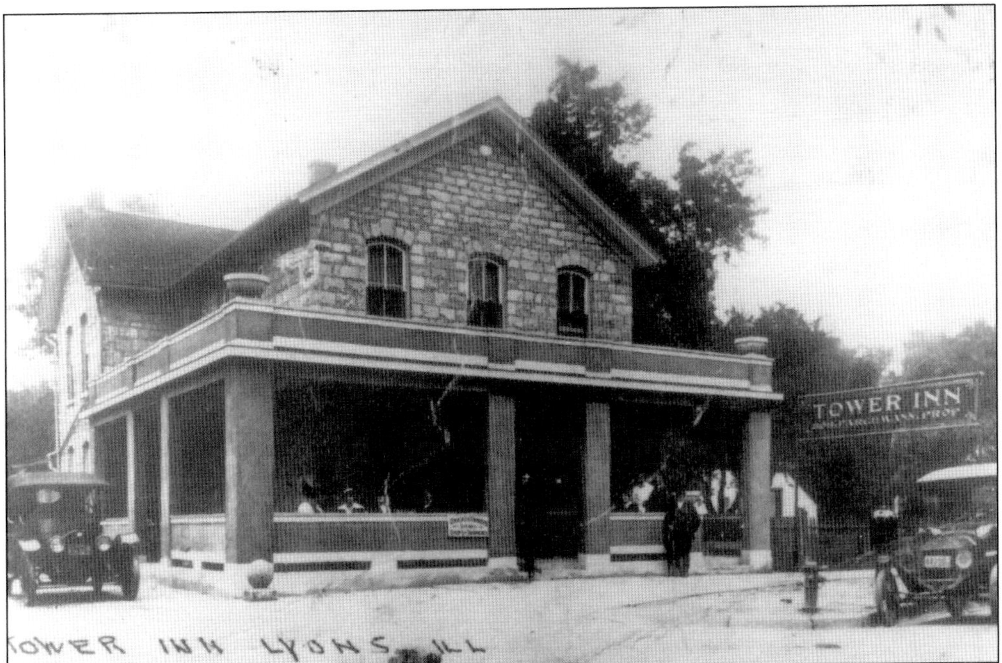

Built from bricks from the Fox Mill, the Tower Inn was opened in 1910 by Robert Parchmann on property owned by Hofmann just south of his offices. Parchmann served as Lyons's mayor from 1915 to 1919; in 1937 Frank and Helen Mangam would come to run the Tower Inn and then their own Mangam's Chateau on the former Chateau Des Plaines site.

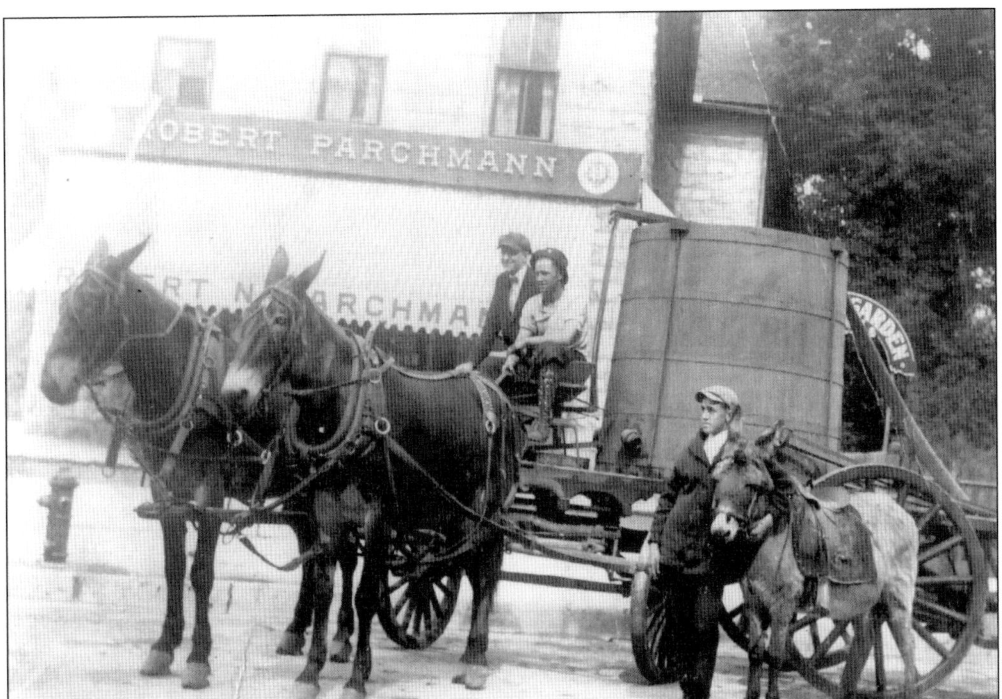

A water wagon, stationed in front of the entrance to Parchmann's beer garden at the Tower Inn.

The boathouse that was built alongside the Hofmann Tower is to the right of this picture from 1910. The river was the key attraction to the tower, as an item in the July 17, 1909, edition of the *Lyons Herald* explains: "All motor boats, launches, and canoes are invited to decorate their respective crafts with Japanese lanterns. . . . Music and singing no doubt will be in abundance, as

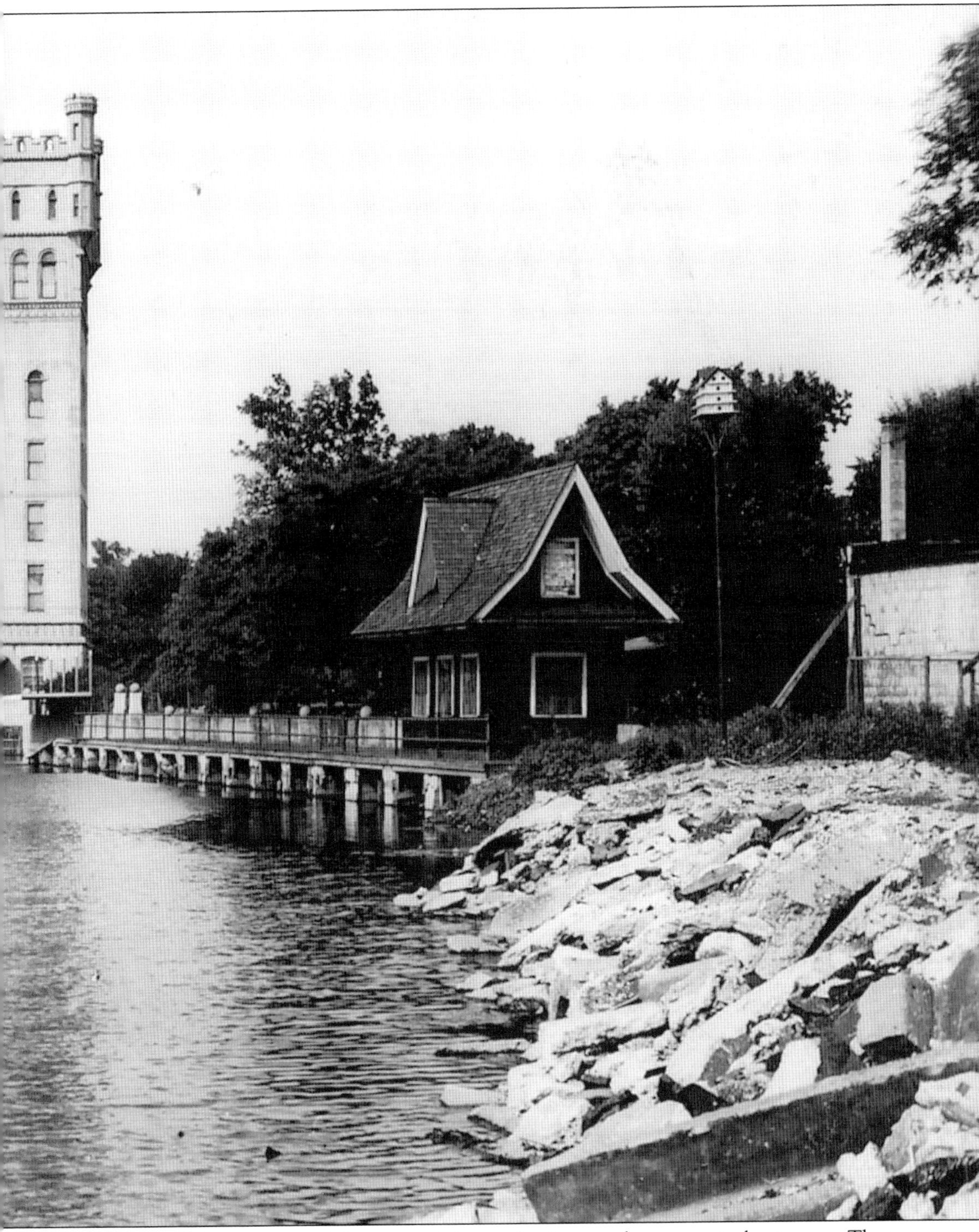

a great many of the young people have mandolins and guitars, and some musical voices. . . . There are some spots along the Des Plaines that equal in beauty anything in the Alps or any scenic river in the world."

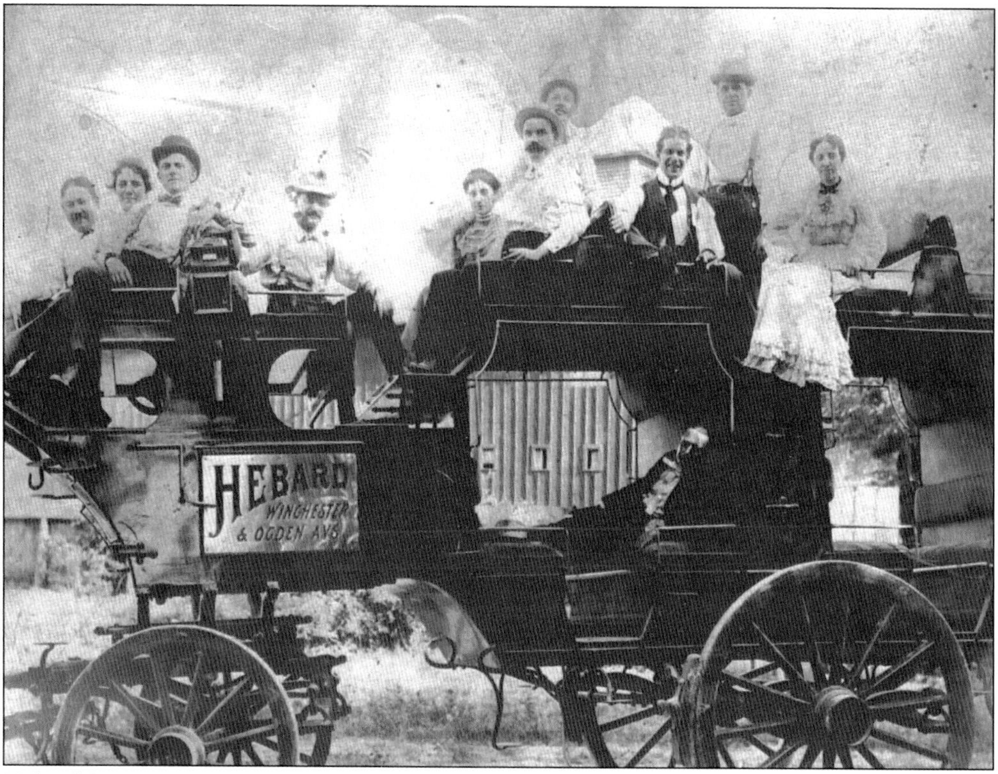

Hebard Spencer, an area resident, owned a "tally-ho" carriage that transported revelers to events in Lyons. The sponsor of the event, usually a tavern, rented the carriage.

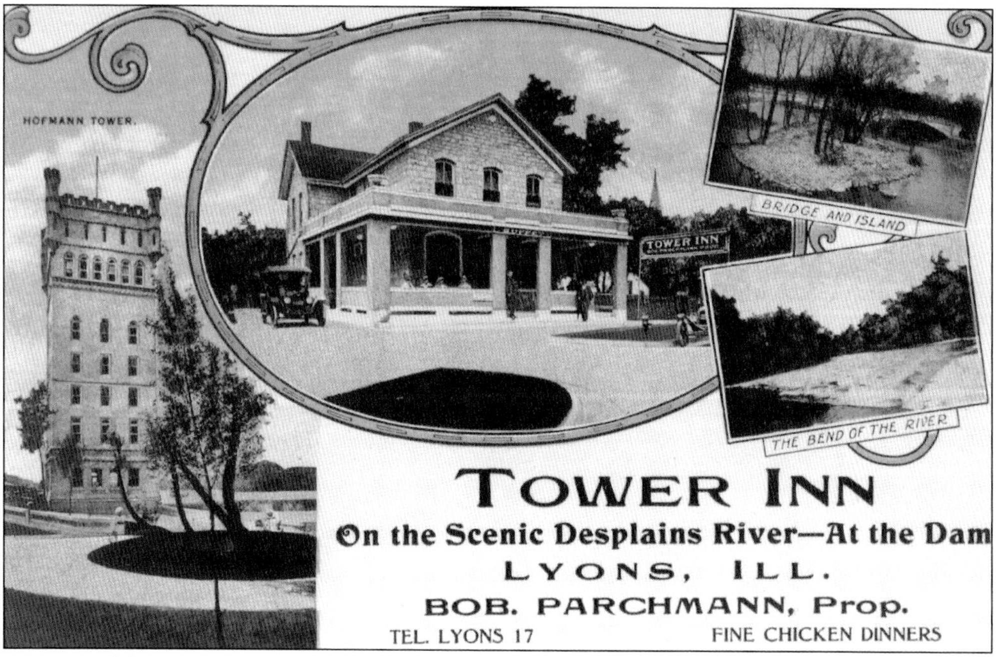

A postcard from the Tower Inn promoted the site's various amenities, including the tower and the river views from the beer garden.

An unidentified group enjoys a winter stroll past the tower and its boat landings.

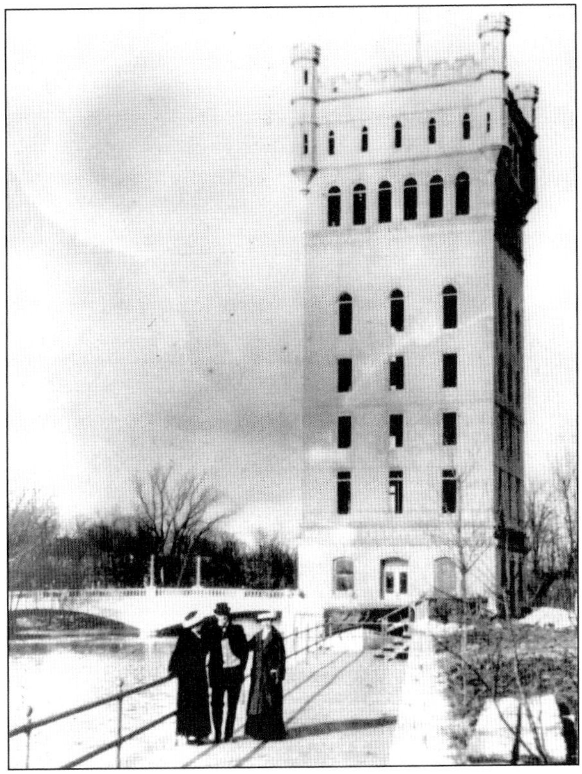

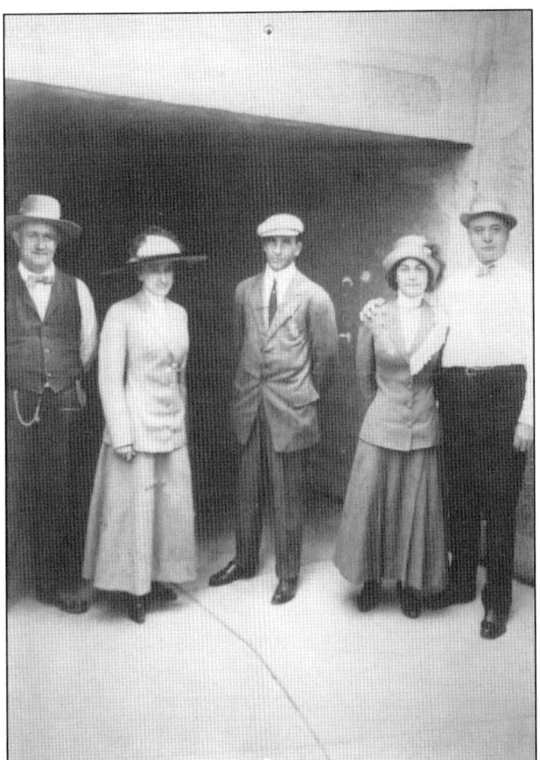

An underground passageway ran beneath Thirty-ninth Street, allowing patrons of the tower to reach it while avoiding streetcars. George Hofmann Jr. is shown here at the far right in this photograph; his caretaker, Joe Dow, is at the far left.

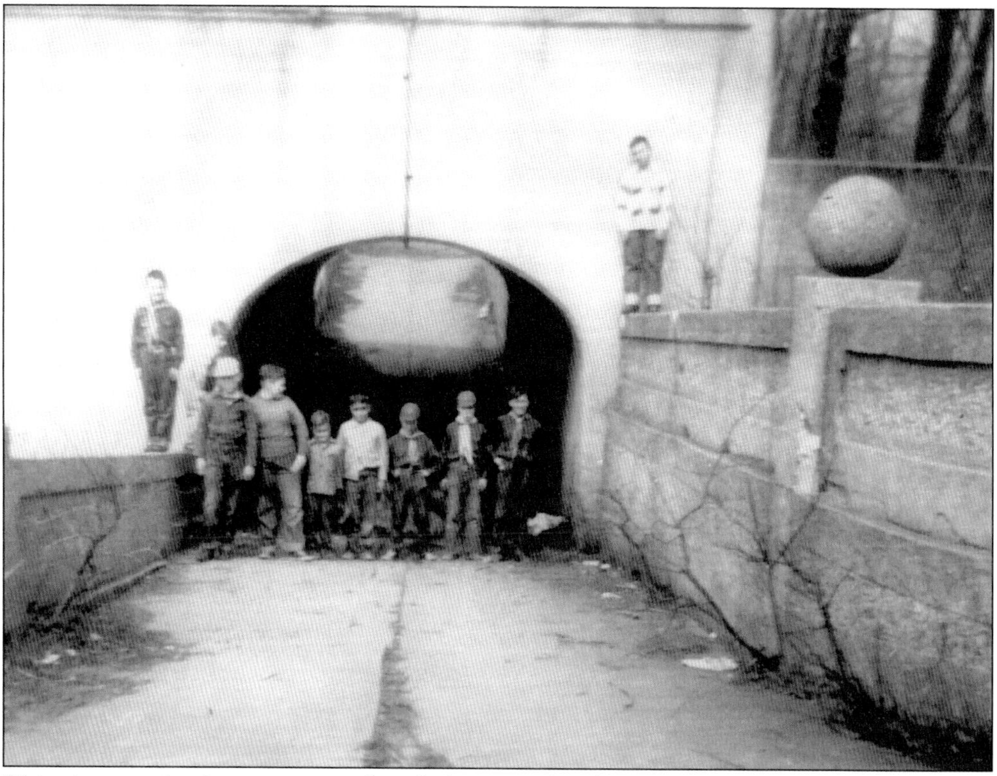

This photograph, showing an unidentified group of Cub Scouts, offers a clearer view of the underground passageway. It was sealed shut in the 1970s.

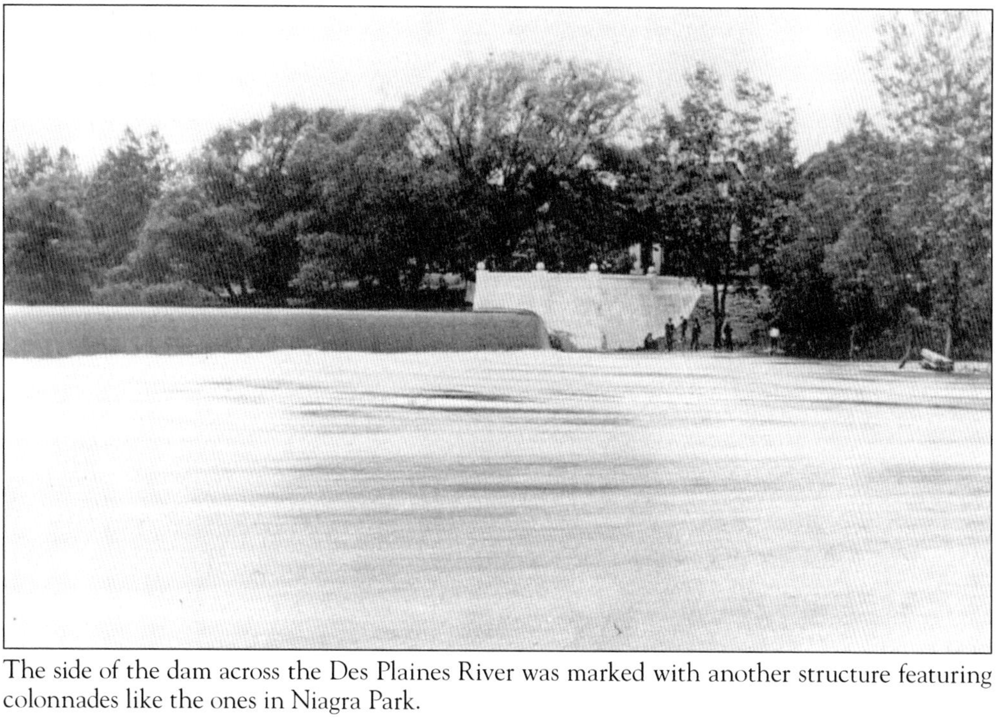

The side of the dam across the Des Plaines River was marked with another structure featuring colonnades like the ones in Niagra Park.

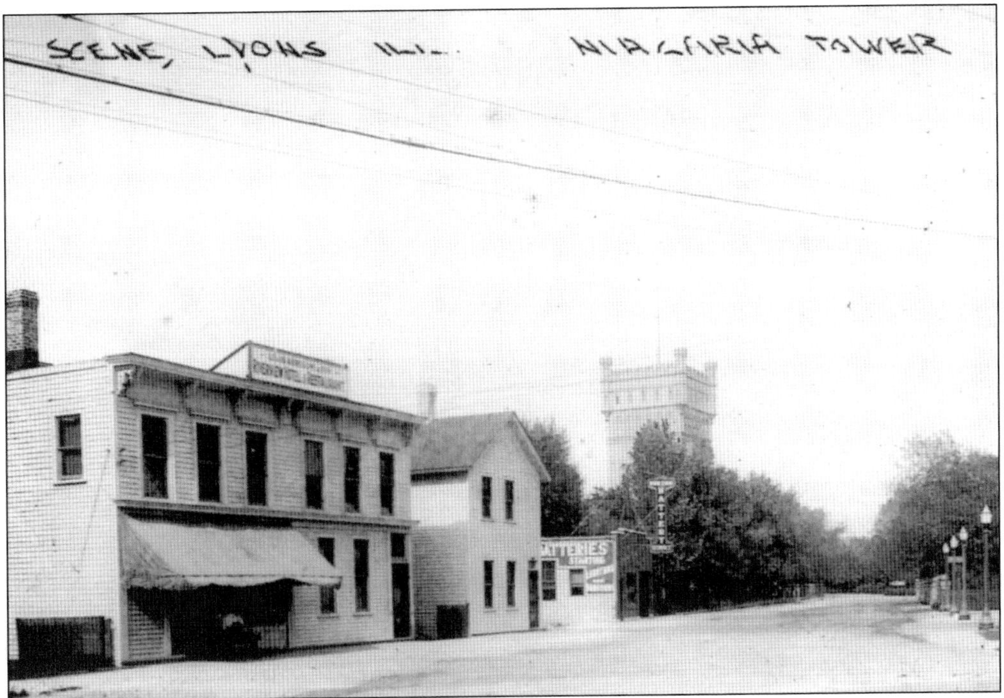

The serene wooded pathway leading north up to the tower was flanked by Hofmann's triangle property at right and the Riverview Hotel and Restaurant, operated by Louis Arrigoni, at left.

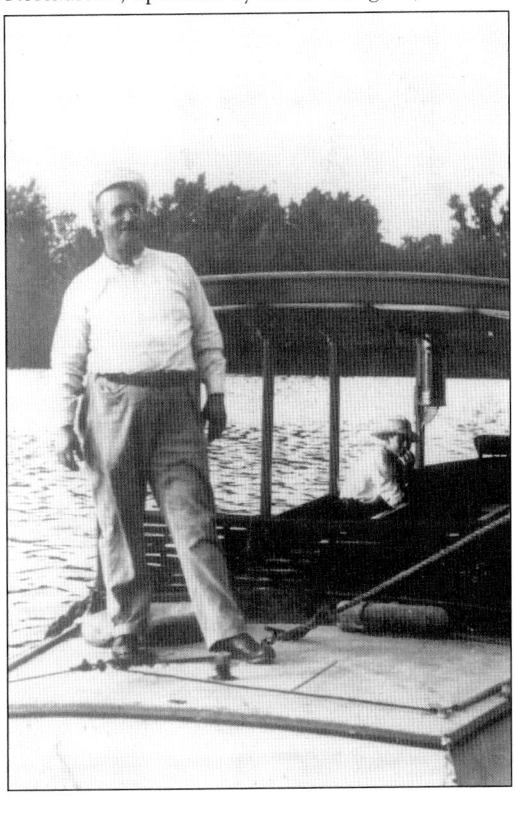

Two canopied boats offered trips up the river to Forest Avenue. One was named *Niagra*, the other *Al Hofmann*, after George Jr.'s brother. Joe Dow is shown here standing on the stern of one of them.

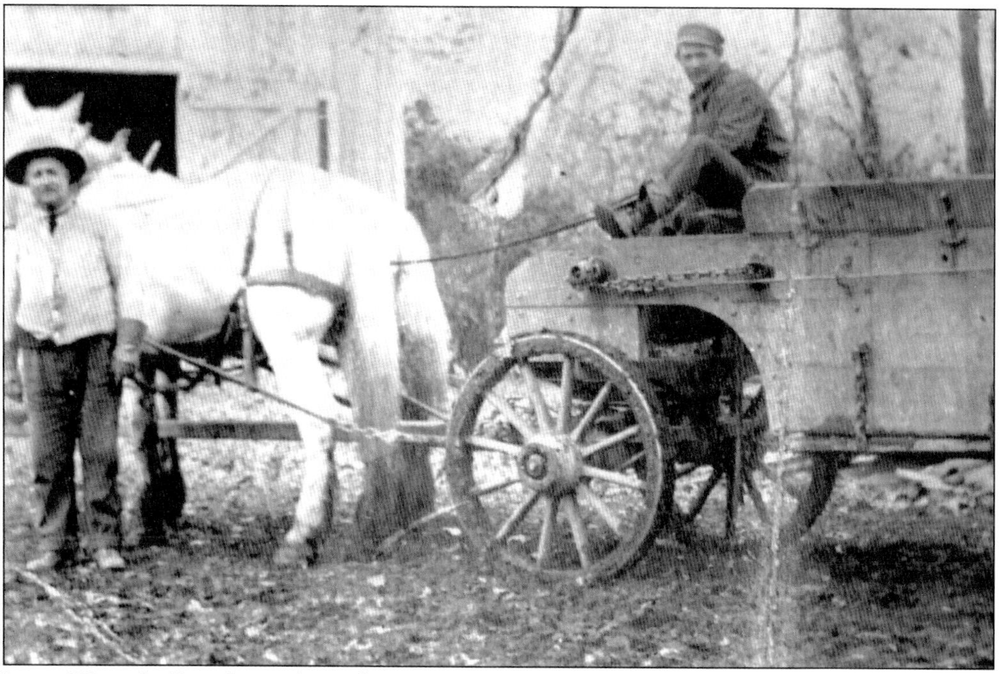

Louis Westerhoff is shown here driving a Lyons garbage wagon near the Tower Inn in the early 1900s.

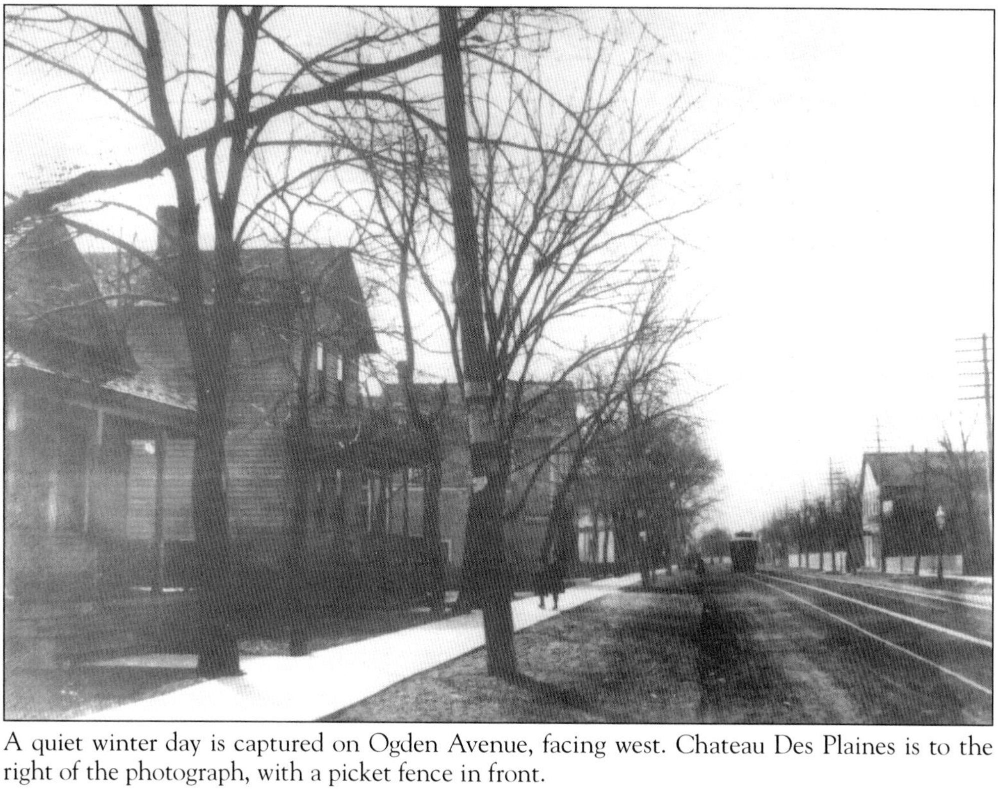

A quiet winter day is captured on Ogden Avenue, facing west. Chateau Des Plaines is to the right of the photograph, with a picket fence in front.

Although George Hofmann Jr. primarily owned property within Lyons, he continued to run a brewery in the city. The reverse of this postcard depicting the towers lists an address for the "Wm. G Hofmann Pub" at 4340 Jackson Street. The Hofmann Brothers Brewery operated at 2606 West Monroe Street until 1925.

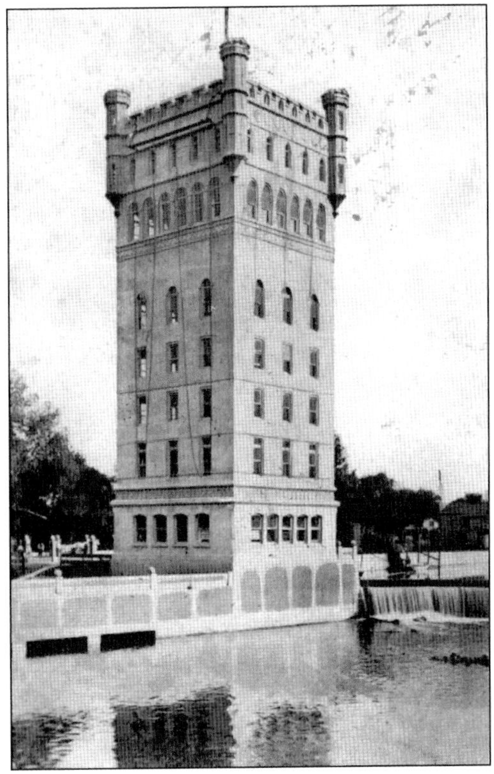

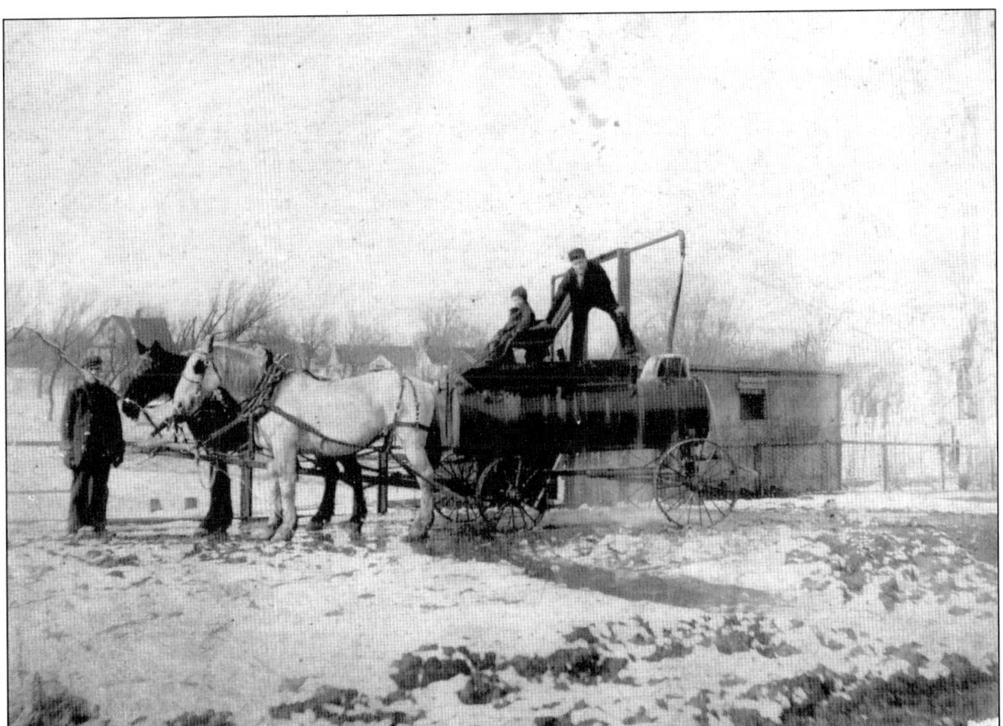

A water wagon is pictured in front of the Hofmann tower boat house, around 1915.

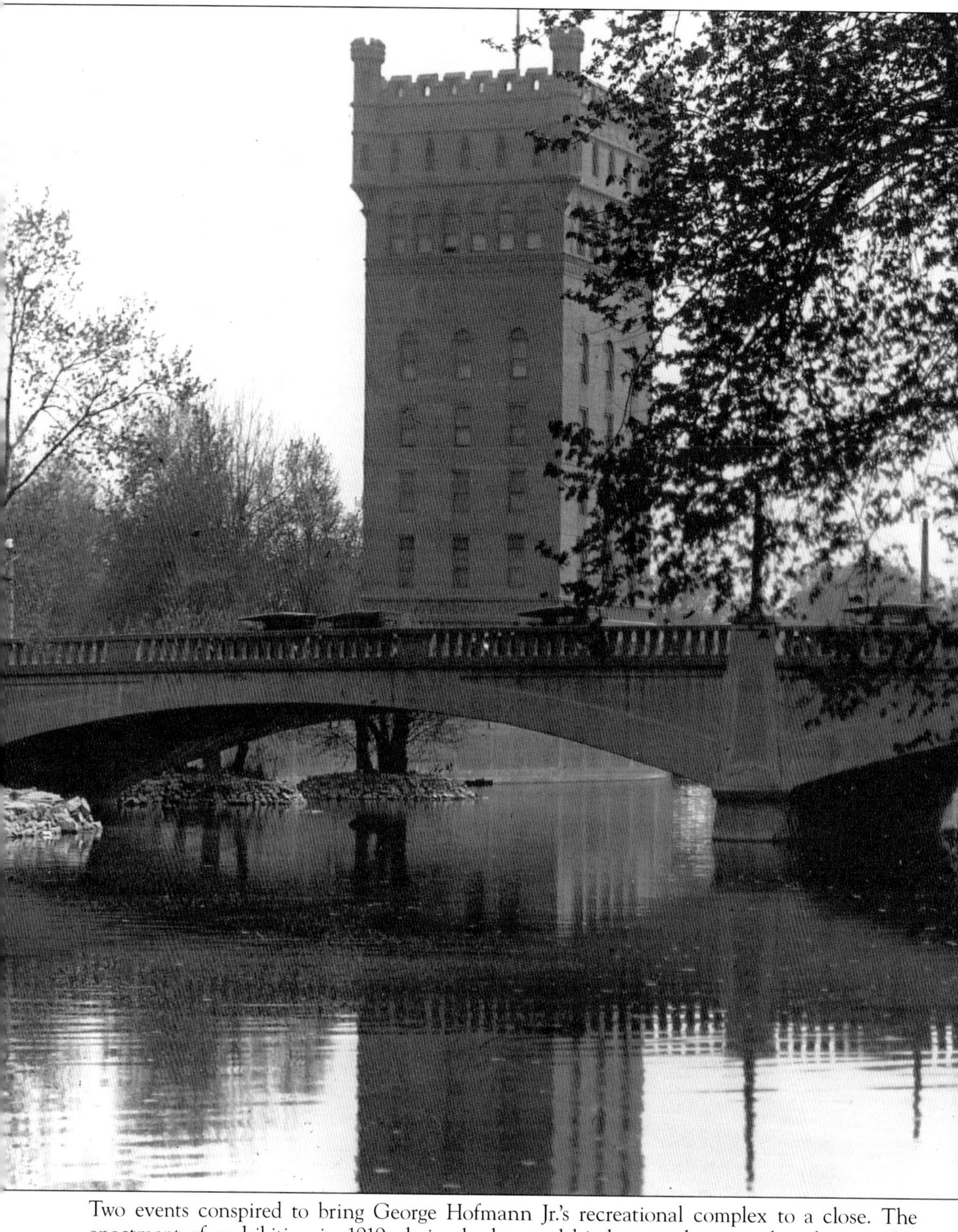

Two events conspired to bring George Hofmann Jr.'s recreational complex to a close. The enactment of prohibition in 1919 obviously damaged his brewery business, but the site also suffered from increased dumping of raw sewage into the Des Plaines River. Hofmann, in an effort to keep the area near the tower clean and open for boating and recreation, refused requests

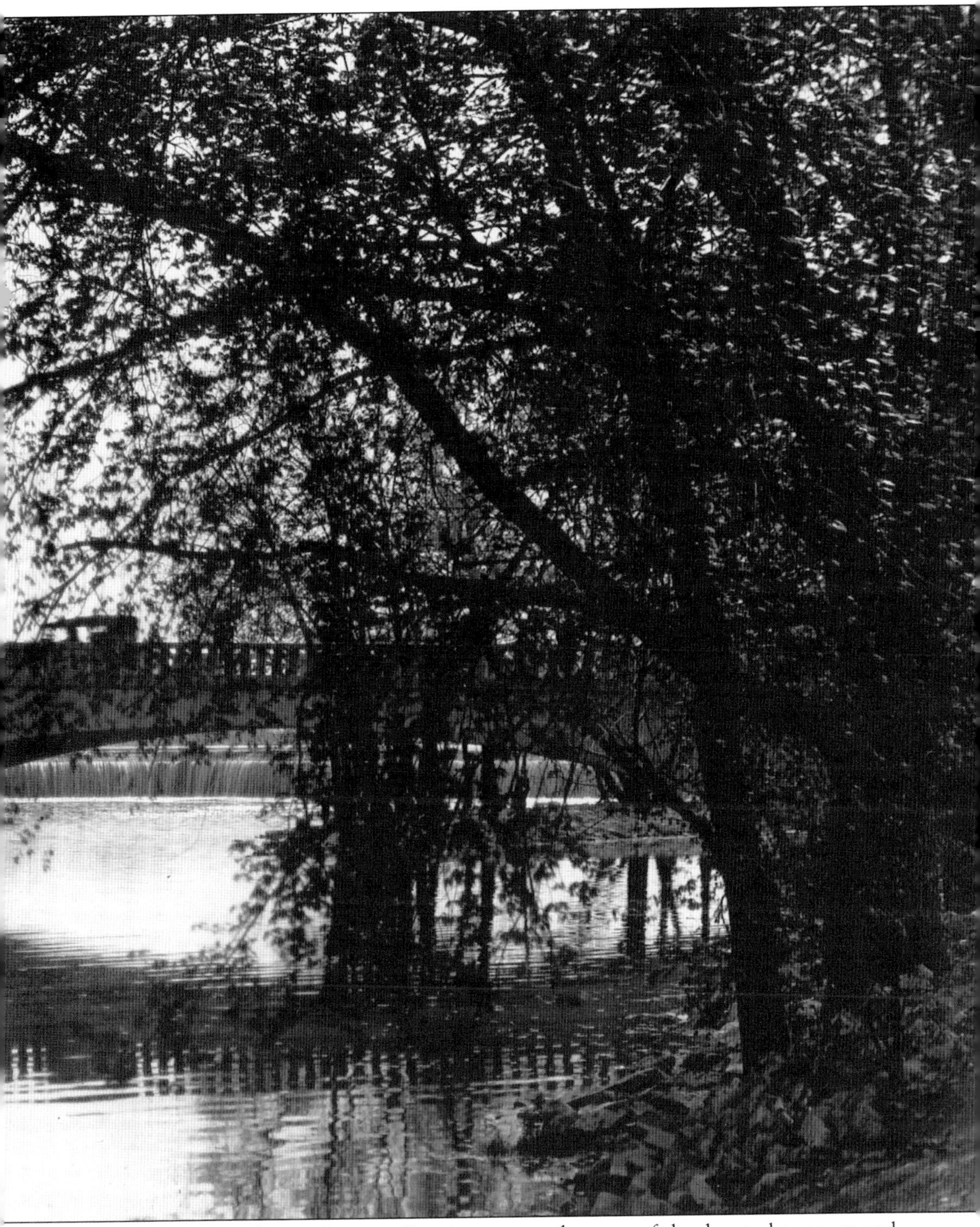

by residents and the Chicago Sanitary District to open the gates of the dam to let sewage and sludge pass through. Amid the tussling about who owned the rights to the dam, fewer and fewer patrons attended the park, and the Chicago Sanitary District sidestepped Hofmann by building a sewage bypass in 1928. This photograph shows the tower area after its closure.

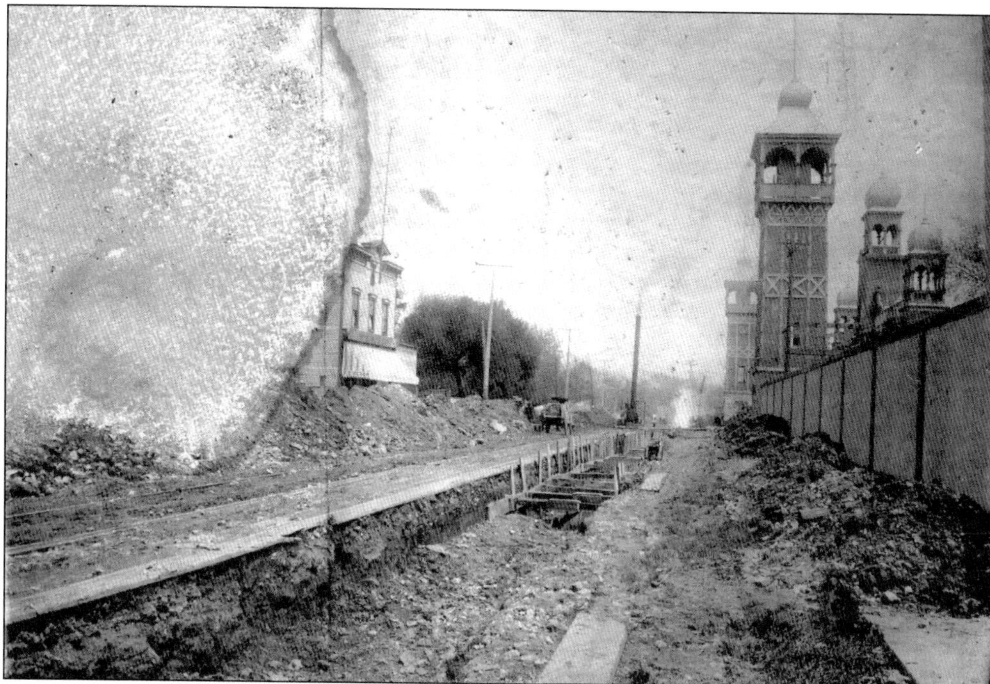

This photograph from 1908, despite its water damage, clearly shows the process of sewer installation in Lyons. Neher's Tavern is on the left; the shuttered Cream City Amusement Park is on the right.

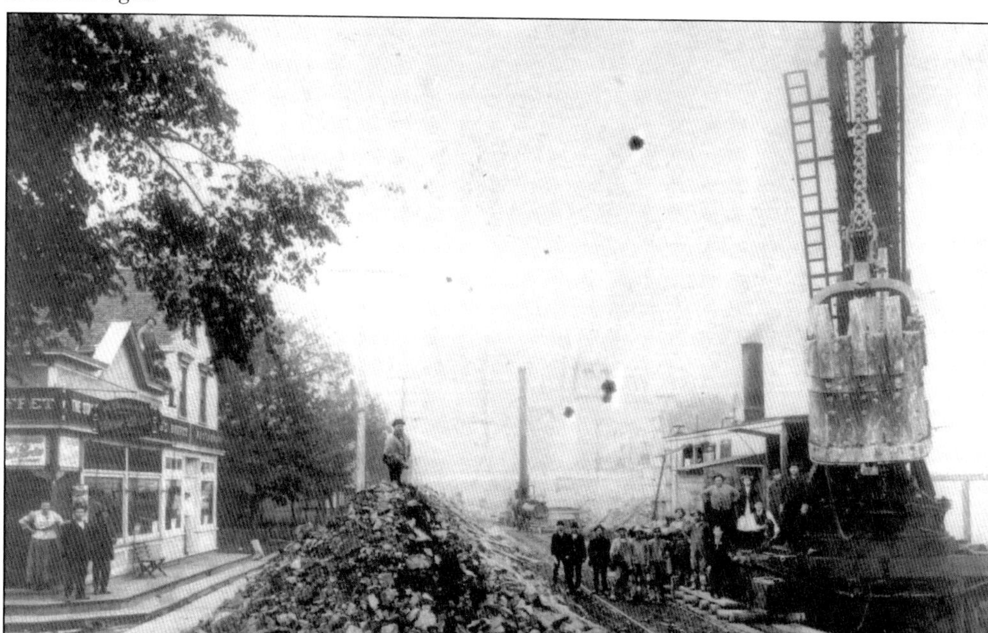

Workmen kept busy installing Lyons's sewers in 1908. The Cream City towers can be seen in the background.

Three

Work and Play in Lyons

Lyons has always been a working-class town. Its earliest residents helped build the Illinois and Michigan Canal, worked in the quarries and mills, or worked in a service roles for the well-to-do families to the north in Riverside. And the growing network of trains and trolley cars made access to downtown Chicago much easier than the carriages that ran up old Plank Road—which itself was paved in 1914.

By the early 1900s, its residents were taking part in the industrial boom. In 1905, the Western Electric Hawthorne Works, which manufactured telephones for Bell System, opened in Cicero. Although the Great Depression hit after the stock market crash of 1929, many Lyons residents were employed by the Electro-Motive diesel engine plant in neighboring McCook, which opened during the mid-1930s. McCook was also home to the Reynolds Aluminum factory, which opened during World War II to manufacture airplane parts.

By the 1950s, Lyons was fully a residential town, with well-established schools, churches, a health center, and, of course, the taverns—which would become increasingly notorious in the following decades.

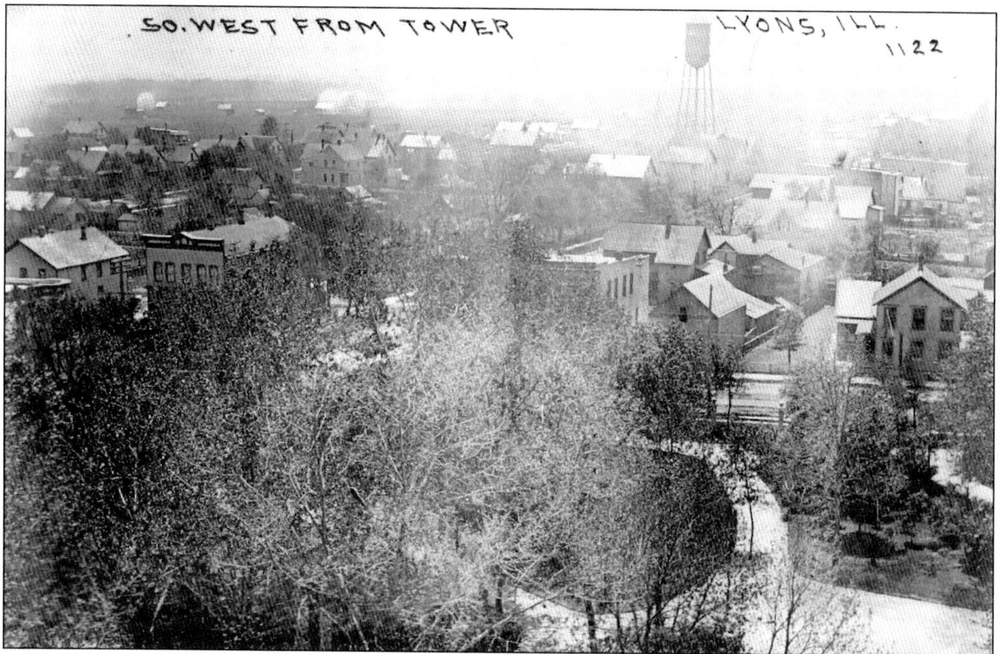

This view is southwest from the Hofmann Tower in 1910. As the photograph shows, much of the town south of Ogden Avenue remained undeveloped at this time.

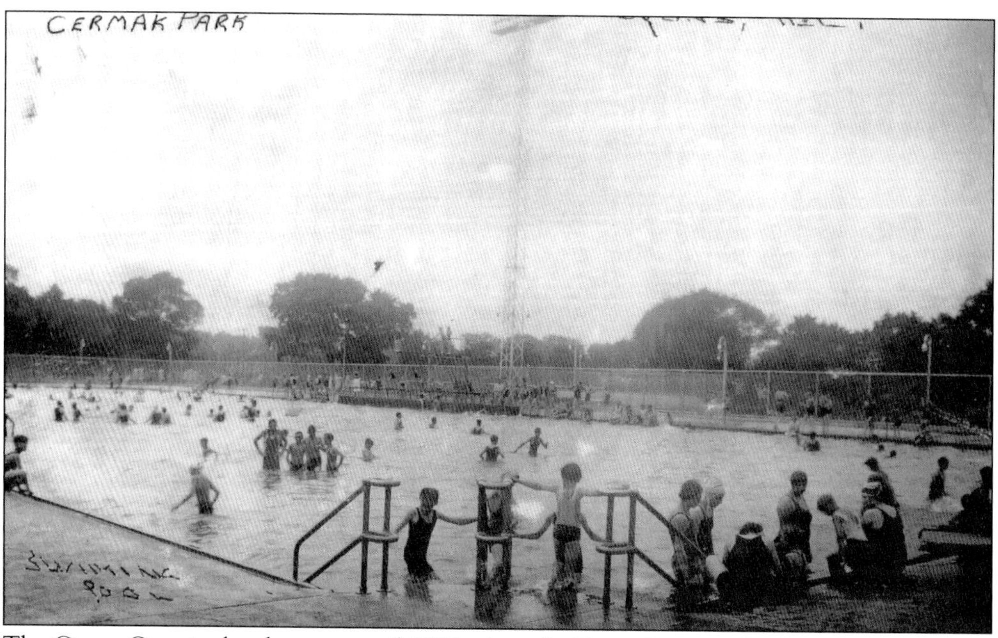

The Cream City site lay dormant until 1927, when the Forest Preserve District opened Cermak Pool on the property, which became a summer gathering spot for many of the village's families.

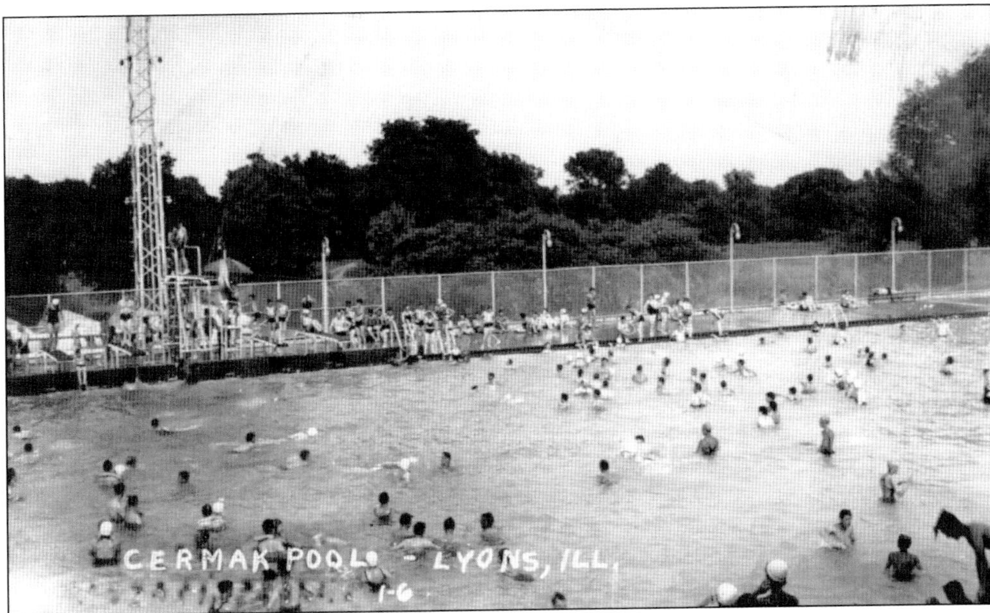

When the million-gallon Cermak Pool opened in 1927, it was the largest public pool in Illinois. The pool was named after Anton Cermak, who at the time was the president of the board of Cook County Forest Preserve Commissioners; he became mayor of Chicago in 1931.

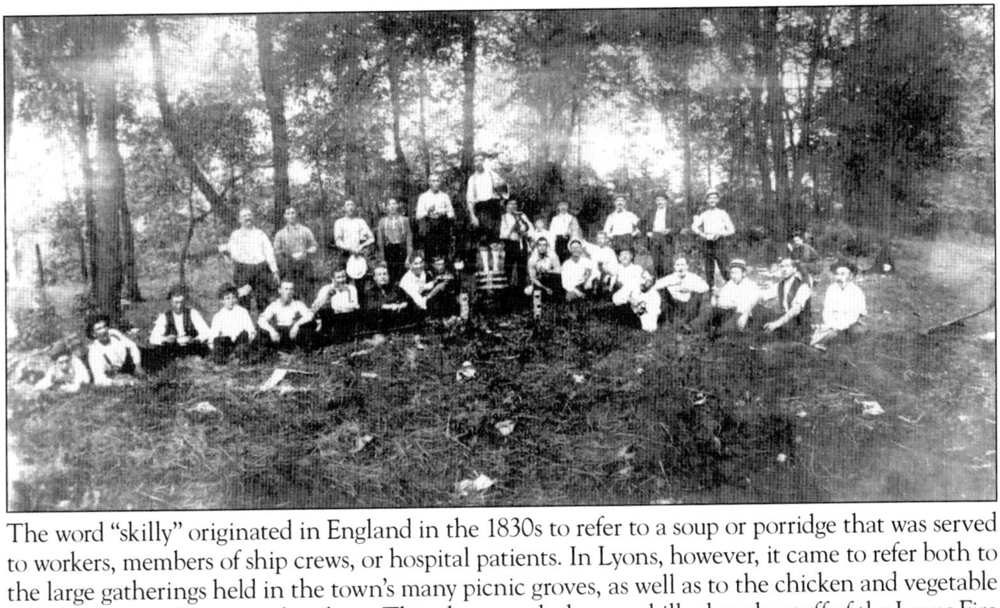
The word "skilly" originated in England in the 1830s to refer to a soup or porridge that was served to workers, members of ship crews, or hospital patients. In Lyons, however, it came to refer both to the large gatherings held in the town's many picnic groves, as well as to the chicken and vegetable stews that were often served at them. This photograph shows a skilly that the staff of the Lyons Fire Department held in Schultz's Woods—soon to be the location of Cream City—in 1905.

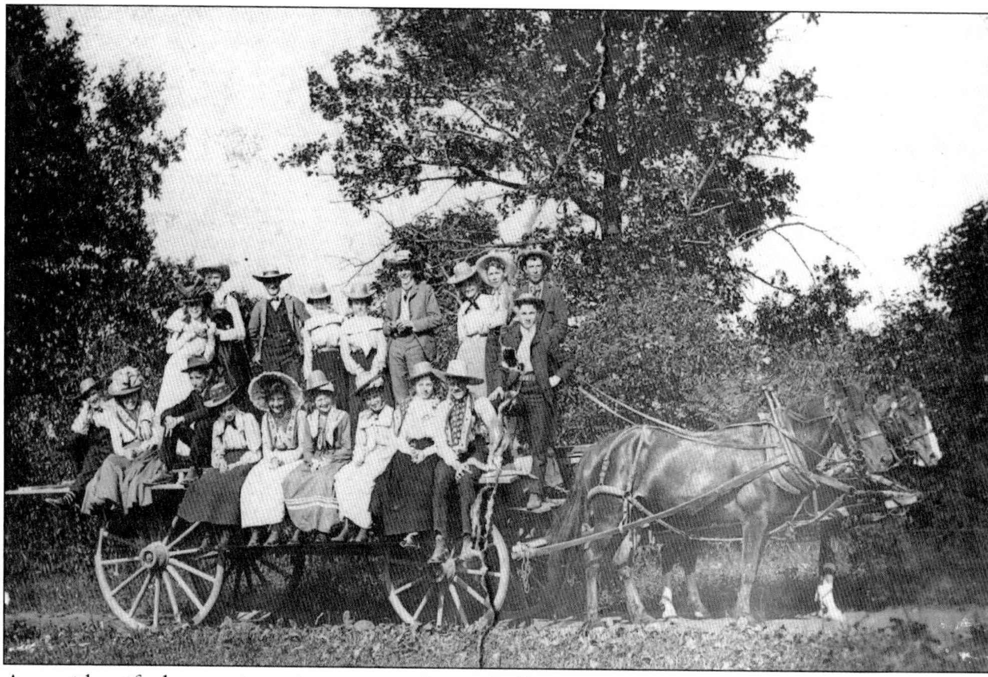

An unidentified group is on its way to a Lyons skilly.

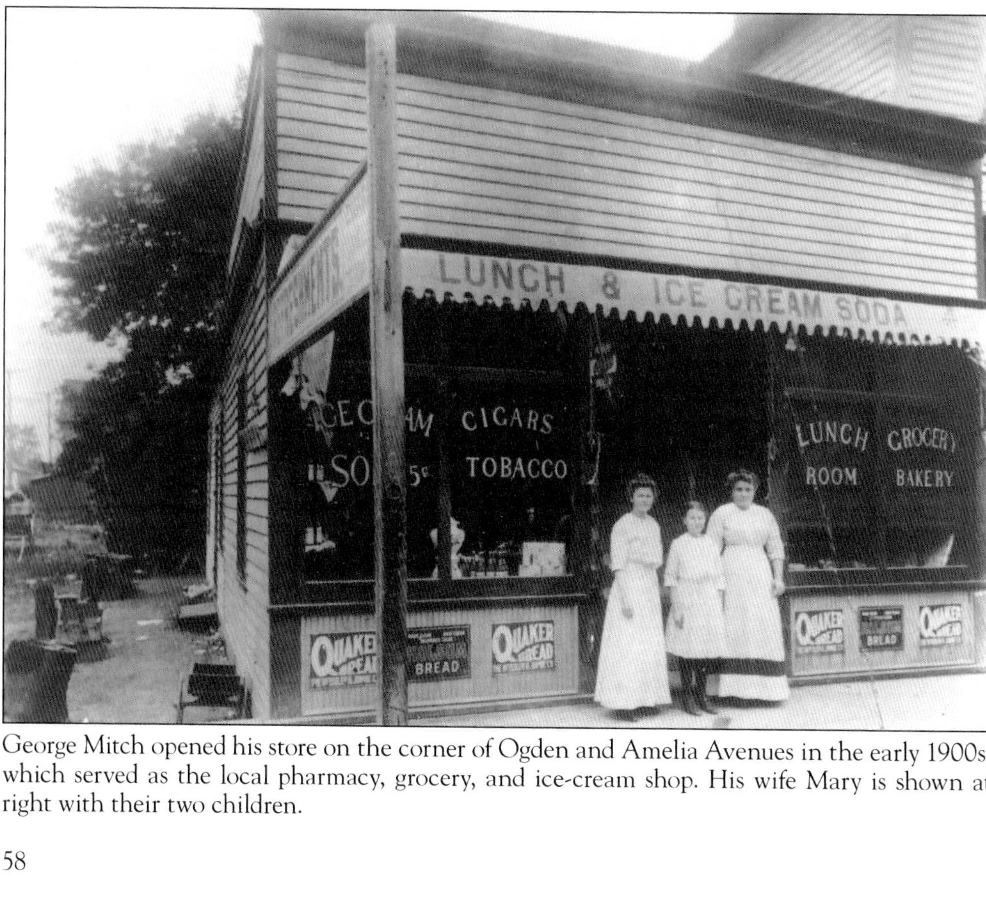

George Mitch opened his store on the corner of Ogden and Amelia Avenues in the early 1900s, which served as the local pharmacy, grocery, and ice-cream shop. His wife Mary is shown at right with their two children.

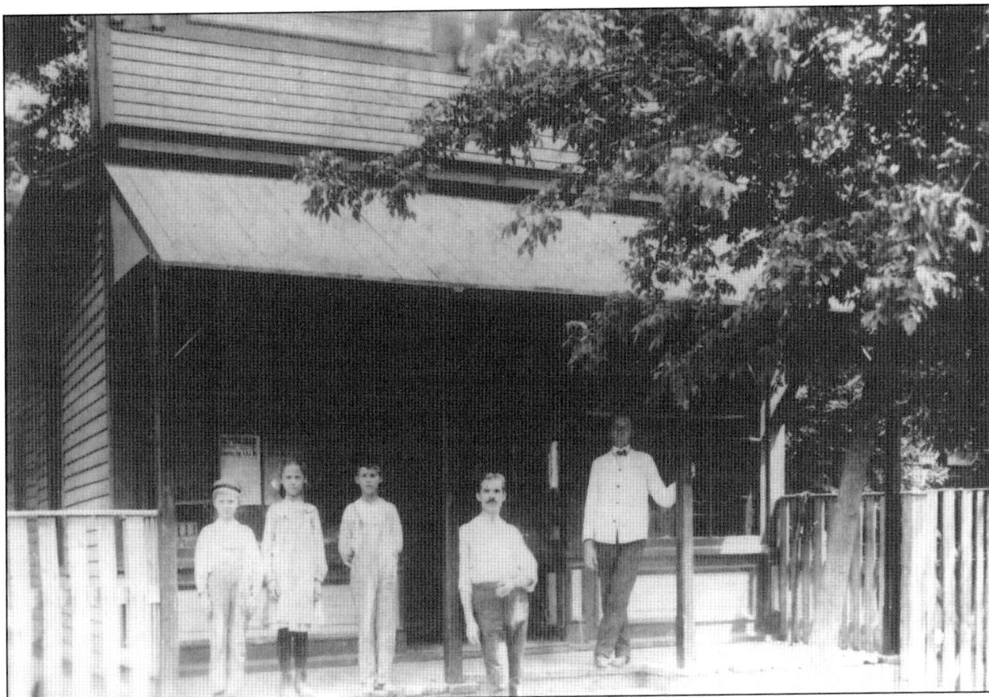

This photograph shows the front of the Mitch General Store in 1906. George Mitch is the man with the mustache standing against a pole.

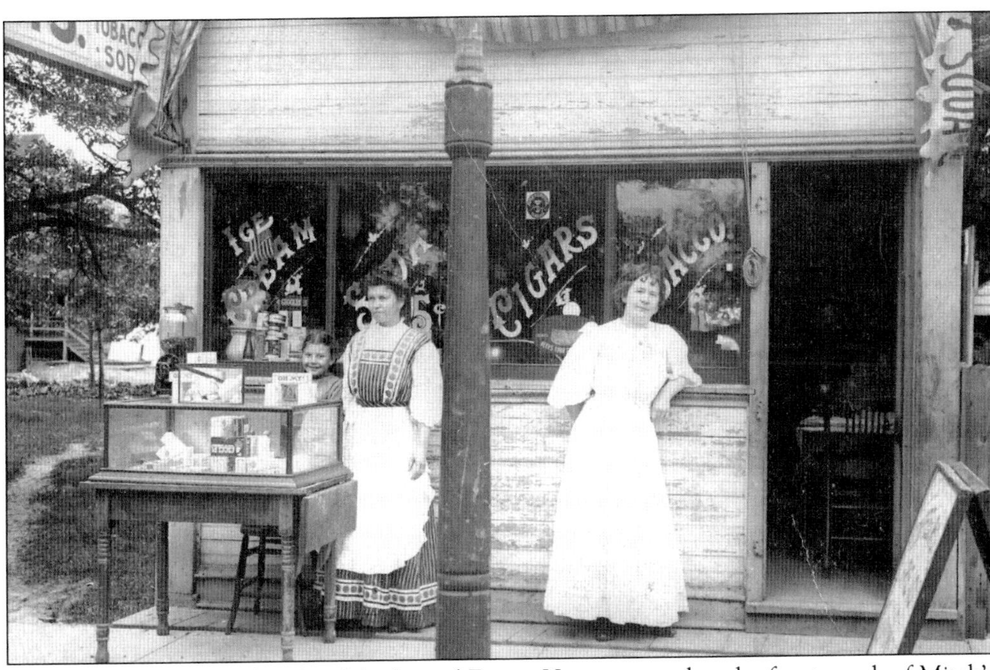

Mary Mitch Hoppenrath, Mary Mitch, and Emma Hennen stand at the front porch of Mitch's. Cracker Jack, which was introduced at Chicago's Columbian Exposition in 1893, is among the snacks for sale.

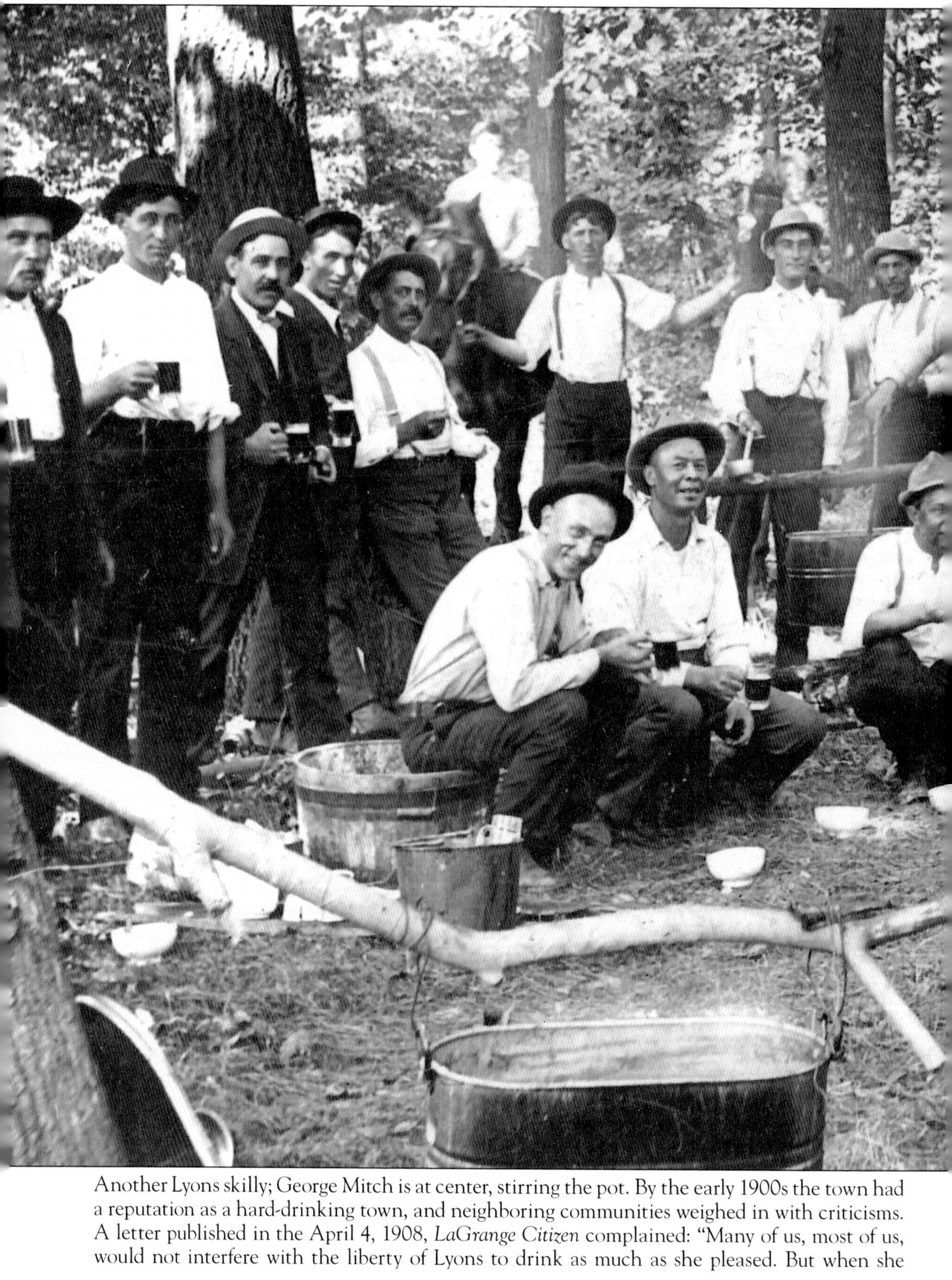

Another Lyons skilly; George Mitch is at center, stirring the pot. By the early 1900s the town had a reputation as a hard-drinking town, and neighboring communities weighed in with criticisms. A letter published in the April 4, 1908, *LaGrange Citizen* complained: "Many of us, most of us, would not interfere with the liberty of Lyons to drink as much as she pleased. But when she

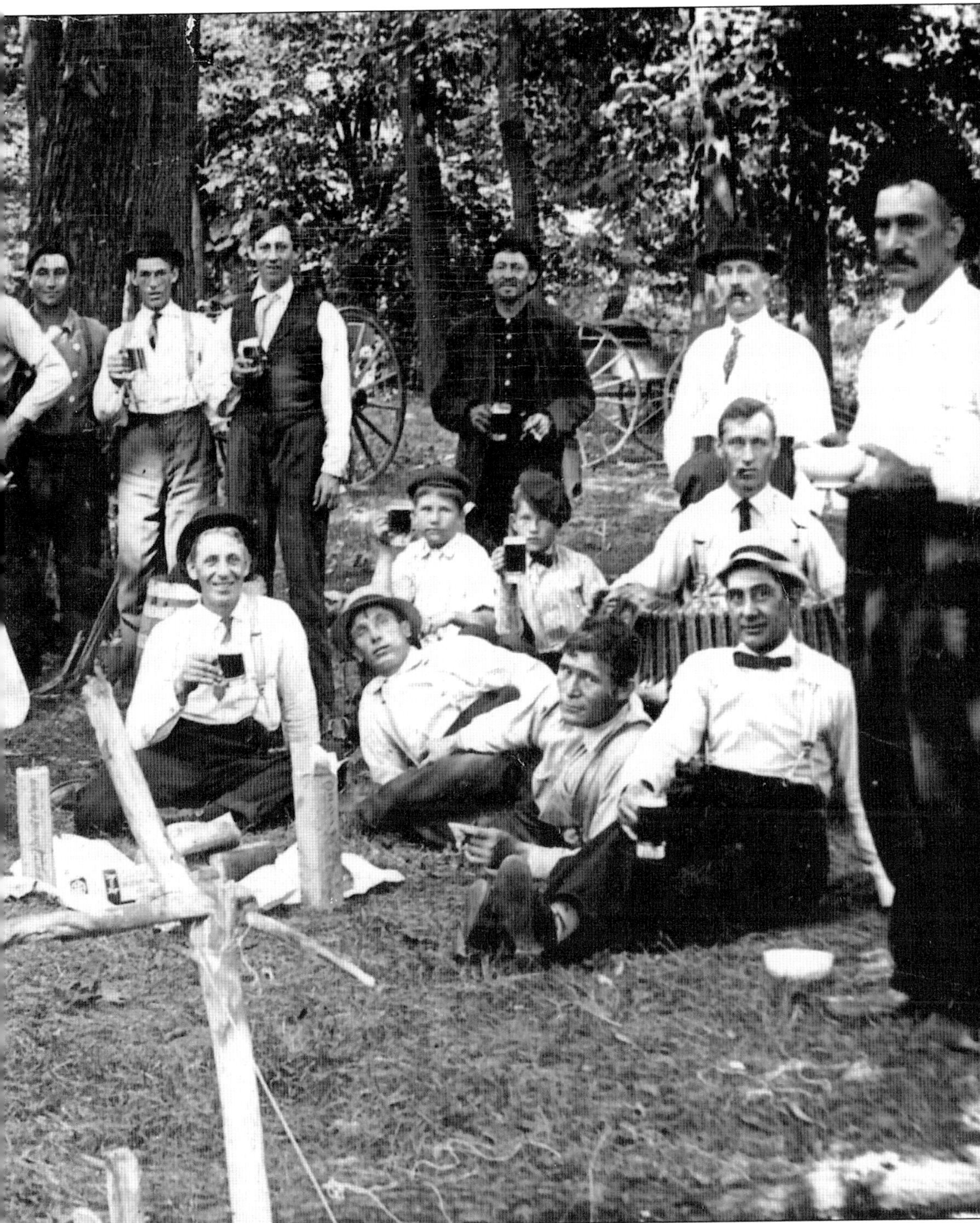

invites all of underground Chicago to join in a continuous debauch and sets enticements in her pleasure parks for the young and ignorant of our community as well, we should be much less than men if we did not use every instrument at hand to fight back in self-defense."

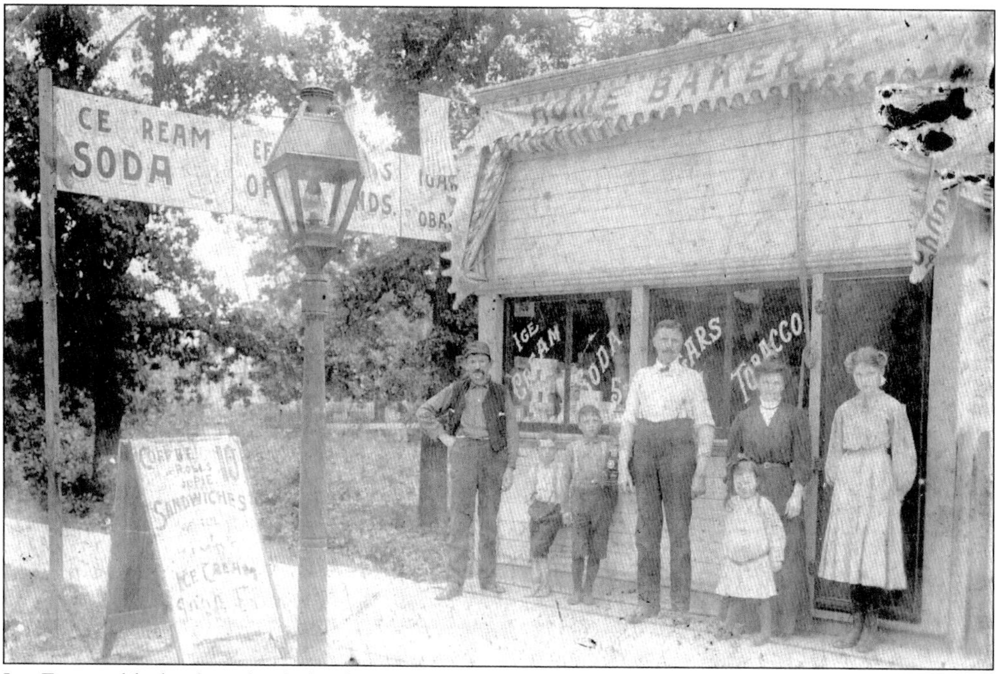

Joe Fitzgerald, the first chief of police in Lyons, is at the left of this photograph, standing in front of George Mitch's general store. Mitch is at center; his wife Mary is the second from right, next to Mitch.

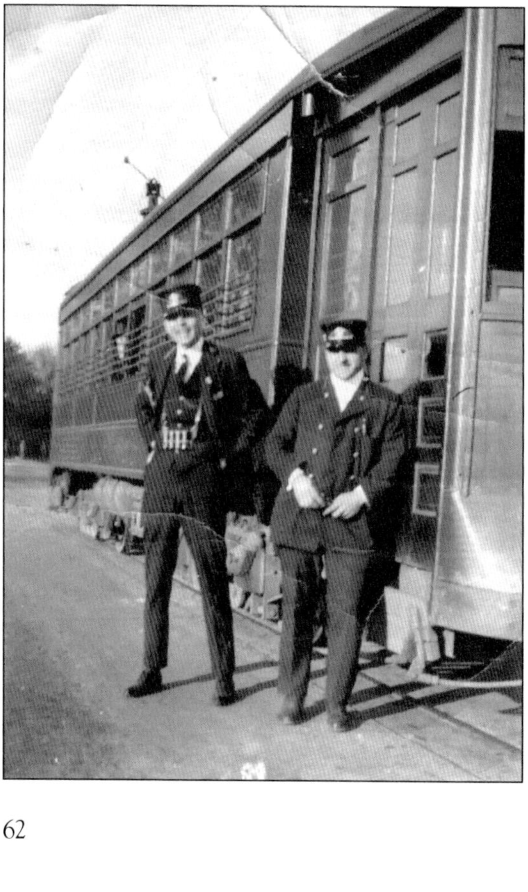
James Villna (left) and Frank Toman, two Lyons streetcar conductors, are pictured here.

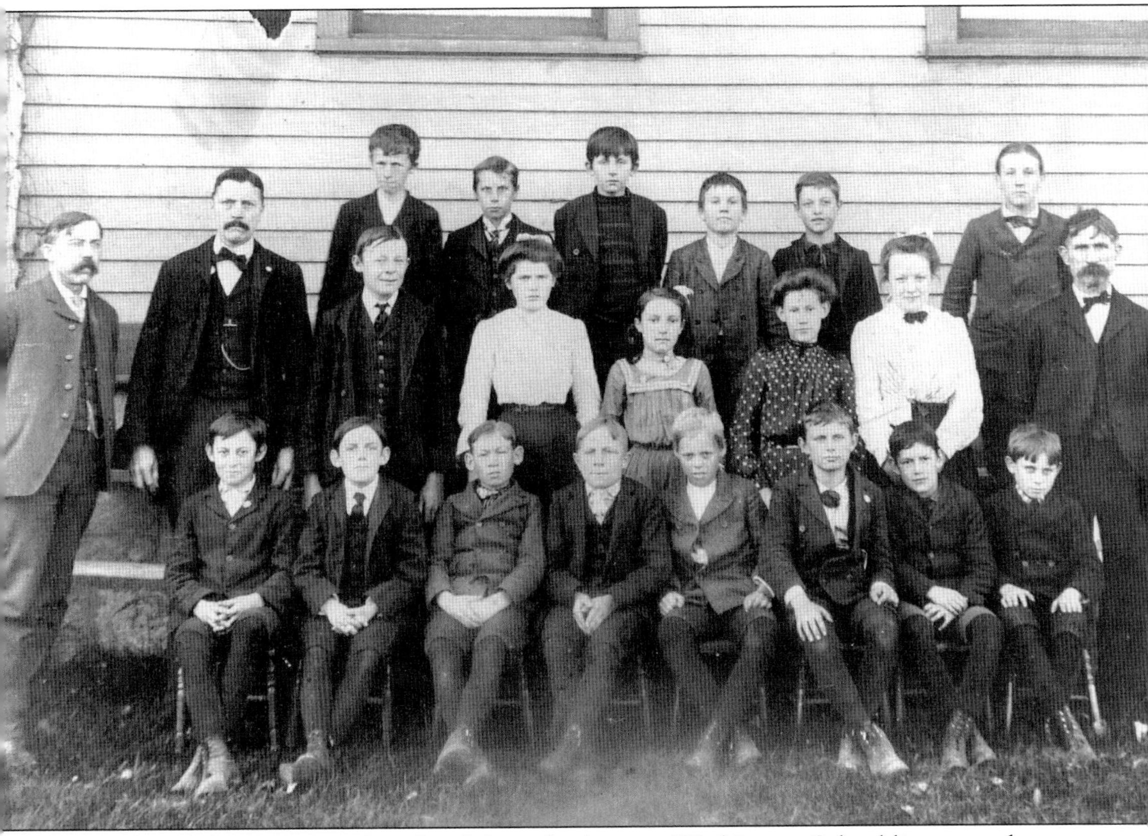

The roster of the 1903 seventh and eighth grade classes at Washington School lists more than a few familiar names. The adults at left are Augustus Haley, principal and teacher, and George Mitch, a member of the school board. From left to right are (first row) Frank Neher, George Neher, George Lange, Frank Sweitzer, Gilbert Nelson, Fred Waller, Roy Frank, and Albert Stubbings; (second row) William Gieseler, Jennie Madsen, Alvina Gerny Reuss, Mamie Frank, Helen Ryan (teacher), and William Bentgen (member of the school board); (third row) Jim Donnelly, Leo Kennedy, Harold Clark, William Darnstadt, Henry Neher, and Carl Darnstadt Jr.

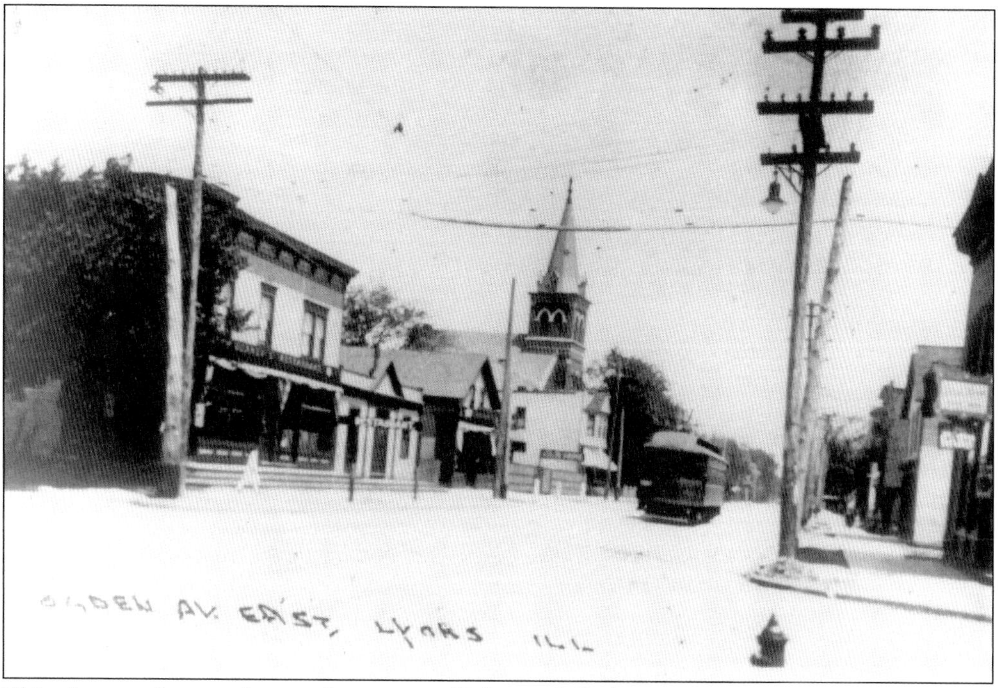

This photograph was taken at the corner of Joliet and Ogden Avenues around 1909 when Zion Lutheran Church was built. John Berner's restaurant, seen at left, later became Grosse's Pharmacy.

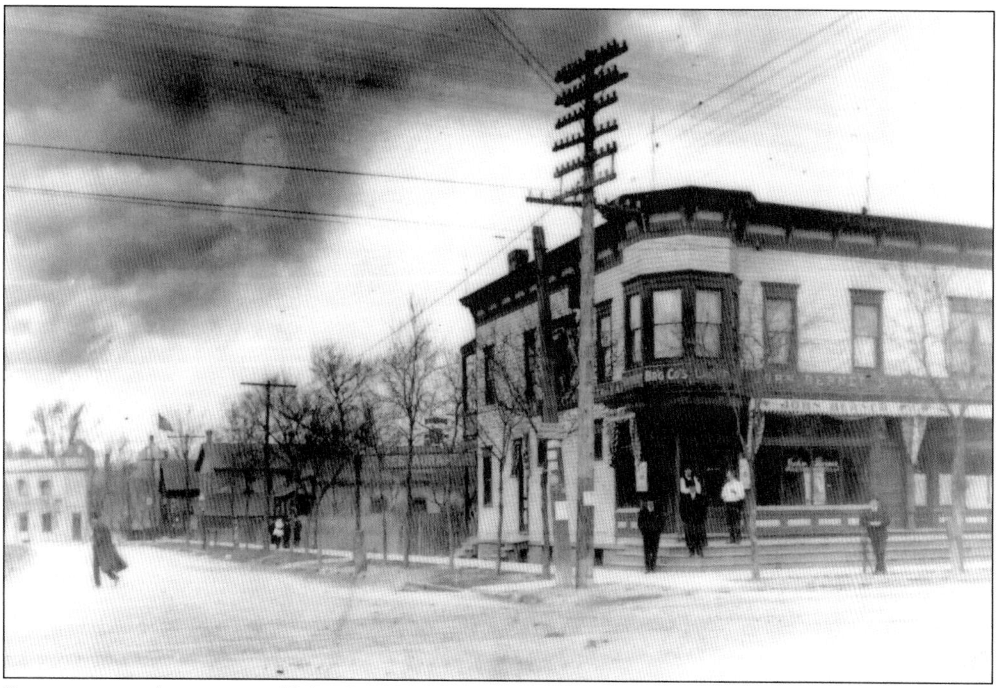

You can get a closer view of John Berner's restaurant in the 1890s in this photograph. The ruins of the Fox Mill, torn down in 1893, can be seen behind Hofmann's building at left.

Bill and Catherine Darnstadt are pictured here in Neher's Grove in the late 1800s. Their twin sons, Ray and Bill Jr., are likely in the buggy.

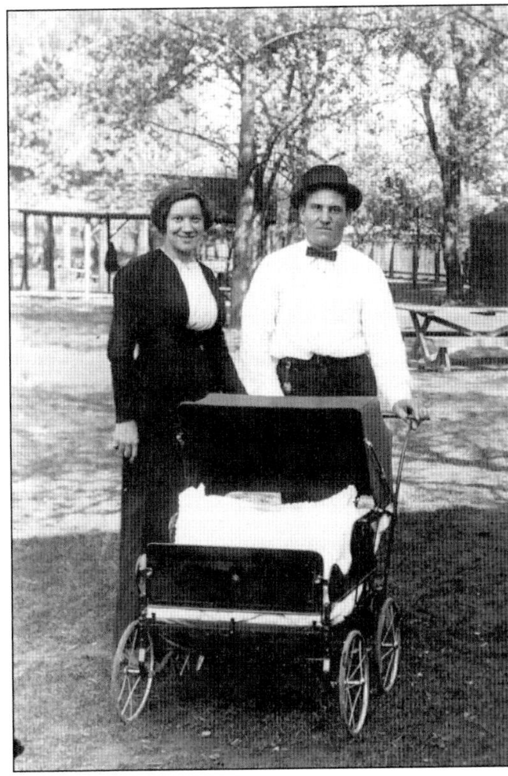

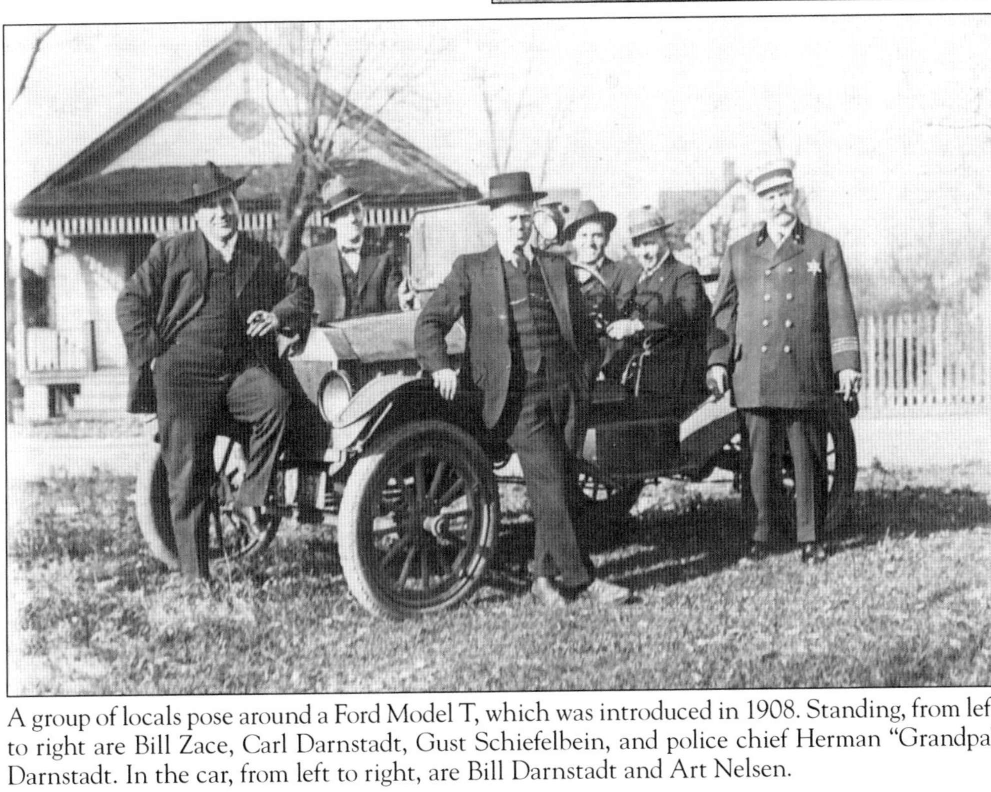

A group of locals pose around a Ford Model T, which was introduced in 1908. Standing, from left to right are Bill Zace, Carl Darnstadt, Gust Schiefelbein, and police chief Herman "Grandpa" Darnstadt. In the car, from left to right, are Bill Darnstadt and Art Nelsen.

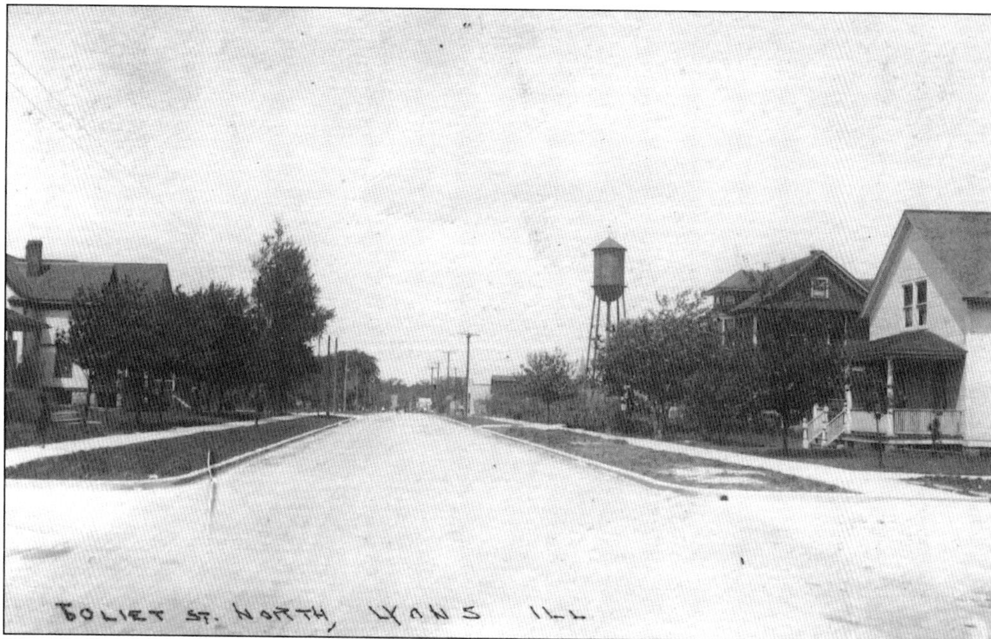

This photograph offers a view north up Joliet Avenue. The first Lyons water tower, with a 100,000-gallon capacity, was built in 1908; it would remain in place until the new one was constructed in 1973.

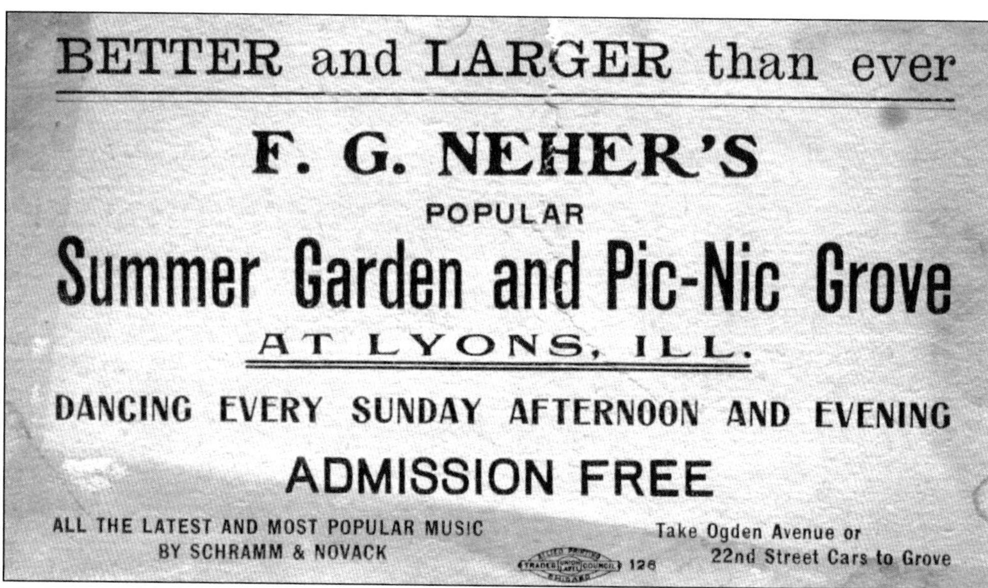

This postcard from 1908 promotes a dance party at Neher's Grove, which was located alongside the Neher's Tavern toward the Des Plaines River.

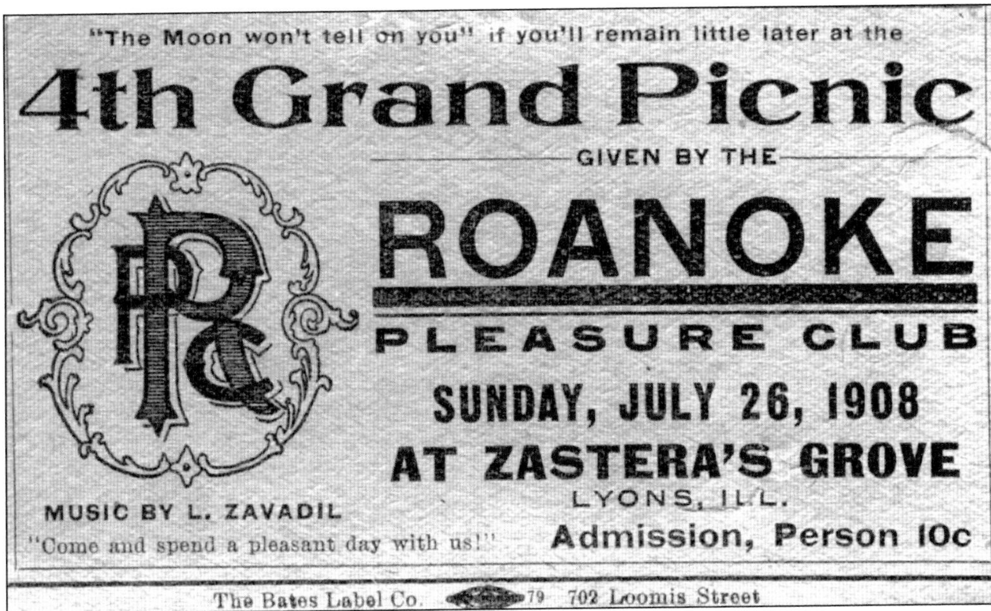

By 1908, Lyons had fewer than 1,000 residents. Tavern owners took advantage of undeveloped areas in town to set up picnic groves. This is a promotional card for an event at Zastera's Grove, which was located between the Reuss and Virzine properties on Ogden Avenue. Many such cards included song lyrics on the back, and this one included the words to "The Moon Won't Tell on You," written by Joseph Barton and Frank Klickmann.

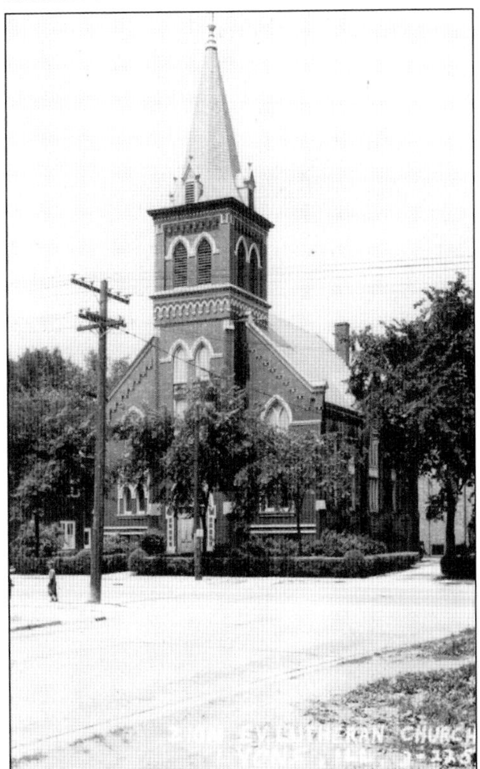

Traveling Lutheran pastors performed the first church services in Lyons starting in 1859, and a group called the First Religious Society of Lyons and Riverside held services in a chapel on the Plank Road in 1874. The congregation was officially recognized by the Lutheran Church in 1878. By the early 1900s, it had outgrown its chapel space; a new building, shown here, was constructed in 1909.

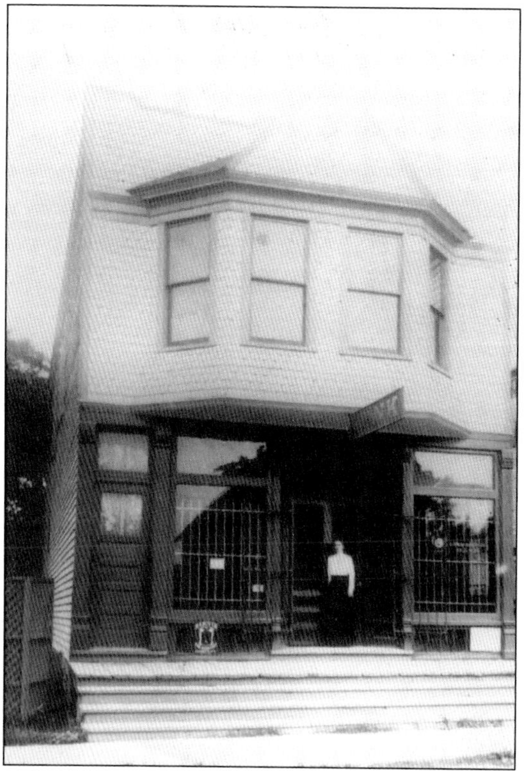

The German American Bank, the first bank in Lyons, opened just west of Zion Lutheran Church on the north side of Ogden Avenue.

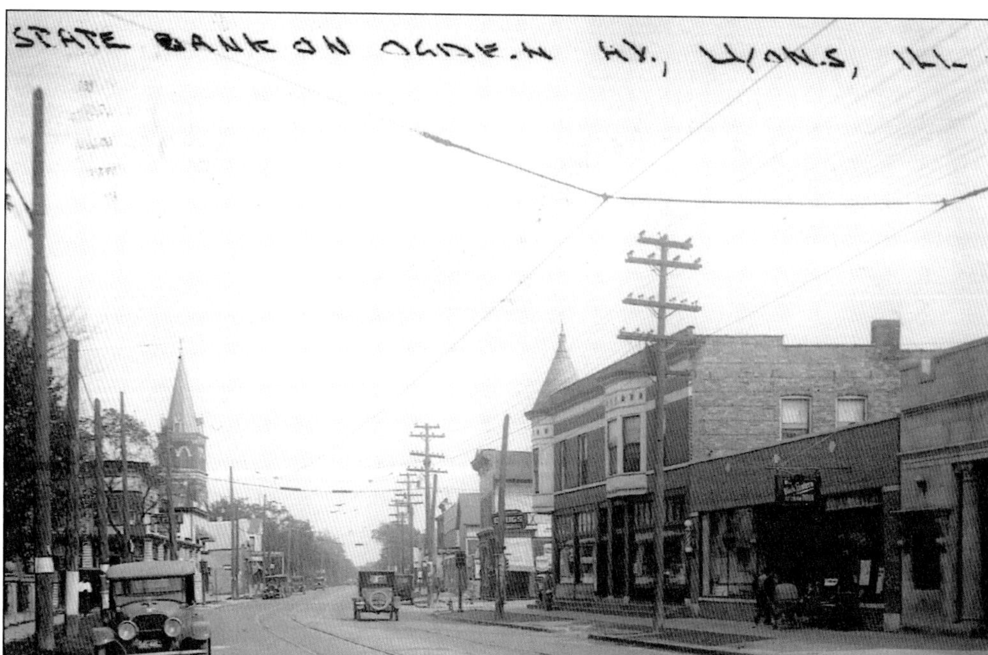

At the far right is the State Bank of Lyons, which opened in 1922 on Ogden Avenue with the opening of the Lyons Loan and Building Association to spur home ownership in town. Locals on the street gather in front of the Black Lantern Ice-Cream Parlor.

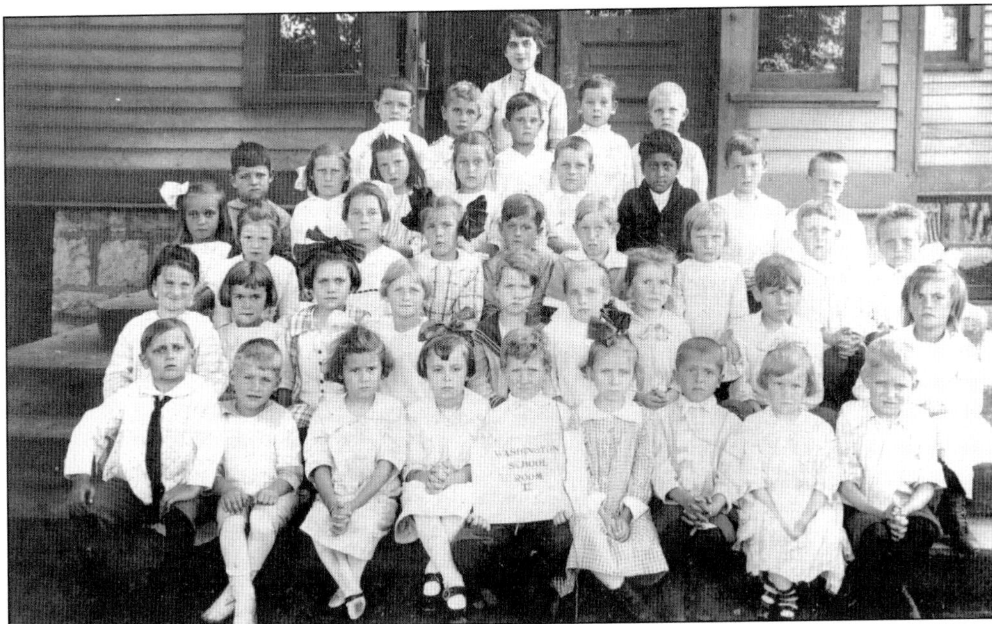

Pictured is Washington School's second-grade class of 1914. From left to right are (first row): Joe Novak, Raymond Nelson, Hazel Frank, Margaret Metz, Charles Ditman, Caroline Labusch, Tony Masalewnis, Marie Melbon, and Fred Bergman; (second row) Rose Worik, Ethel Nitzel, Ella Sembera, Antoinette Horalek, Amy Schieve, Annie Adamijech, Jessie Polich, Lawrence Frank, and unidentified; (third row) Anna Doblevich, Anna Frietak, unidentified, unidentified, Frank Shilhivek, Joe Bartels, unidentified, William Gerny, and August Gumtow; (fourth row) Ralph Puntzel, Anna Kuban, Anna Lekovish, unidentified, Frank Mack, Gust Stanley, Herbert Hill, and unidentified; (fifth row) Ed Szumski, George Votruba, Ralph Deverny, Arnold Giesler, and Chester Zimmerman. The teacher at rear is unidentified.

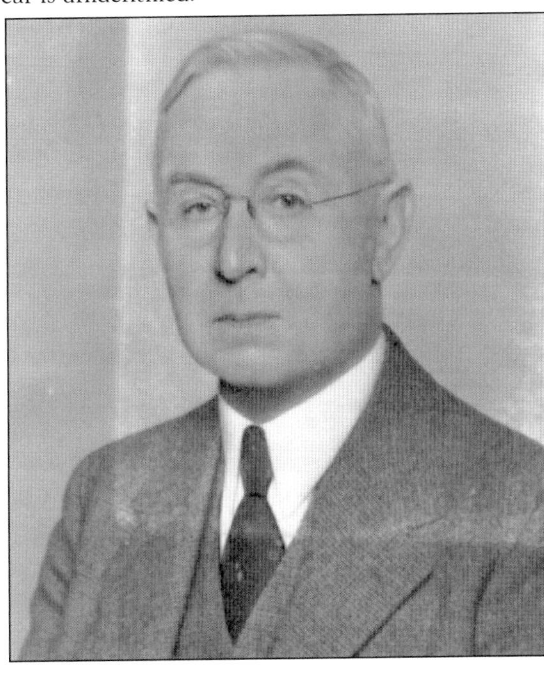

John W. Costello, for whom Costello School was named, was the superintendent of Lyons schools from 1912 to 1940. Born in Linden, Ohio, he grew up in Wisconsin and taught in Evergreen Park before moving to Lyons.

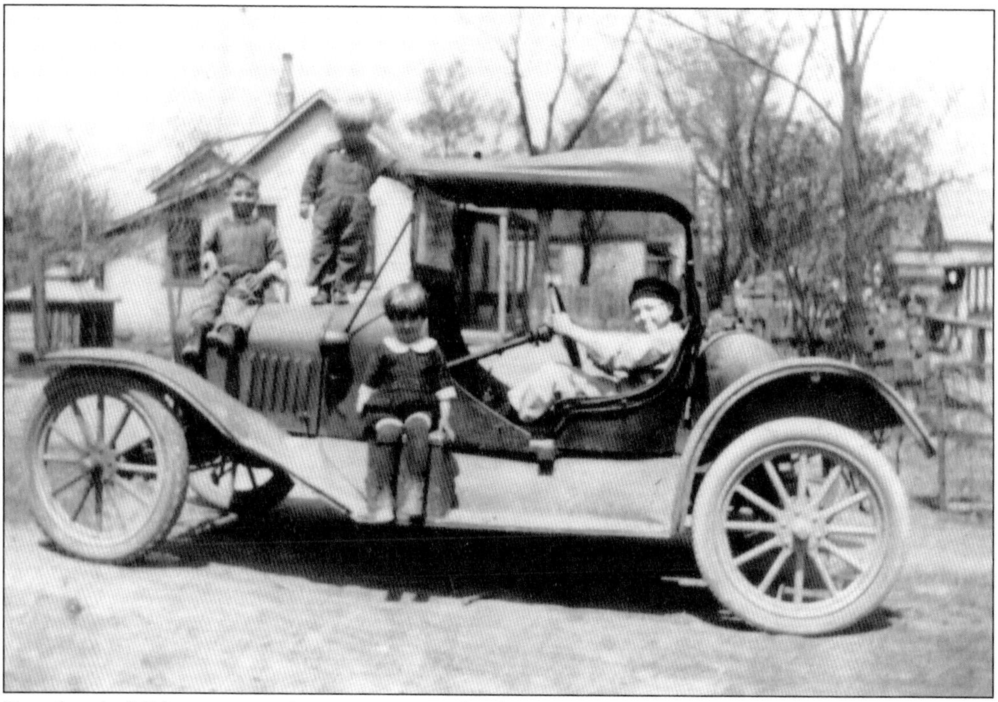

Four local children are road-testing a car of unknown vintage on Gage Avenue; (from left to right) Bud Neher, Debbie Neher, Lorraine "Sis" Neher, and Bill Darnstadt Jr.

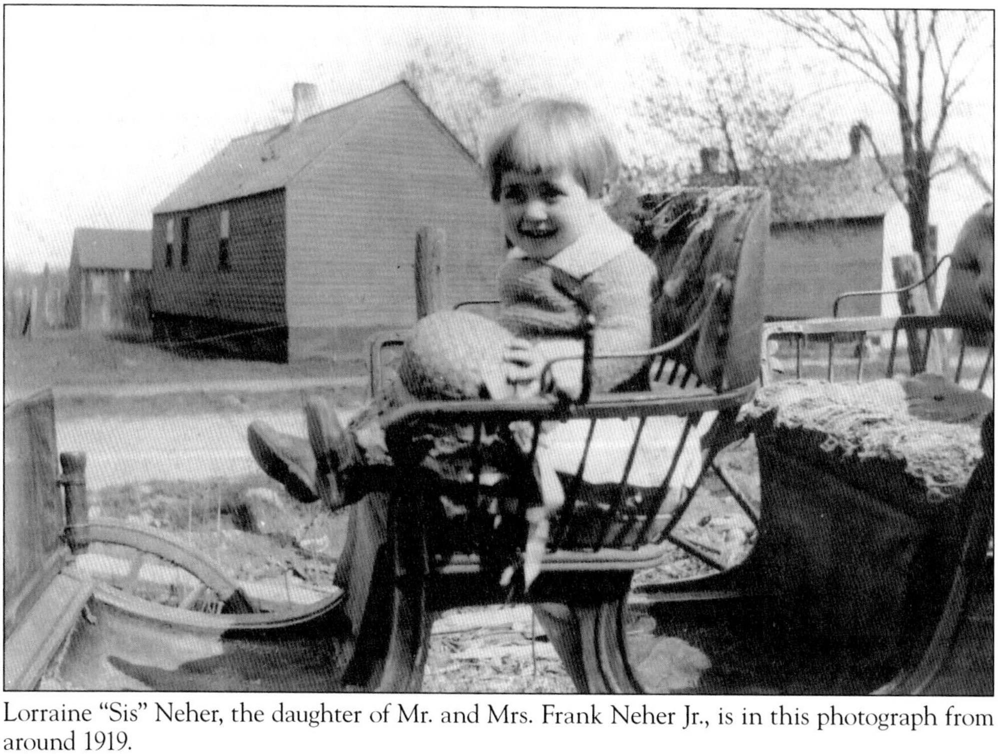

Lorraine "Sis" Neher, the daughter of Mr. and Mrs. Frank Neher Jr., is in this photograph from around 1919.

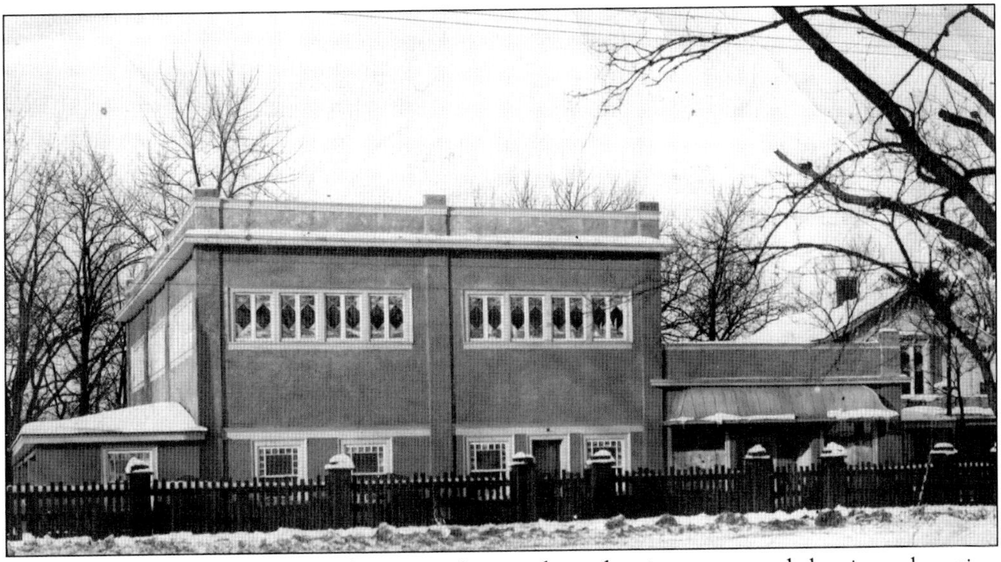

The Chateau Des Plaines opened in 1914. An article at the time promoted the site as boasting "forty acres of private parkings with stone paved roadways and electrically lighted promenades. Everything is exclusive and also conducted in a manner that is above question."

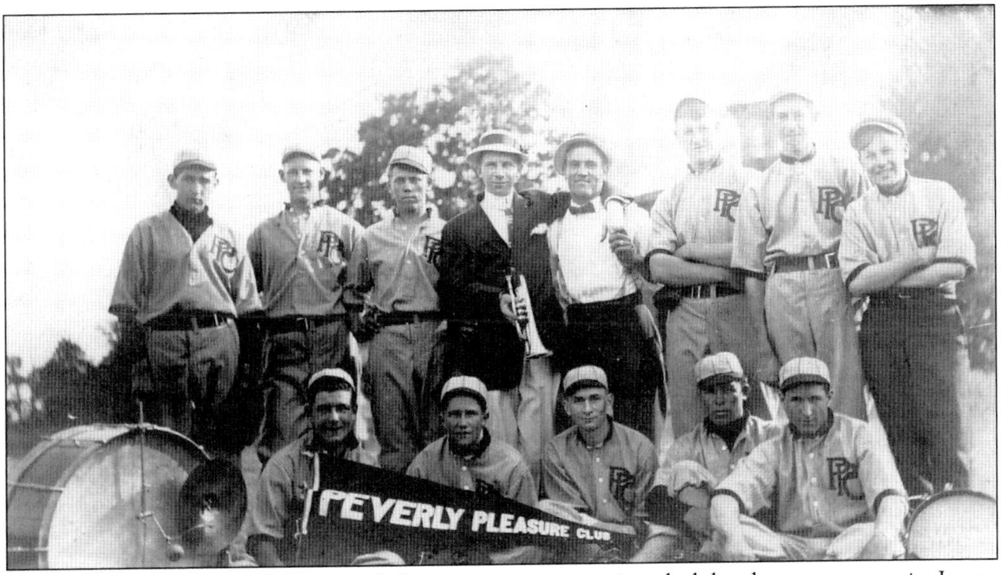

The Peverley Pleasure Club, one of the numerous recreational clubs that sprung up in Lyons to compete in baseball season, had its clubhouse on Joliet and Collins Avenues, near the fire station; it also helped build the Lyons Theater. Standing in uniform, from left to right, are Herman Smith, Henry Melbrown, Bob Schiefelbein, Sandy Schimmelfenning, Bill Darnstadt, and Percy Kuhlman Moody. The seated men are unidentified.

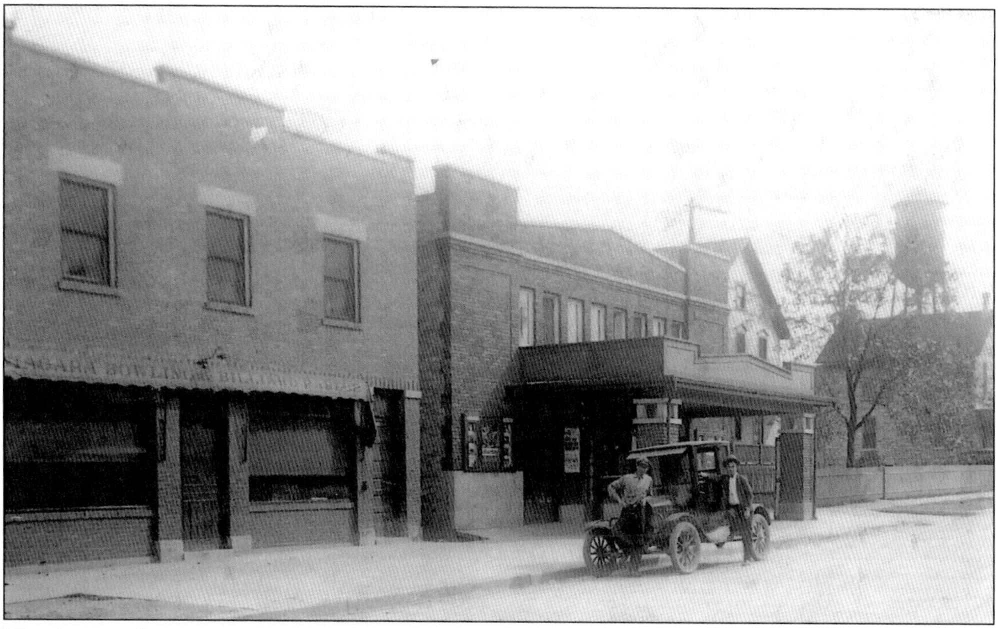

The Lyons Theatre on Joliet Avenue, which opened in the second decade of the 20th century, was one of two theaters serving local moviegoers, and also hosted community events like raffles and children's competitions. It remained open through the late 1960s, when it (along with the tavern and bowling alley next door) became the Tower Home for Funerals. The sample schedule of screenings comes from 1930. (*Abraham Lincoln* was the second-to-last film by pioneering director D. W. Griffith.)

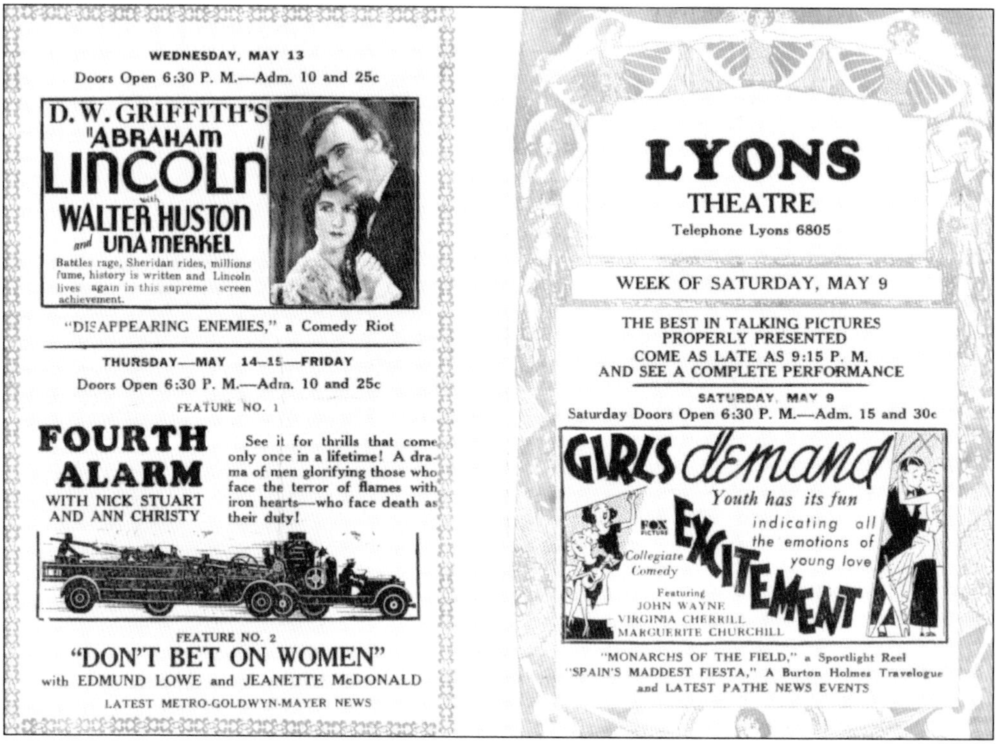

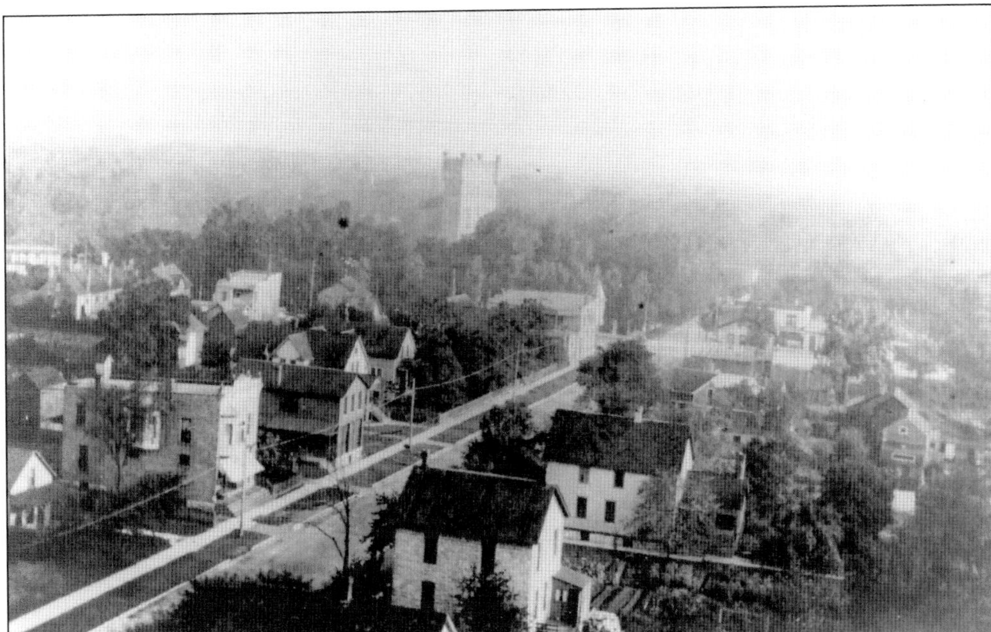

This aerial view shows Lyons, looking north from the water tower, around 1915.

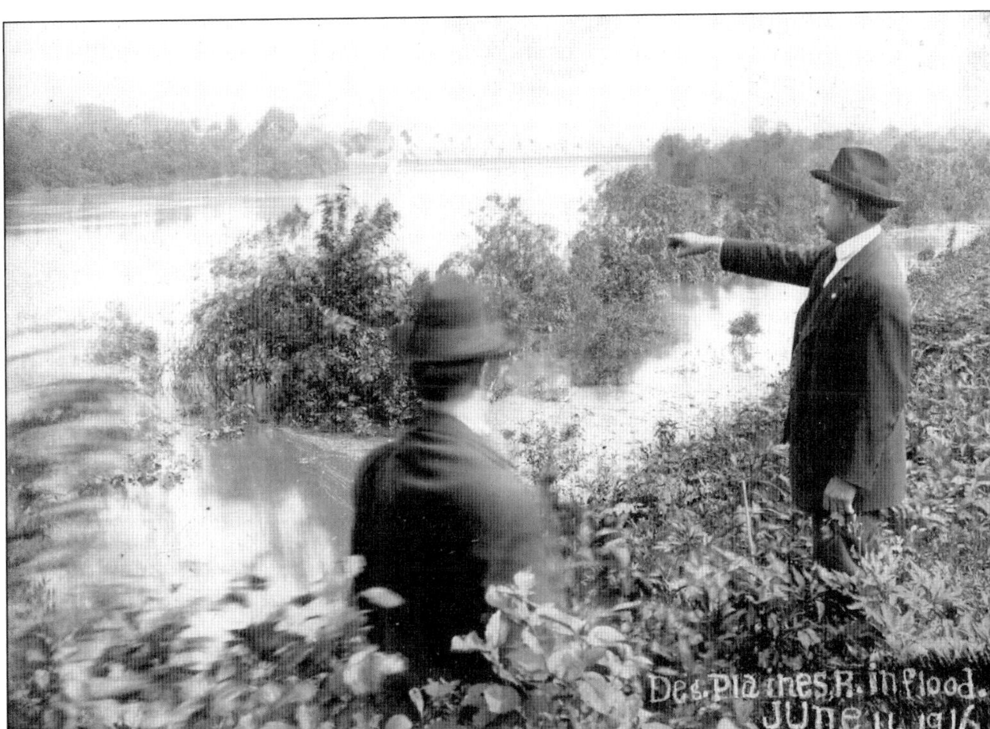

This flooding on the Des Plaines River in Lyons occurred in June 1916.

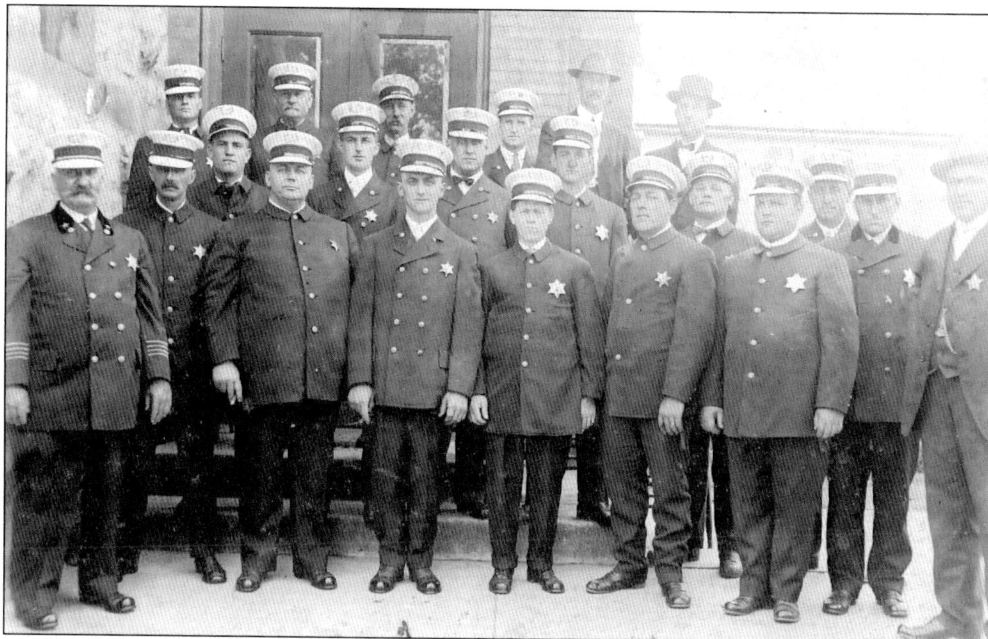

This photograph shows the Lyons Police Department from 1916. Lyons police first operated its calaboose on Joliet and Collins Avenues, with an outdoor area to hold stray pets and livestock. That building burned down in 1892 and was replaced with a new one on Joliet and Salisbury Avenues. It moved into village hall in 1900, where it maintains its offices today. Carl Darnstadt is in the back row, far right; Gust Schiefelbein fifth from left in the first row; and Herman Darnstadt, chief of police, is the far left in the first row, with the mustache.

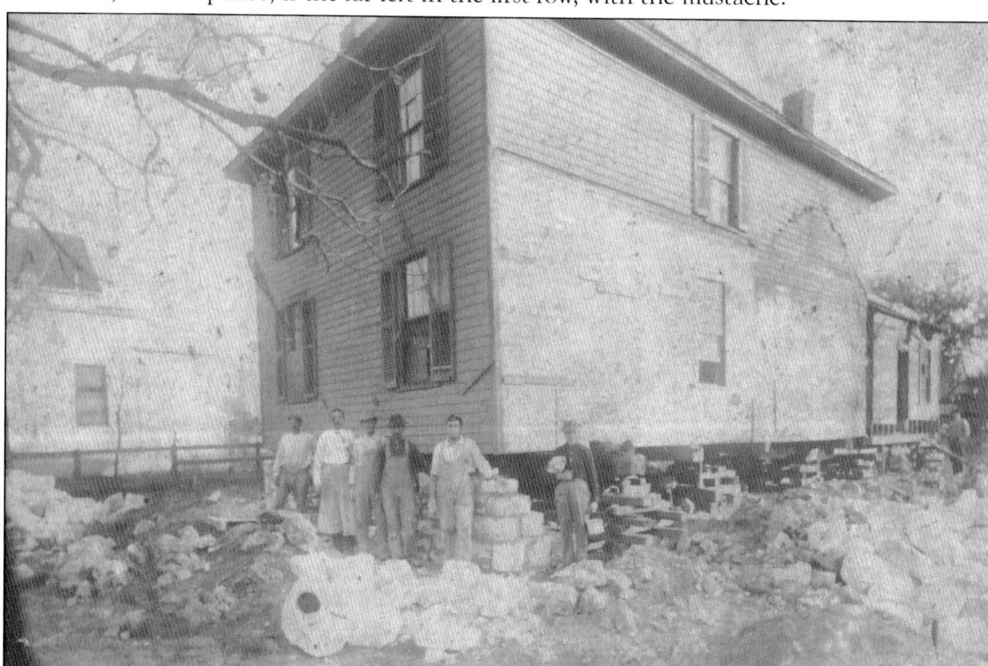

This photograph from 1916 shows a group of workers moving a house from Thirty-ninth Street to Amelia Avenue.

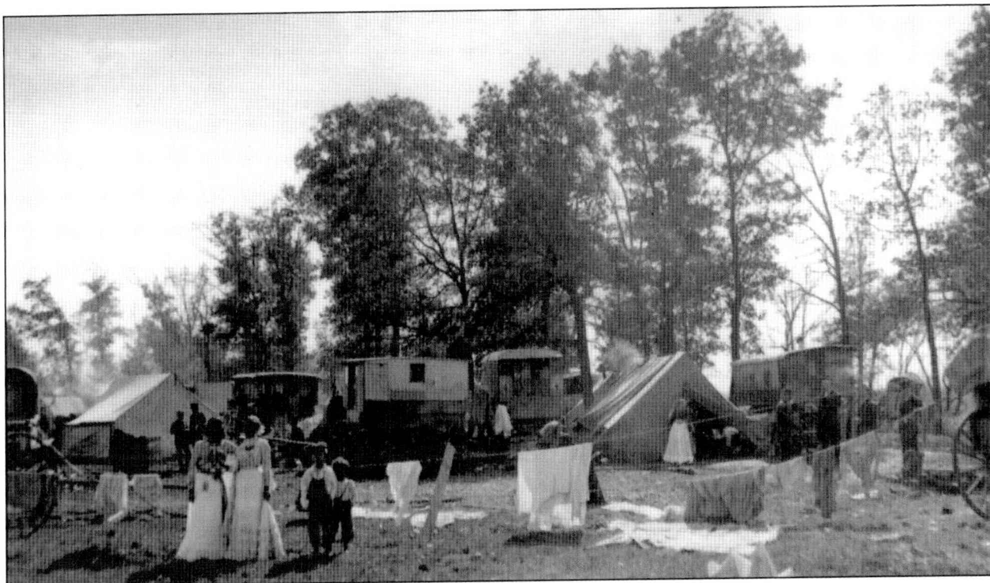

After World War I, the area off Harlem Avenue south of Thirty-ninth Street attracted immigrants from Europe, who formed a camp on the land. The Rom gypsies performed shows in Cermak Woods on Sundays, complete with fortune tellers, live music, and a dancing bear. Kate Leonhardt, who operated a shop in Lyons, lived near the camp and would regularly pick up children living there to have them get checkups from Catherine Brady, a Chicago nurse, who would later become the first nurse of the Lyons Health Center. The gypsy camp dispersed in the late 1930s, when it became the site of Fairyland Park.

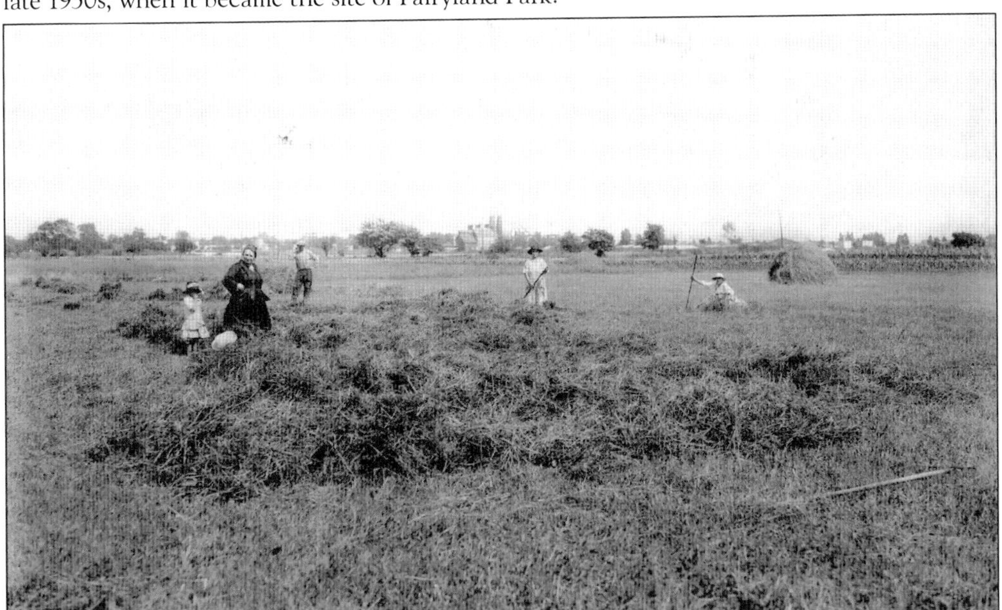

Lyons's second triangle property, bordered by Ogden Avenue, First Avenue, and Plainfield Road, has had many uses over the years; home to bars (the Hayloft, the Mineshaft), a dog-racing track, and (currently) a Starbucks and Walgreens. But in 1920, it was simply an open field, as this image shows; buildings related to quarry work at Materials Service Corporation can be seen in the background.

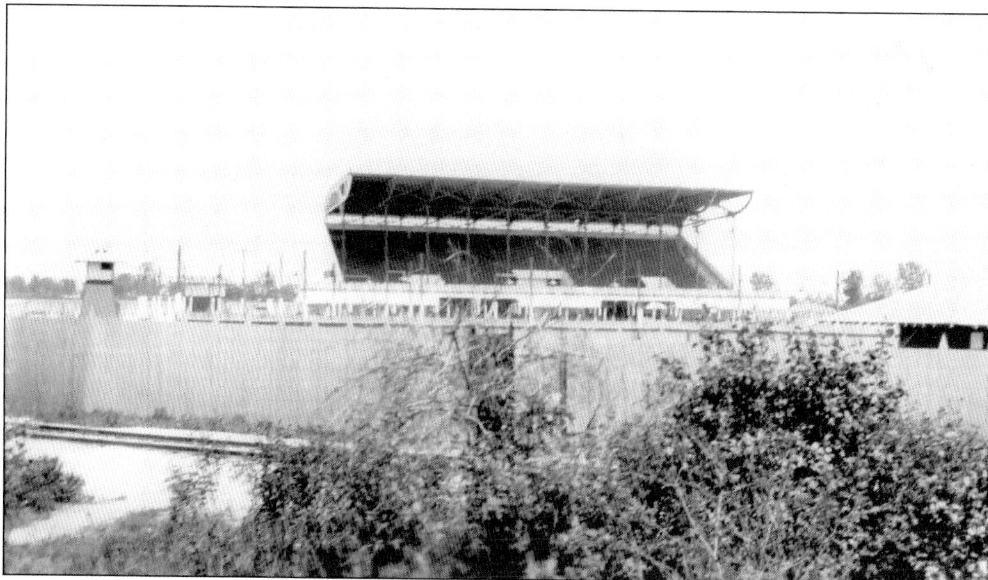

In the early 1920s, Lyons was briefly home to a dog track, the Ogden Kennel Club, located at the intersection of Ogden Avenue, Plainfield Road, and First Avenue.

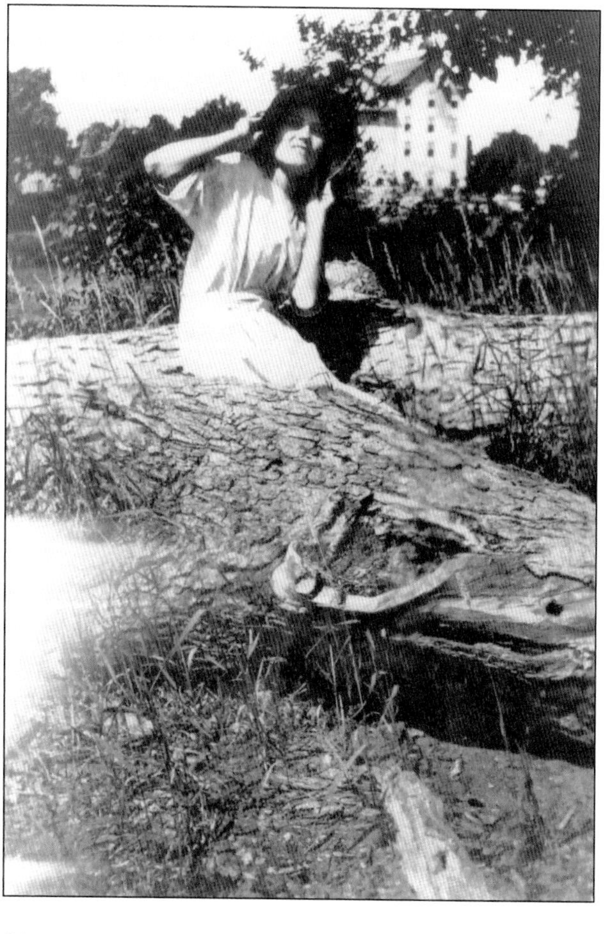

Anna Masek, mother of Lyons Historical Commission cofounder Gladys Yirsa, sits by the banks of the Des Plaines River in 1921.

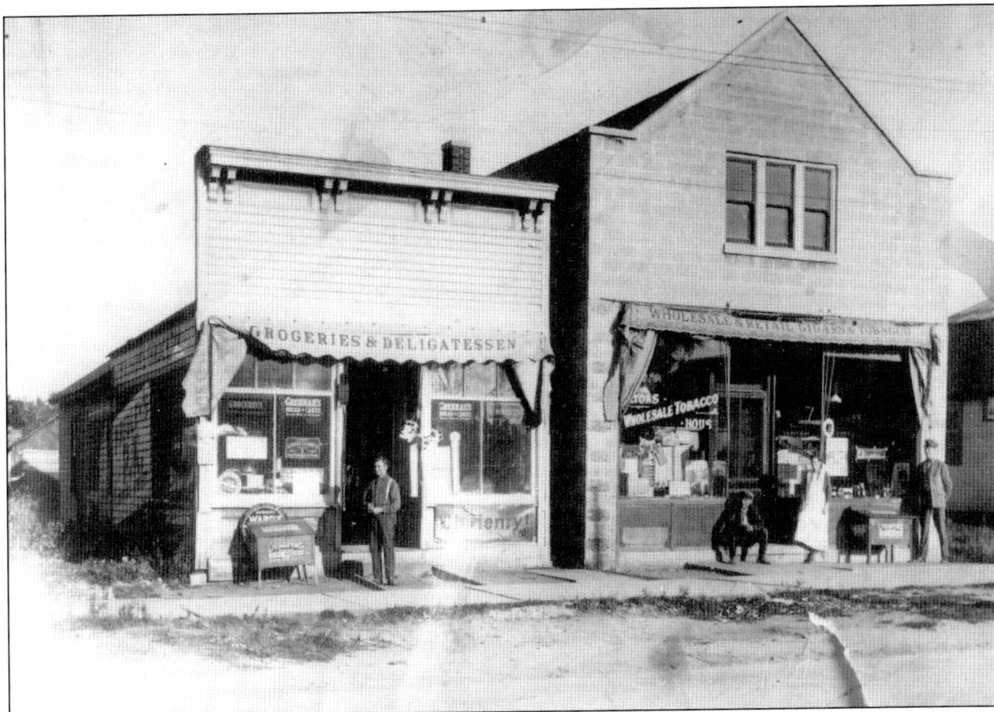

Wilson's Groceries and the Lyons Wholesale Tobacco House operated on Joliet Avenue in the 1920s.

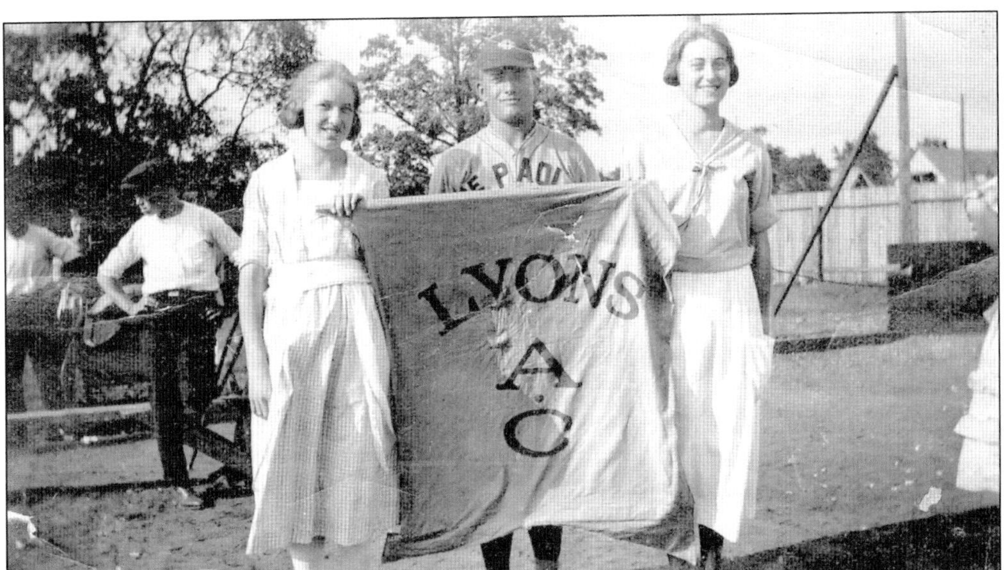

Walter Mitch holds the banner for the Lyons Athletic Club, which held baseball games and other sporting events in Lyons starting in the 1920s, and competed against the Peverley Pleasure Club, the Forest Athletic Club, the Lyons Mustangs Athletic Club, the Lyons Tigers Athletic Club and others.

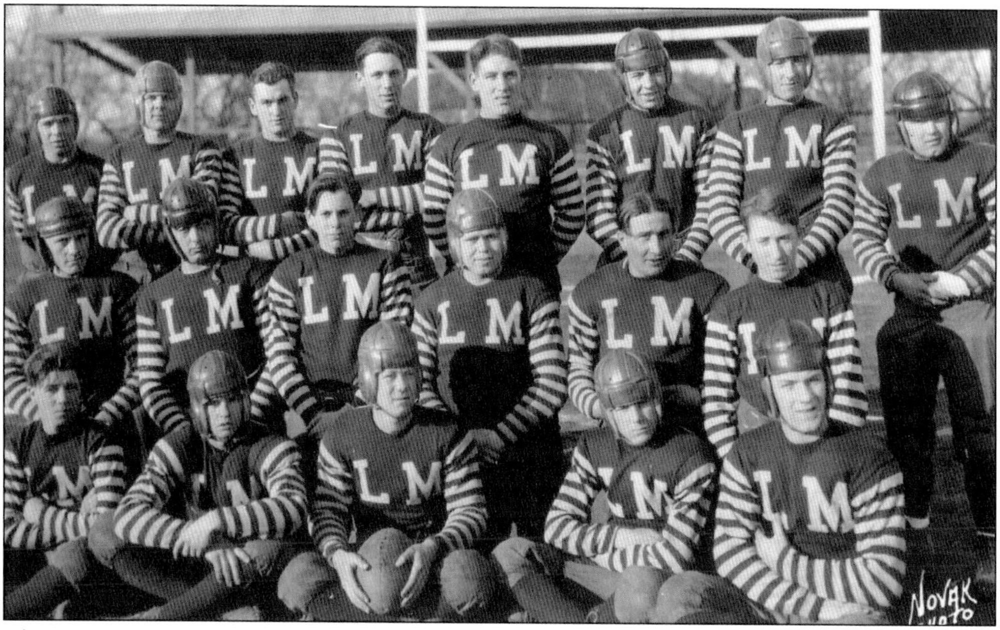

The Lyons Mustangs Athletic Club was founded on August 4, 1923, to host football and baseball games, as well as boxing matches. Pictured here is the 1924–1925 football squad. From left to right are (first row) unidentified, Lawrence "Bud" Fredricksen, Rich Pucci, unidentified, and Norman "Curley" Mitch, unidentified, and George Schiefelbein; (second row) unidentified, ? Bernhagen, S. Maves, and Bill Guerney; (third row) Art "Google" Anderson, C. Gatz, Bobby York, unidentified, Art "Jake" Mitch, Harold "Bush" Gatz, W. Schieve, and Tony Fredricksen.

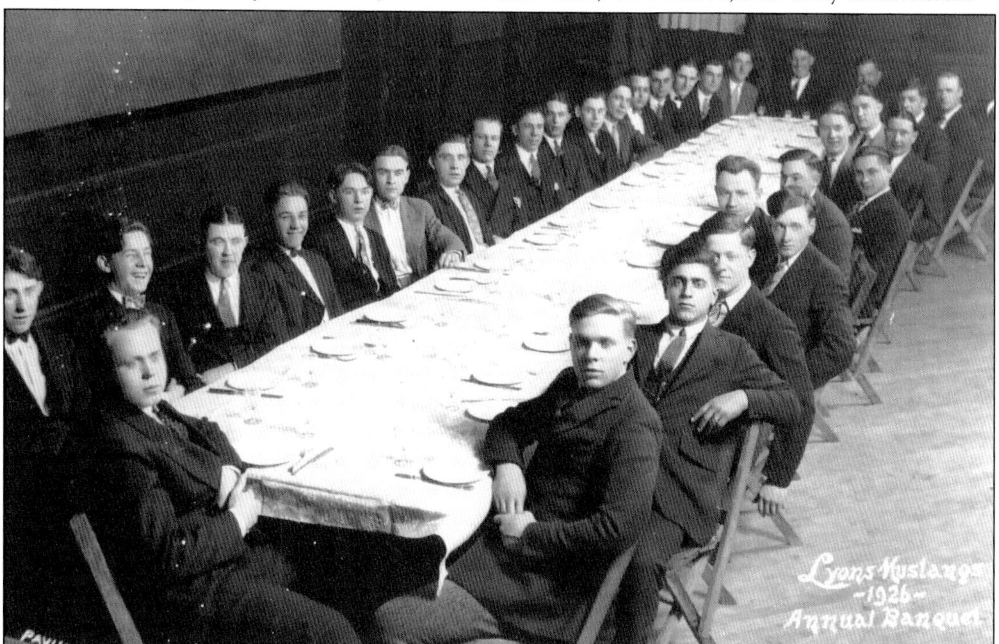

The Lyons Mustangs Athletic Club is shown here assembled for a banquet in 1926. That year, the athletic club sold its lot on Prescott Avenue and bought a new one on Leland Avenue, where the club built its headquarters. The building opened in 1927.

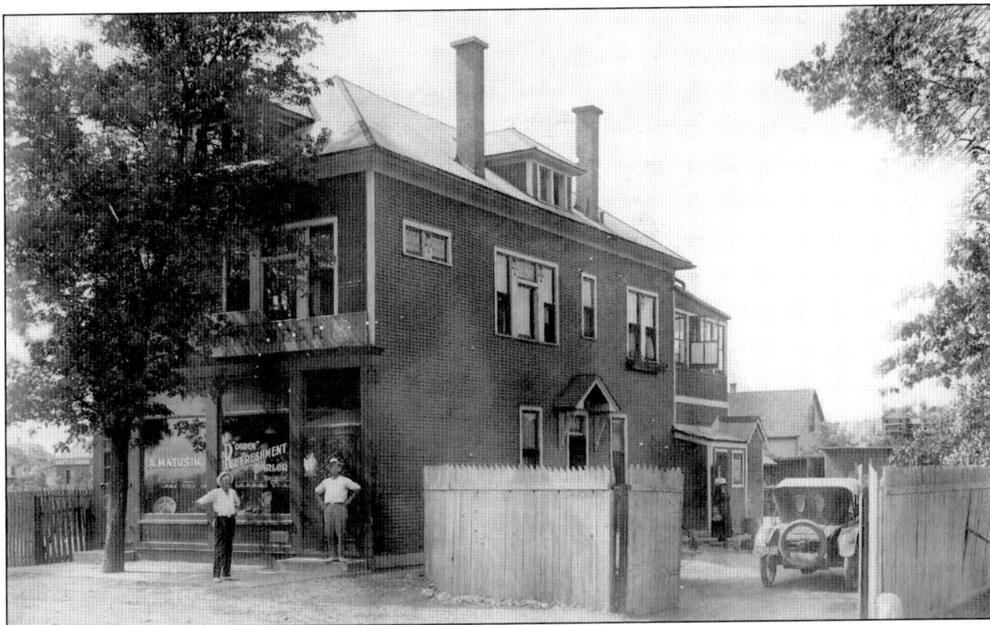

The "refreshment parlor" at 8550 West Ogden Avenue, shown here in 1922, reflects the Czech and Polish community that gathered in Lyons west of First Avenue. Many of the west-end streets have a Polish history: Cracow Avenue is named after the city, and Conrad Avenue is named after the Polish-born novelist Joseph Conrad. There was enough unity among west-end residents to prompt the creation of the West End Improvement Club in 1924.

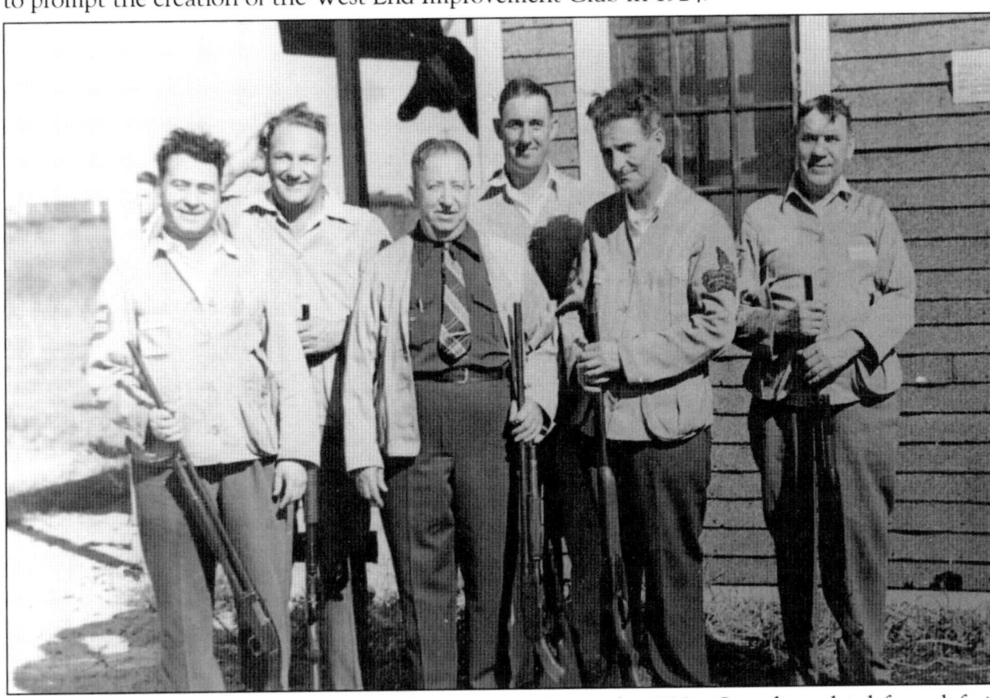

Lyons residents are seen on a gun-club outing in the early 1920s. Standing third from left is O. H. Nelson, who was mayor of Lyons for three non-consecutive terms, from 1913 to 1915, 1923 to 1925, and 1937 to 1938.

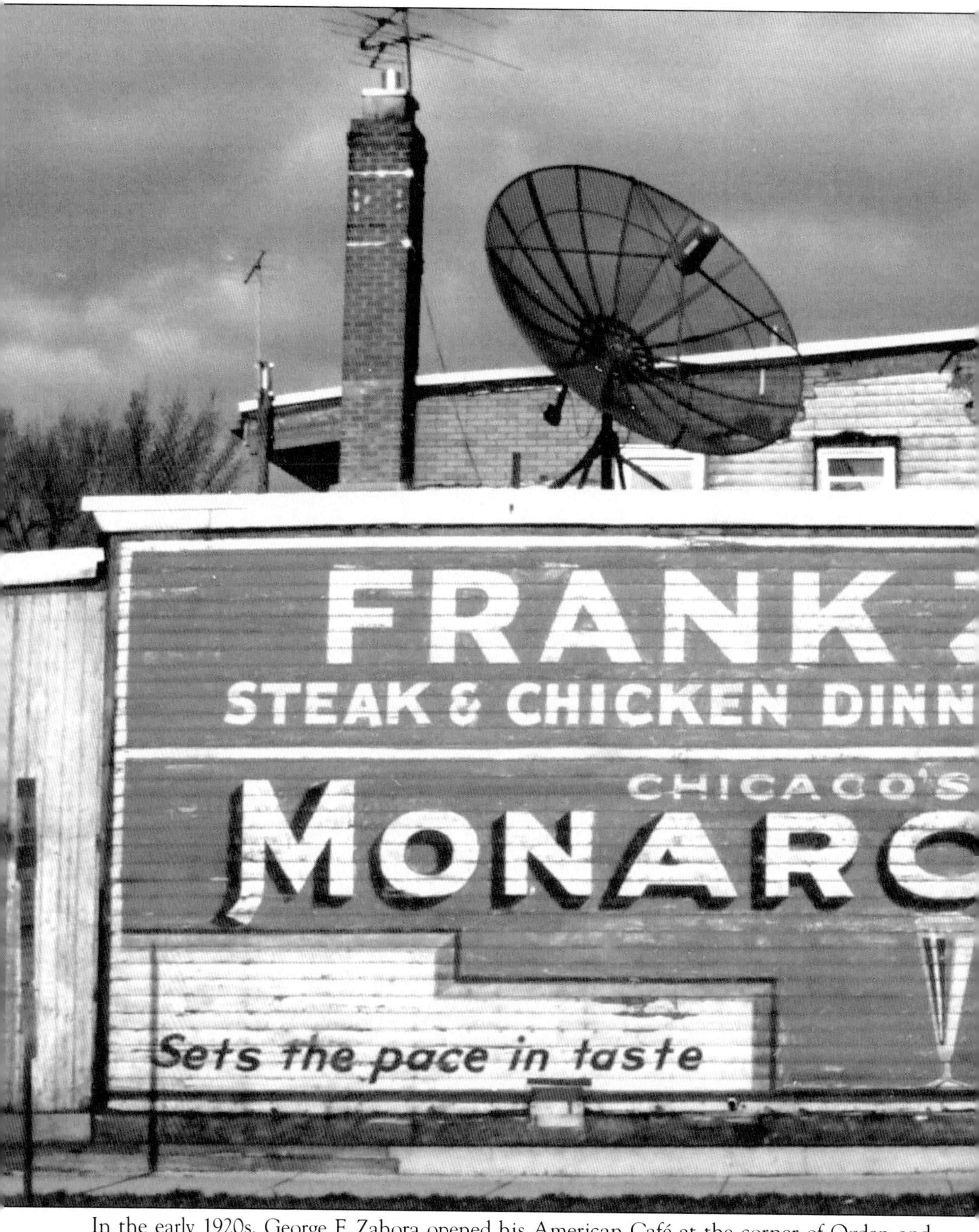

In the early 1920s, George F. Zahora opened his American Café at the corner of Ogden and Custer Avenues, right on the border of Lyons and Brookfield. Like many other Lyons businesses it boasted its own picnic grove. Construction work on the building in the late 1990s exposed this billboard on the wall. The Monarch Brewery Company was founded in Chicago in 1890;

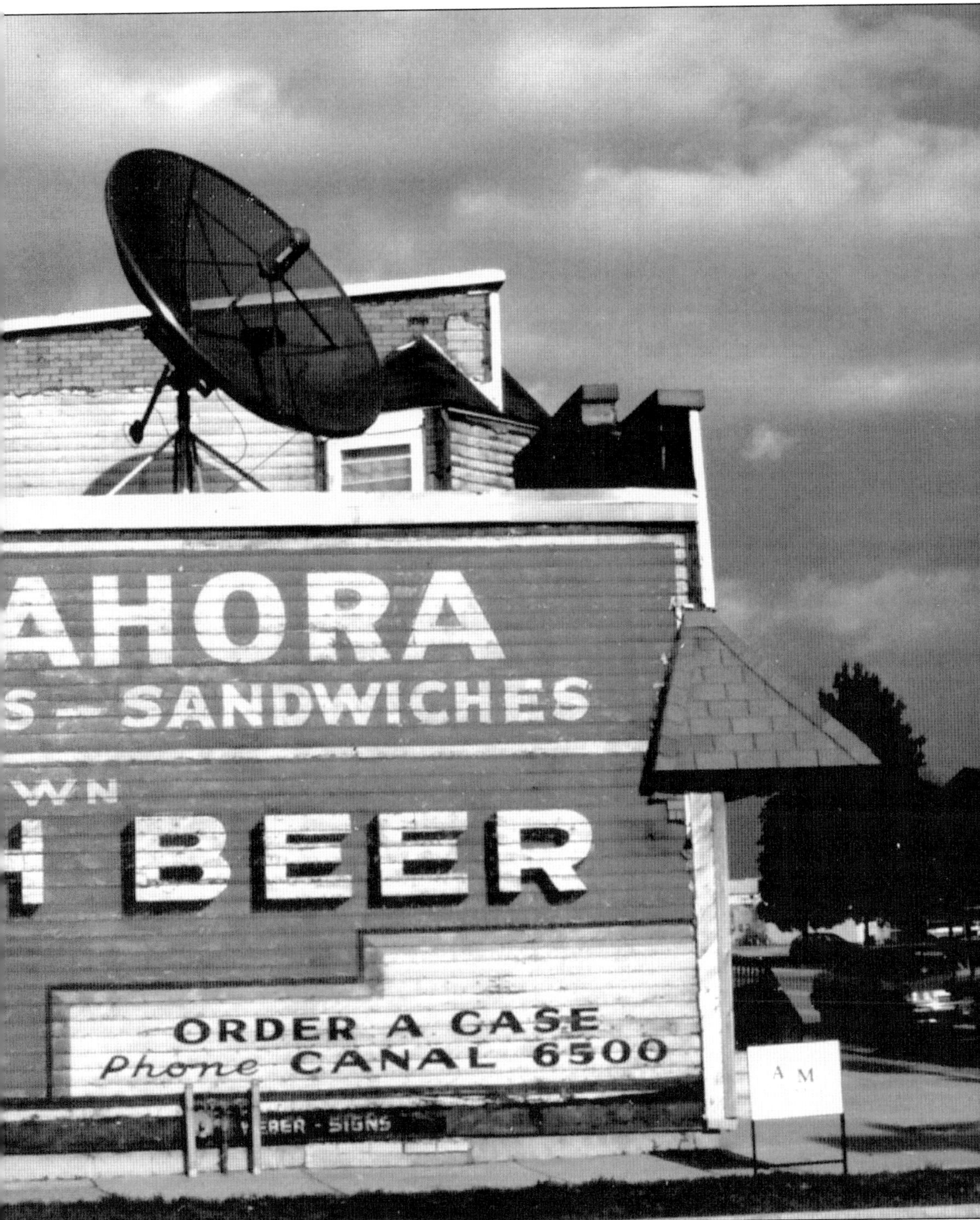

the billboard likely dates from sometime between 1932, when the company reopened after prohibition, and 1952, when it became the Van Merritt Brewing Company. The building itself was torn down in 2003, when it was a club called the Gathering.

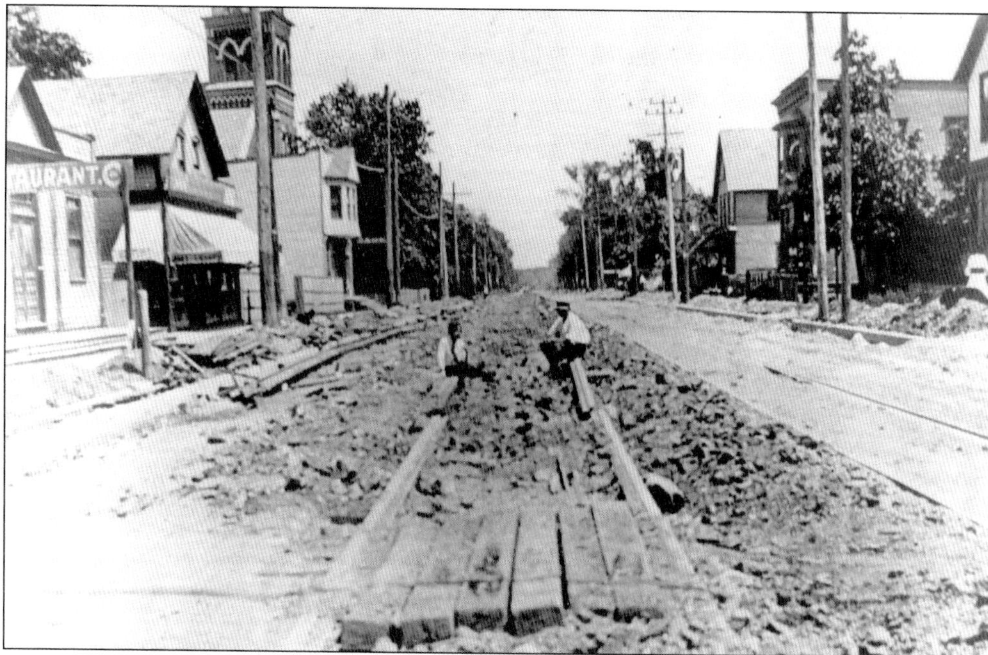

Trolleys began running down Ogden Avenue in the 1850s, but the tracks began falling into disrepair by the 1920s. In 1926, a trolley crossing a trestle over the Des Plaines River derailed and fell into the river with 50 passengers on board. In the 1930s, the tracks were dismantled, as this picture shows, and the trestle running across the Des Plaines River was replaced with the current bridge.

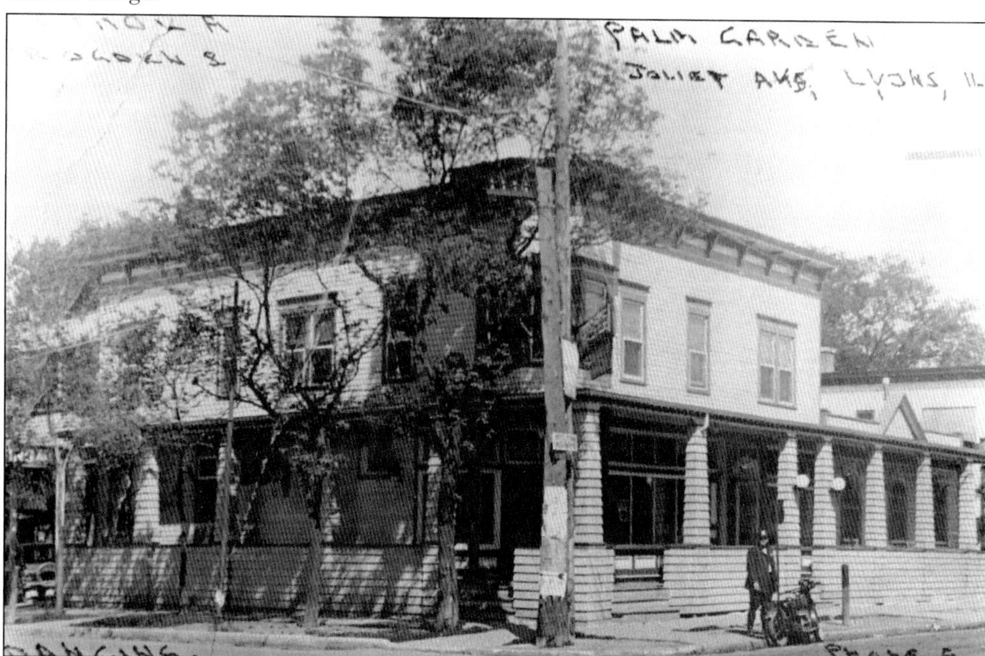

Before it became Grosse's, the building on the northeast corner of Odgen and Joliet Avenues was DePaola's Palm Garden, a tavern. Officer Dirk Huizinga, who was appointed a motorcycle policeman in 1922, is shown standing in front.

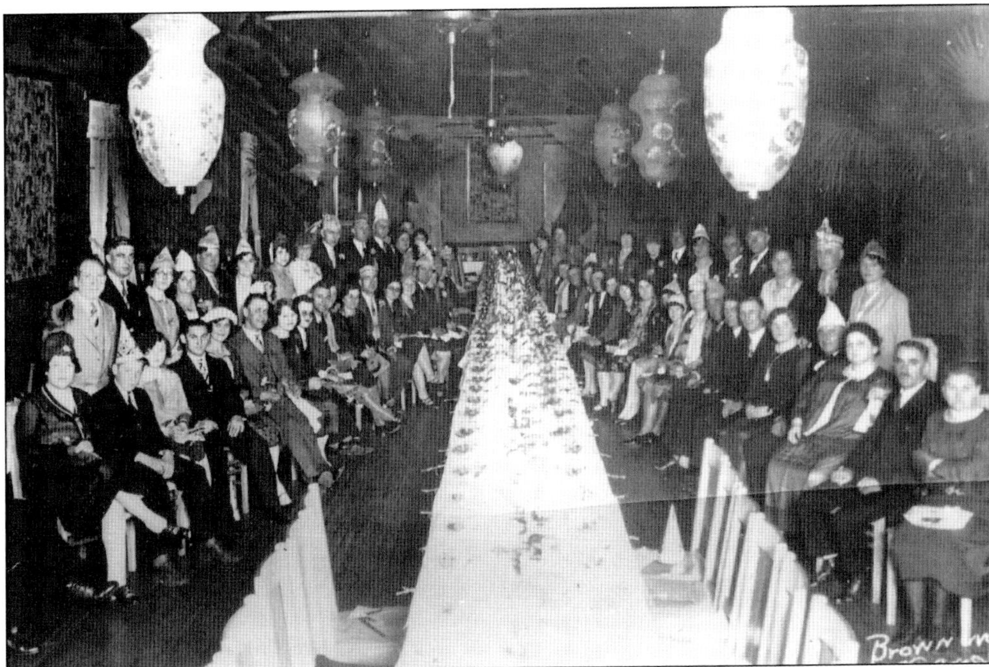

This photograph of a meeting of the Lyons Businessmen's Association from the 1920s shows the interior of DePaola's Palm Garden.

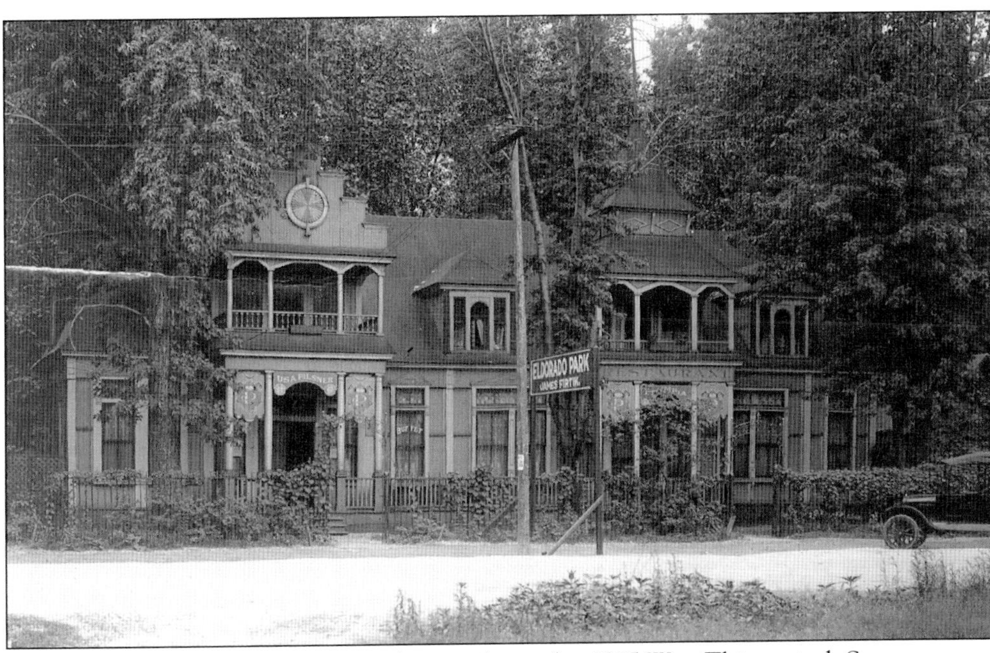

Eldorado Park, an inn, restaurant, and tavern located at 7325 West Thirty-ninth Street, was run by James Firtik in the 1920s through the late 1930s.

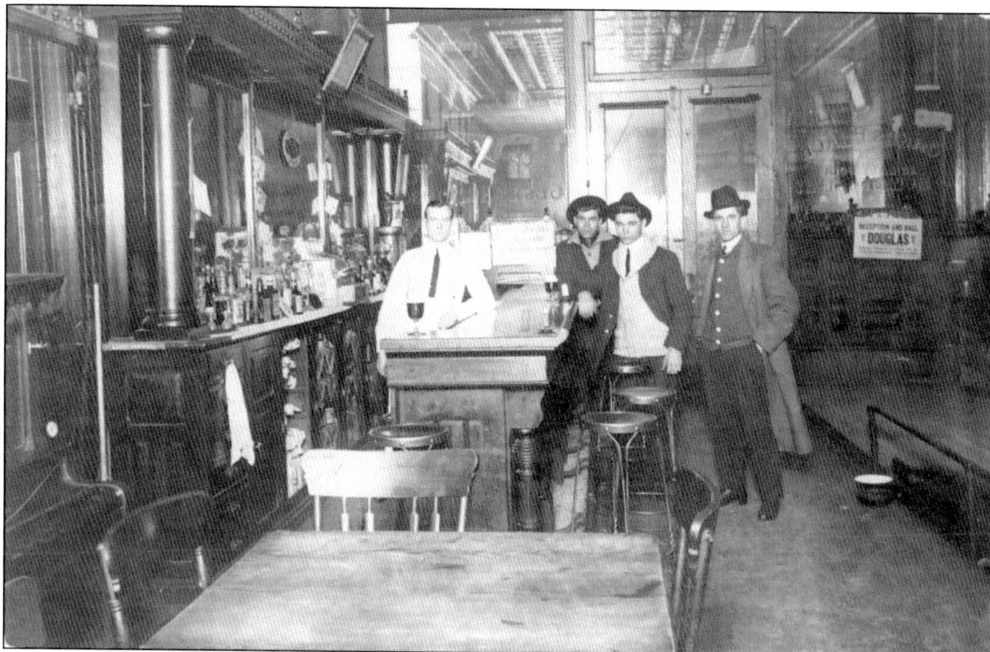

The interior of the tavern at Eldorado Park is seen here. James Firtik is standing behind the bar.

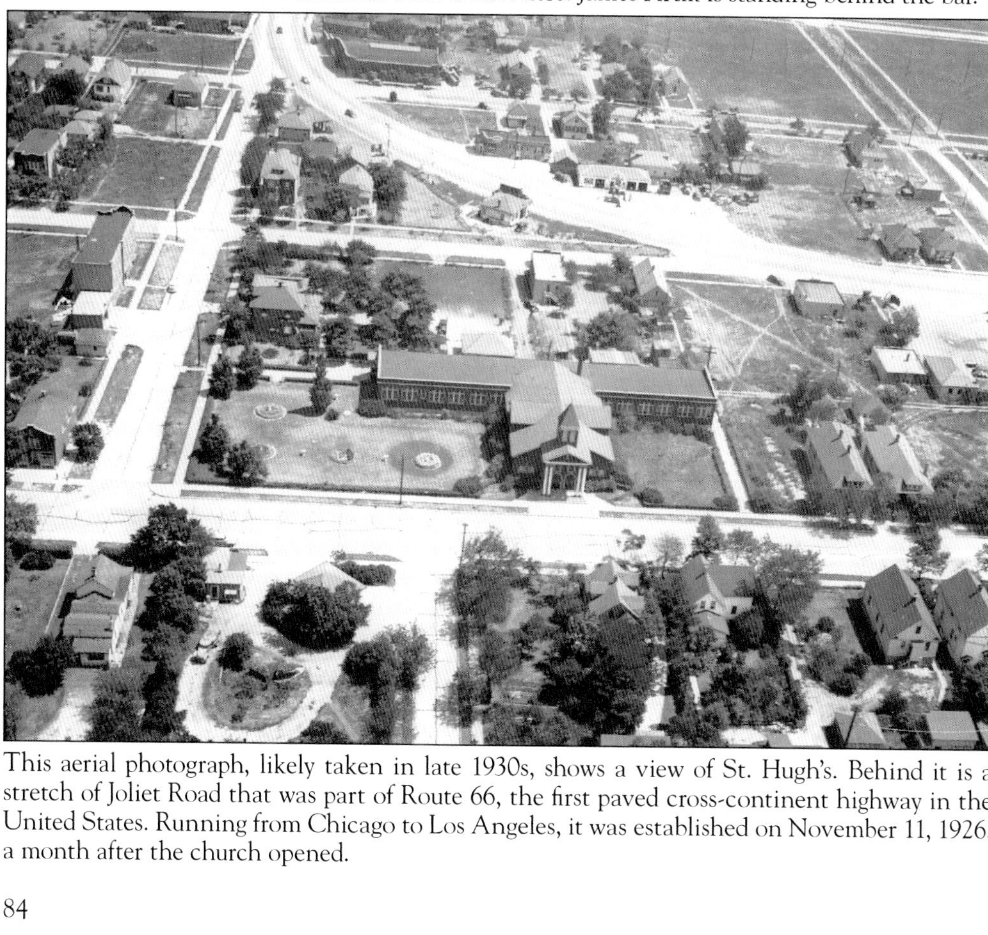

This aerial photograph, likely taken in late 1930s, shows a view of St. Hugh's. Behind it is a stretch of Joliet Road that was part of Route 66, the first paved cross-continent highway in the United States. Running from Chicago to Los Angeles, it was established on November 11, 1926, a month after the church opened.

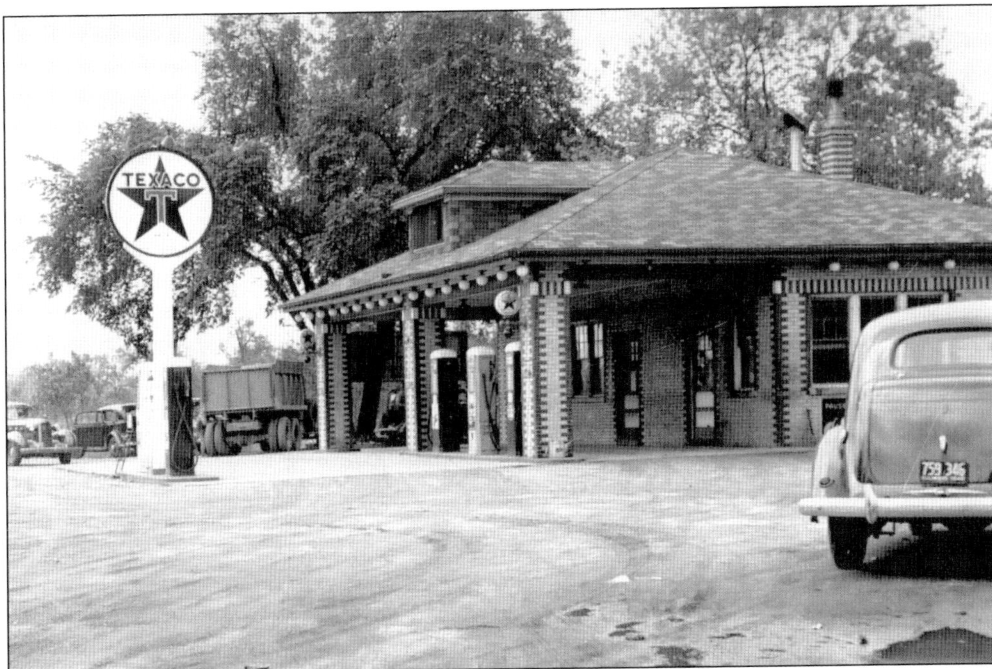

The establishment of Route 66 brought a new influx of road-trippers through Lyons, which prompted a slew of full-service gas stations to spring up on and around Joliet Road. Kerpec's Texaco station, located on Harlem Avenue just north of Joliet Road, featured cabins for resting travelers.

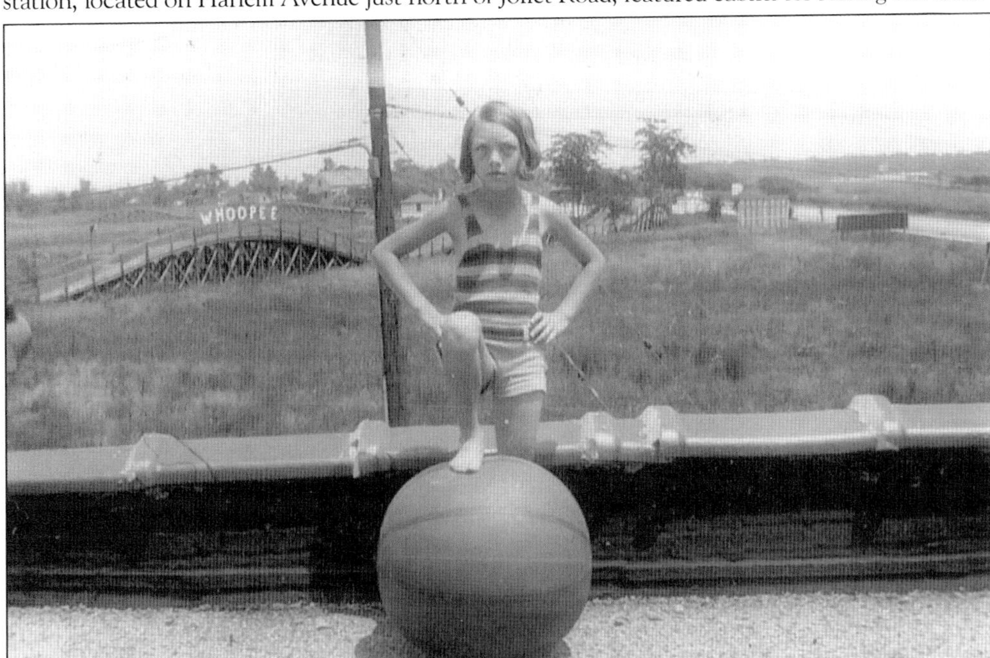

Route 66 also reflected the increasing role of the automobile as more than just a mode of transportation and a source for entertainment in itself. Behind the child in this picture one can see the Whoopee Coaster, an amusement park for local joyriders, located on Lawndale Avenue south of Forty-seventh Street in McCook from the late 1920s to the mid-1930s.

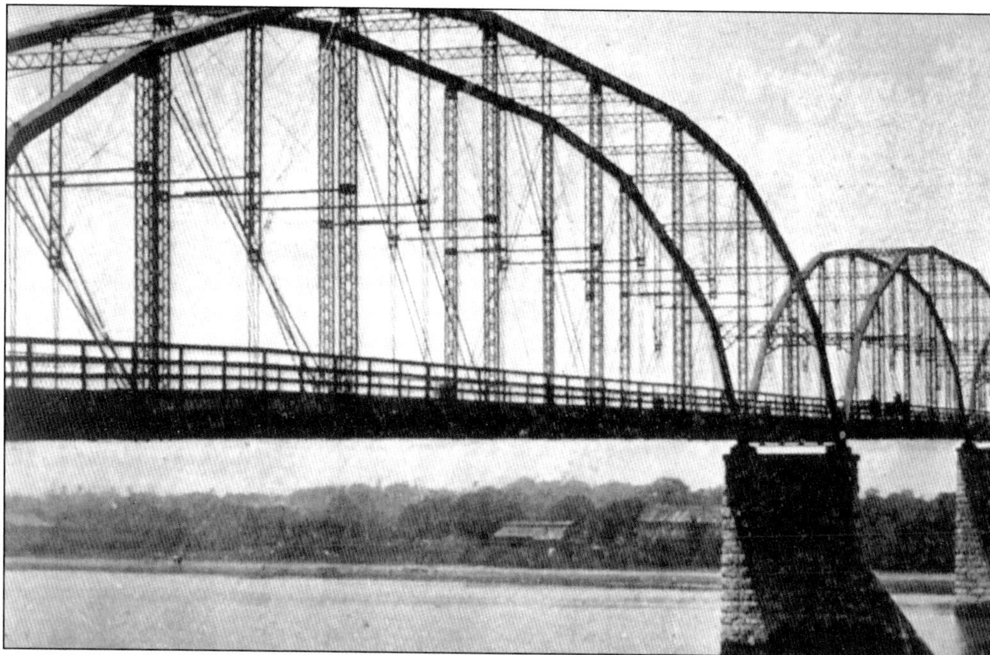

In the late 1800s, construction began on the Chicago Sanitary and Ship Canal, which was designed to reverse the flow of the Chicago river and send the city's waste away from Lake Michigan instead of toward it. The canal opened in 1900, running alongside the Des Plaines River until reaching Joliet to the southwest. The nearby Illionis and Michigan Canal had fallen in to disuse by the time; the section cutting through Lyons was later paved over as part of Stevenson Expressway (I-55). This postcard shows the "high bridge," just south of Lyons, crossing the river and leading into Summit.

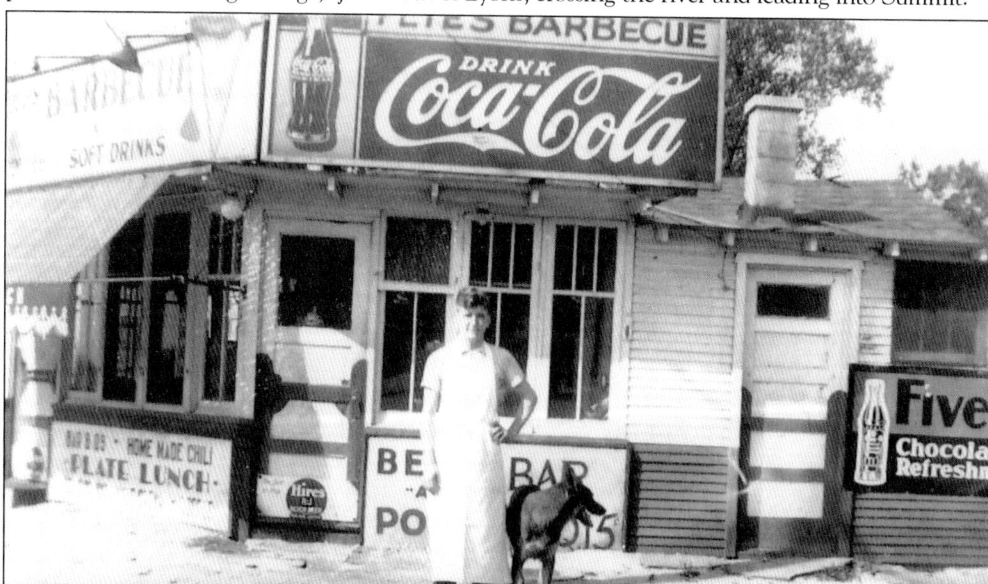

The Stathakis family ran a barbecue restaurant in Lyons since 1928. Pete Stathakis's son, George is shown here in the 1950s, when it occupied the corner of Ogden and Lawndale Avenues.

A teacher leads students in a tornado drill at Costello School in the 1950s.

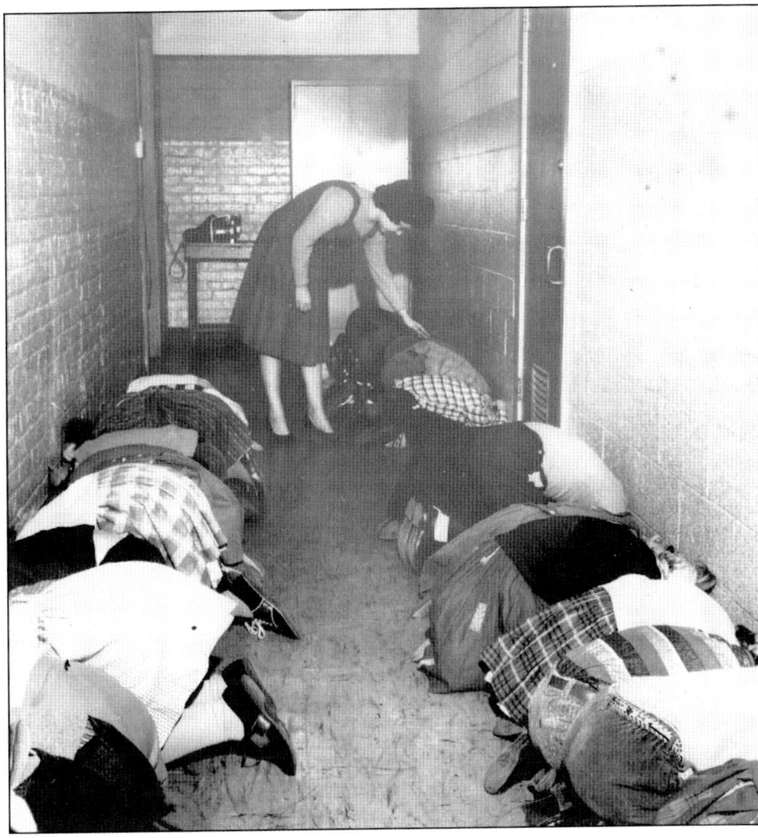

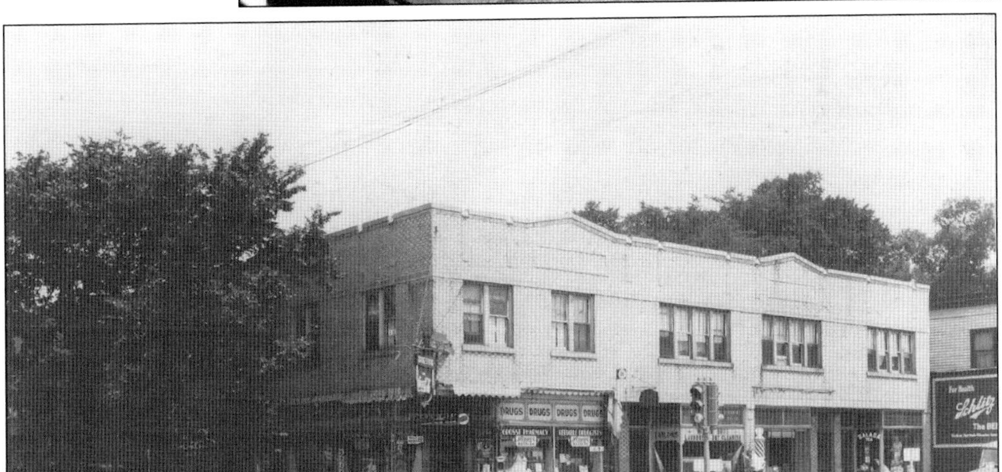

In the 1930s, DePaola's Garden became a pharmacy run by Fritz Grosse. In the 1950s, H. C. Wooley's and Company dime store would open in the spaces occupied by the grocer's and dry cleaners next door.

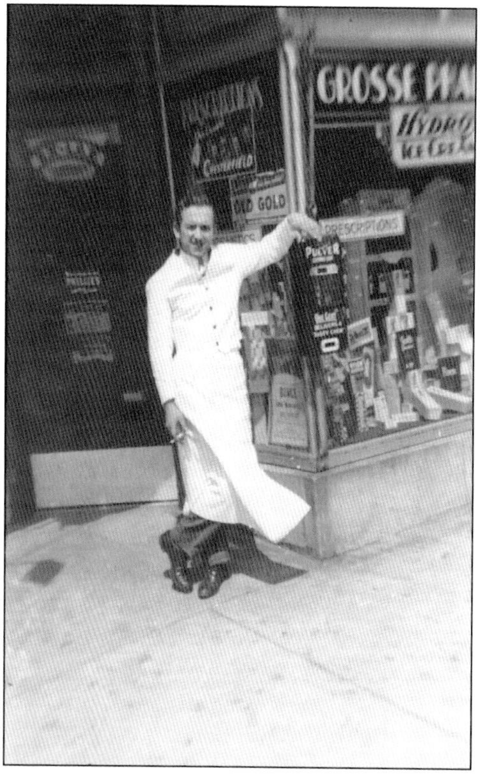

H. Opaka, a soda jerk at the pharmacy, stands in front of the entrance.

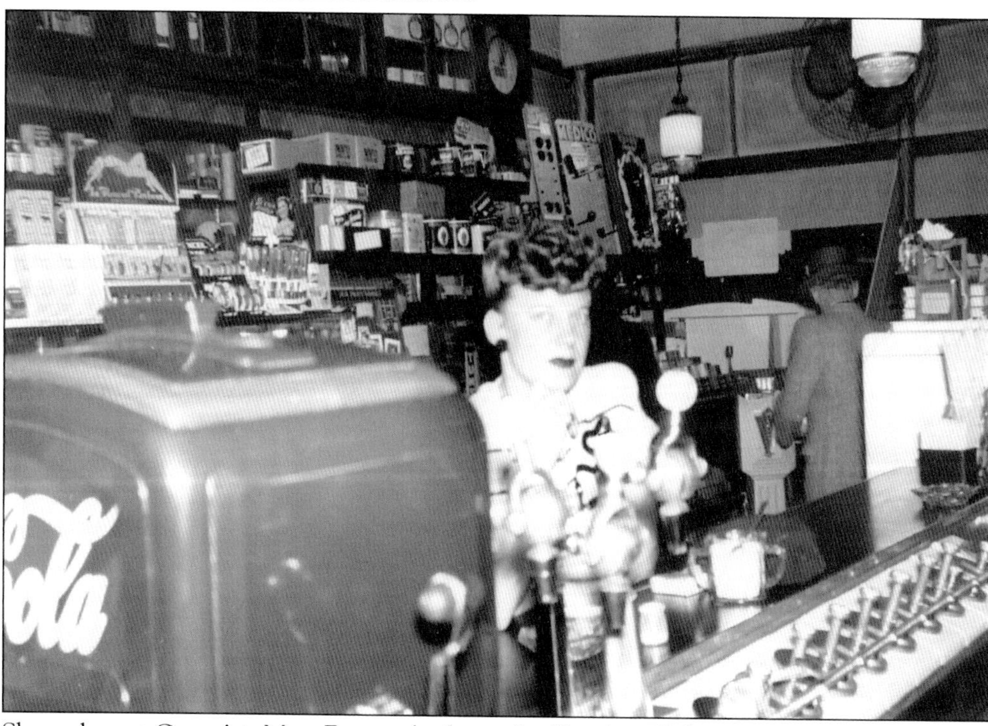

Shown here at Grosse's is Mary Fonter, the first wife of Joachim "Jokes" Fonter, owner of the Mill Bridge Roller Rink.

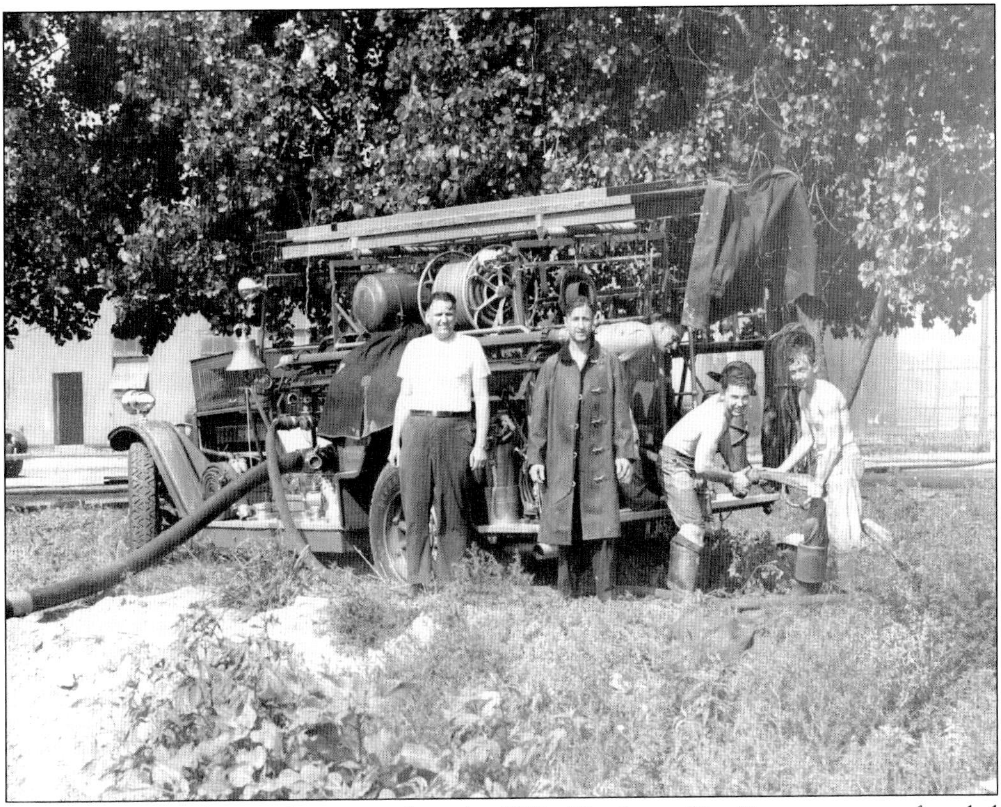

Some of Lyons's volunteer firemen work in the 1930s. The Lyons Fire Department was founded in 1896, and moved into its location at Collins and Joliet Avenues in 1911, near the water tower. At the time this photograph was taken, Lyons had 25 volunteer firefighters.

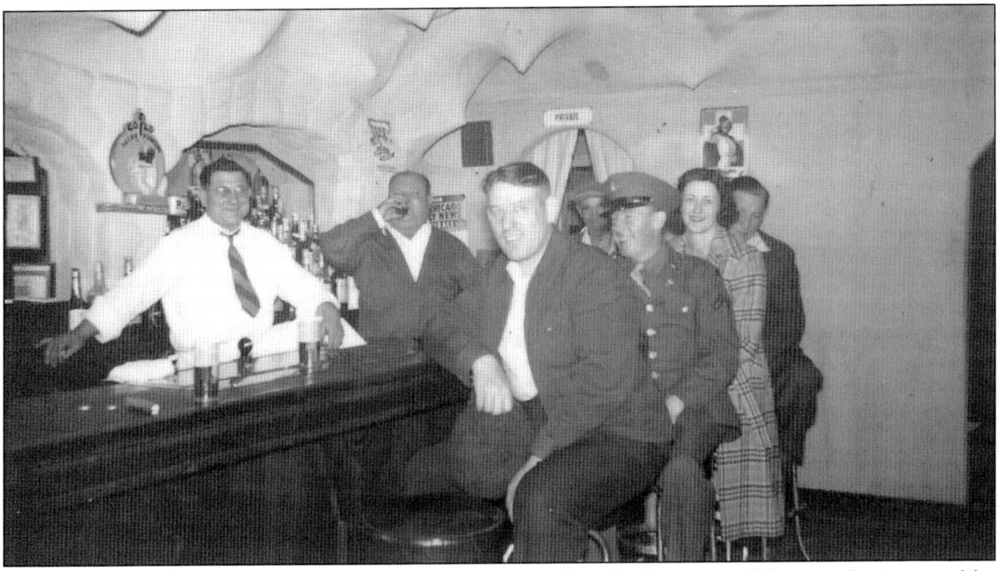

As the name suggests, the Lyons Cave tavern at 8114 West Ogden was well-known for its cave-like interior. Owner Frank Benedetti is shown here behind the bar in a photograph taken around 1940.

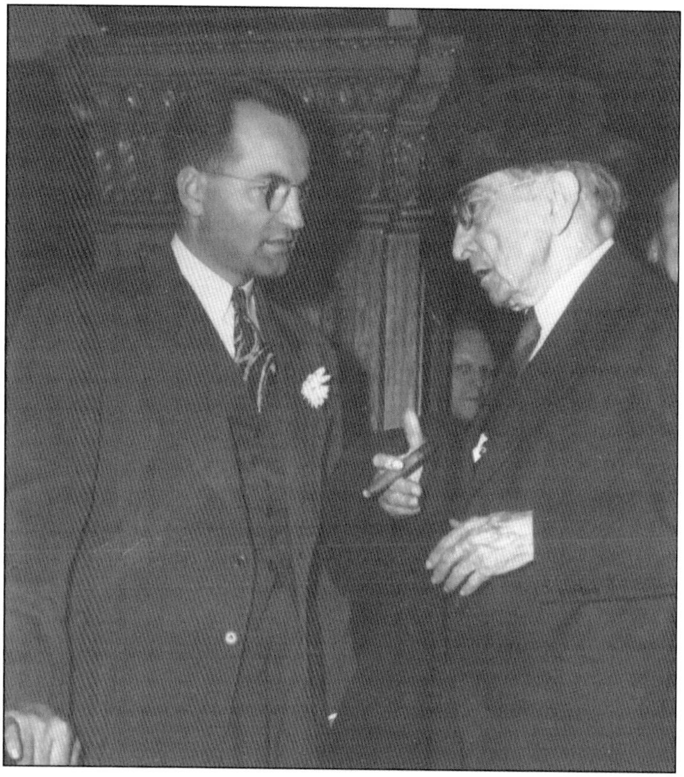

Theofil T. Bulat, left, was mayor of Lyons from 1940 to 1953; he is pictured with Edward Woodruff, mayor of Peoria, who at 80 was the oldest mayor in the state. Bulat died in 1975.

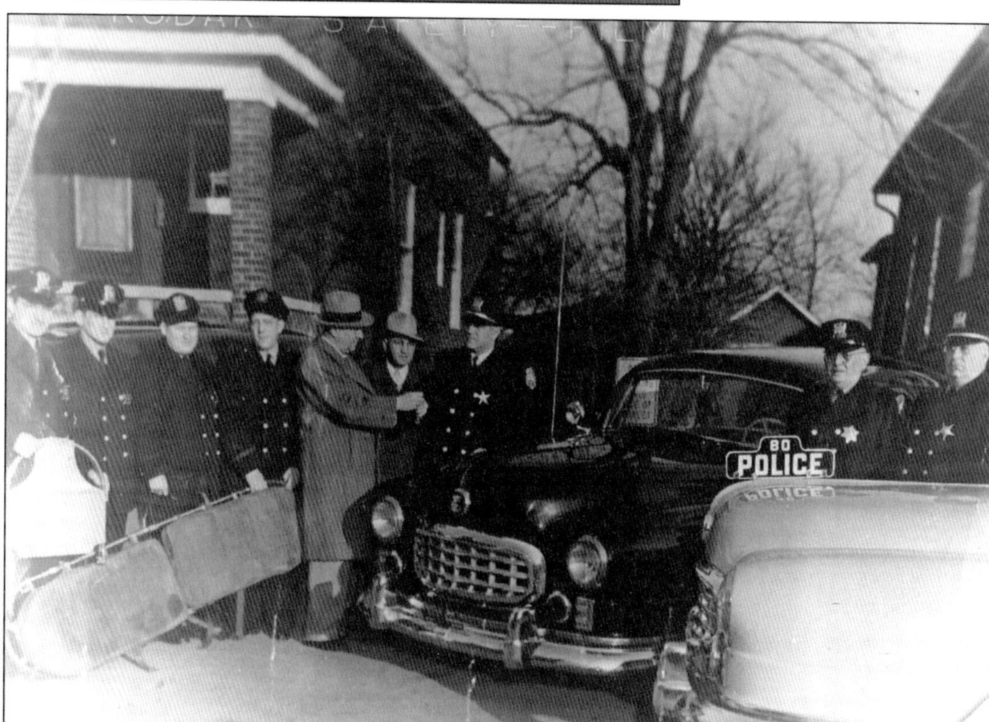

Mayor Bulat is at the center of this photograph, standing with members of the Lyons police.

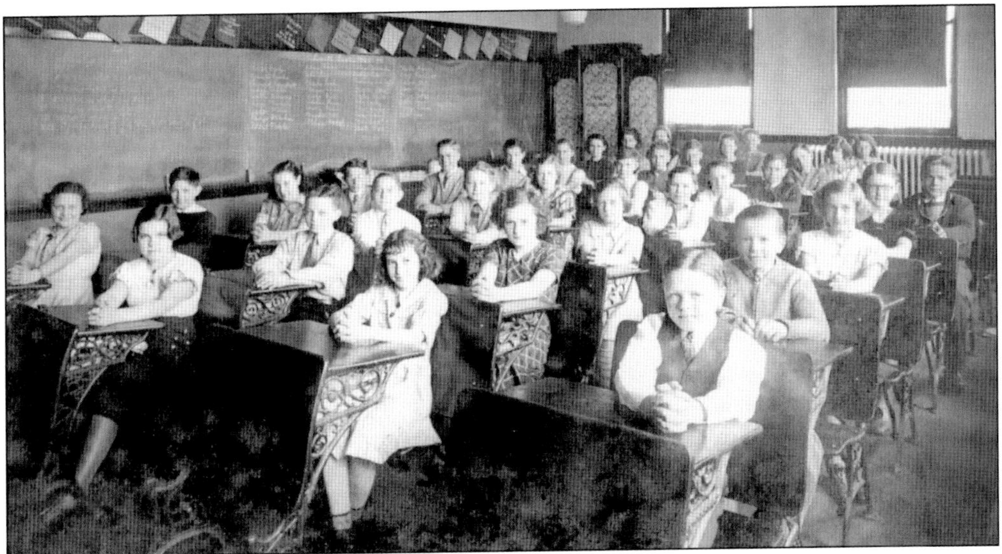

The seventh-grade class at Washington School of 1936 is seen here. The students seen here are Ruth Zace, Richard Gatz, Genevieve Sterday, John Sergo, Kenneth Camden, Arthur Shoreader, Helen Vocelka, Arlean Westerhoff, Jeanette Misher, Dolores Newcanter, Rosemary Sultz, Charles Savacka, Ranyard Darmsted, George Miclous, Dorothy Ericksen, Adolfe Michka, George Mosinik, Clarance Washer, Florence Hokel, Joseph Duffeck, Mary Pukys, Evelyn Peters, Eleanor Waster, Eugene Kanak, Ralph Benes, Charles Blalock, Robert Burkhart, Violet Bull, Margaret Hiedle, Julius Petrik, Alfred Nokala, Pauling Vinichka, Adilian Busnik, and Walter Gasway.

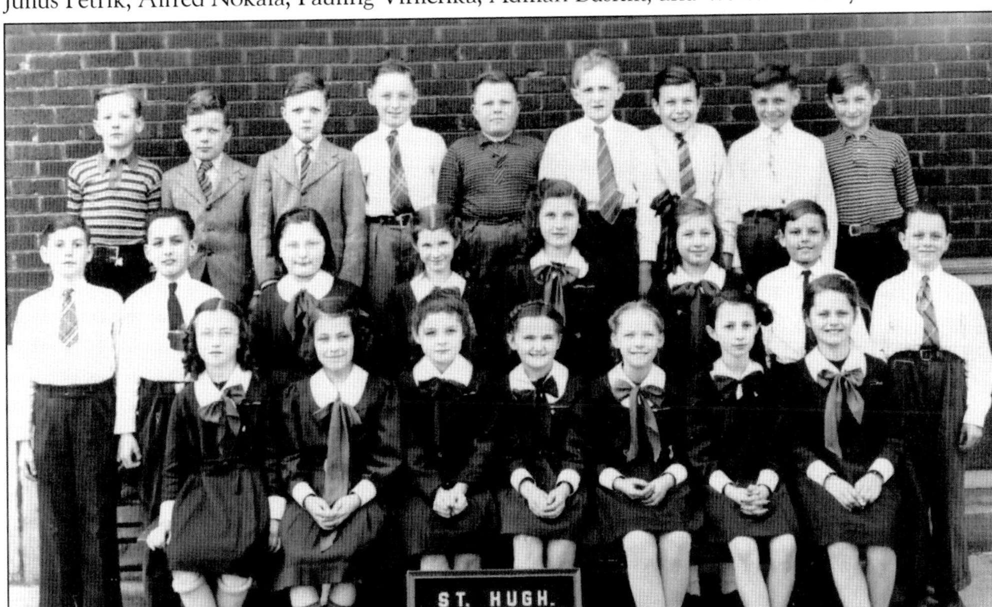

Seen here is St. Hugh's fifth-grade class of 1941. From left to right are (first row) Nora Monaghan, Lorene St. John, Helen Stercay, Rose Zlatich, Dorothy Verba, Evangeline Ferraro, and Gloria Kritzer; (second row) Jack Brocken, Florian Gay, Lorraine Coha, Marlys Ann Chaisson, Margaret Polich, Jo Ann Stupka, Francis Urban, and John Perisich; (third row) John Stemack, Robert Kroll, William Kroll, Clarence Klancer, Leslie Pedersen, William Vavra, Eugene Heslop, Richard Stercay, and James Lucas.

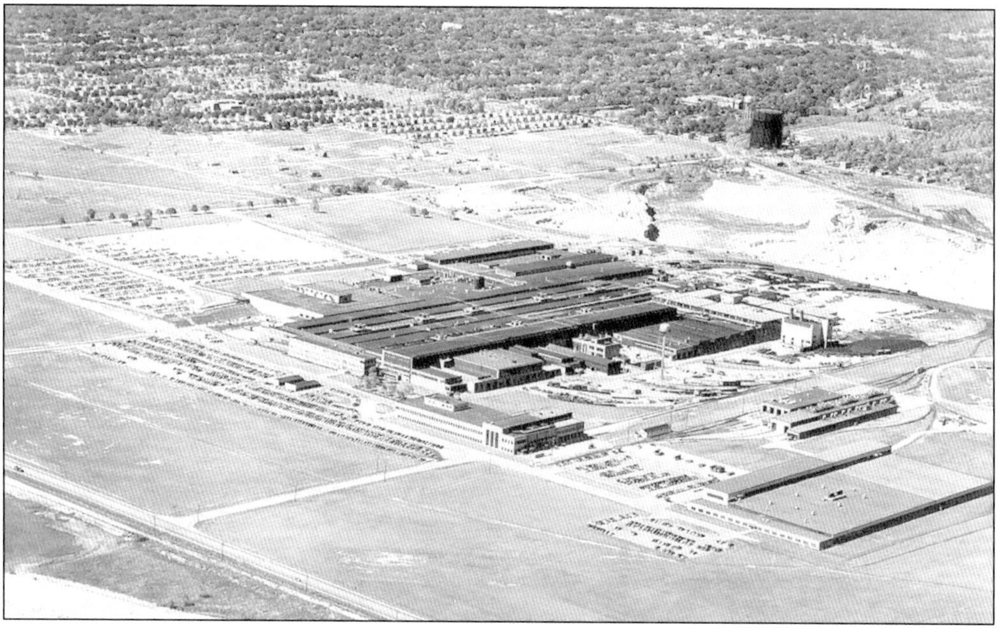

Located in nearby McCook, General Motors's Electro-Motive massive locomotive plant—200,000 square feet on a 74-acre site—was one of the largest employers of Lyons residents, and indeed larger Cook County. At its height, the plant had nearly 15,000 workers. The plant opened in 1926; this photograph shows the plant in 1952 after it expanded. General Motors sold Electro-Motive in 2005.

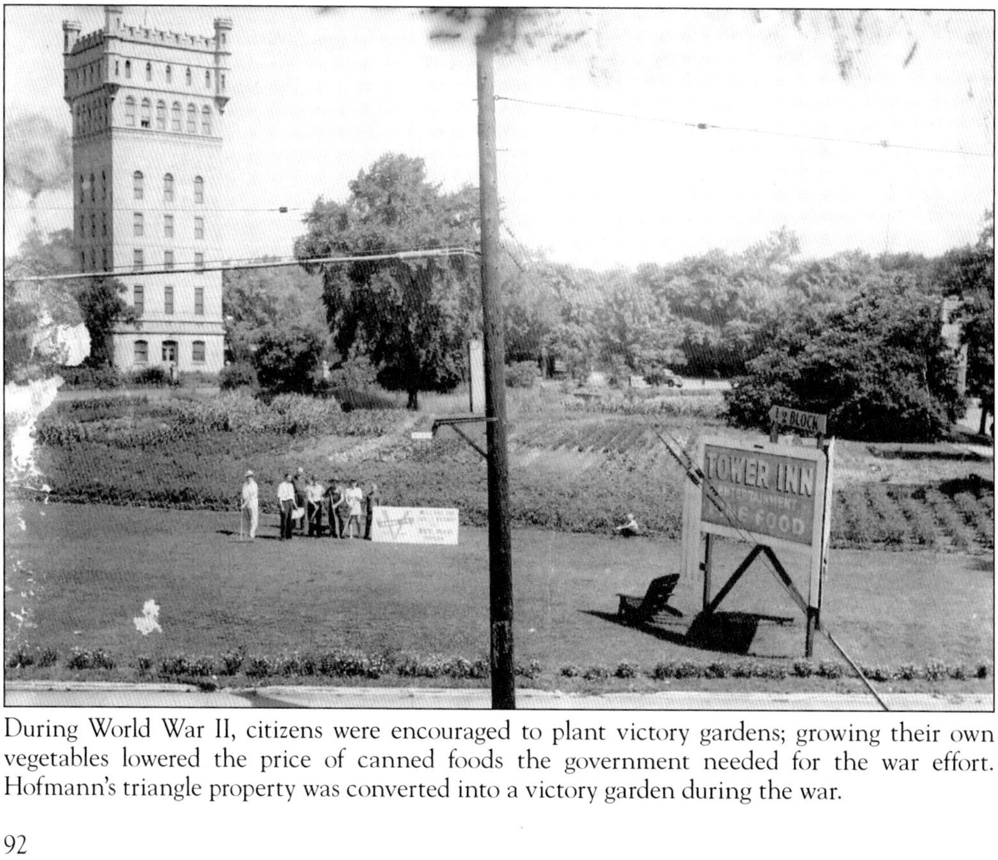

During World War II, citizens were encouraged to plant victory gardens; growing their own vegetables lowered the price of canned foods the government needed for the war effort. Hofmann's triangle property was converted into a victory garden during the war.

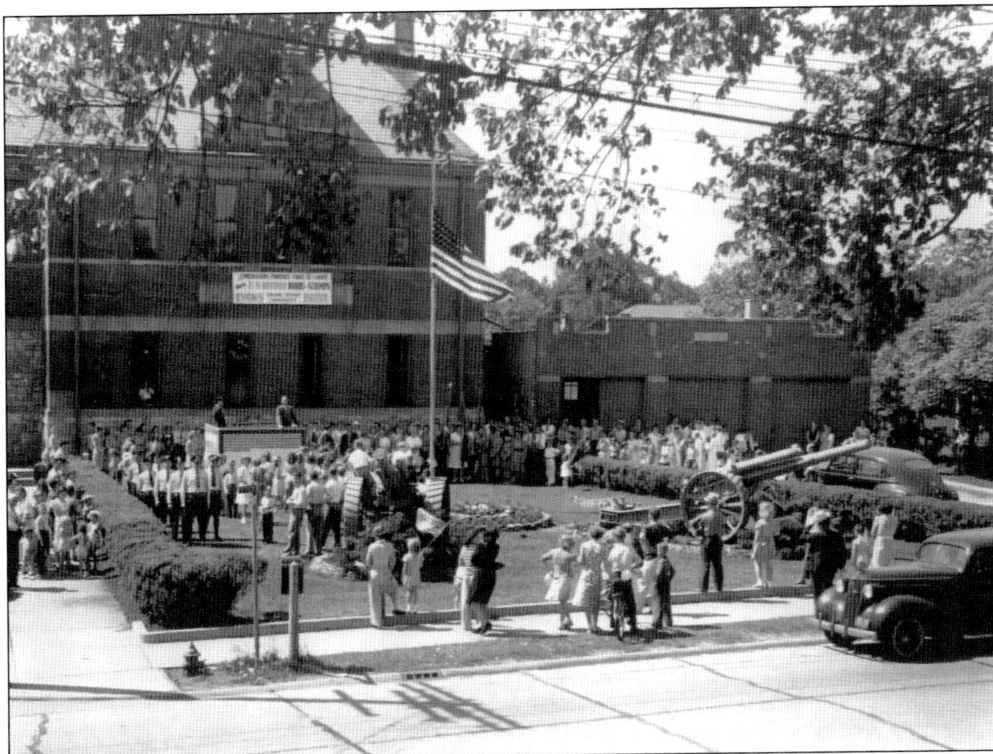

During World War II, Lyons's village hall played host to war-bond rallies like this one.

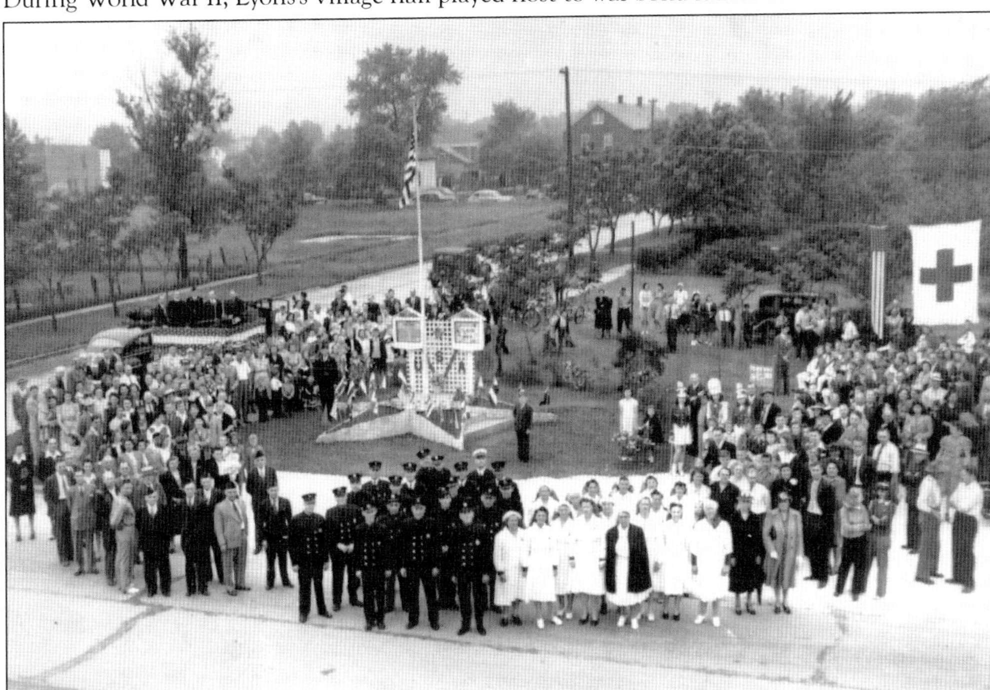

This local World War II rally of nurses, police officers, and volunteers was held at a lot at Forty-fifth Street and Joliet Road.

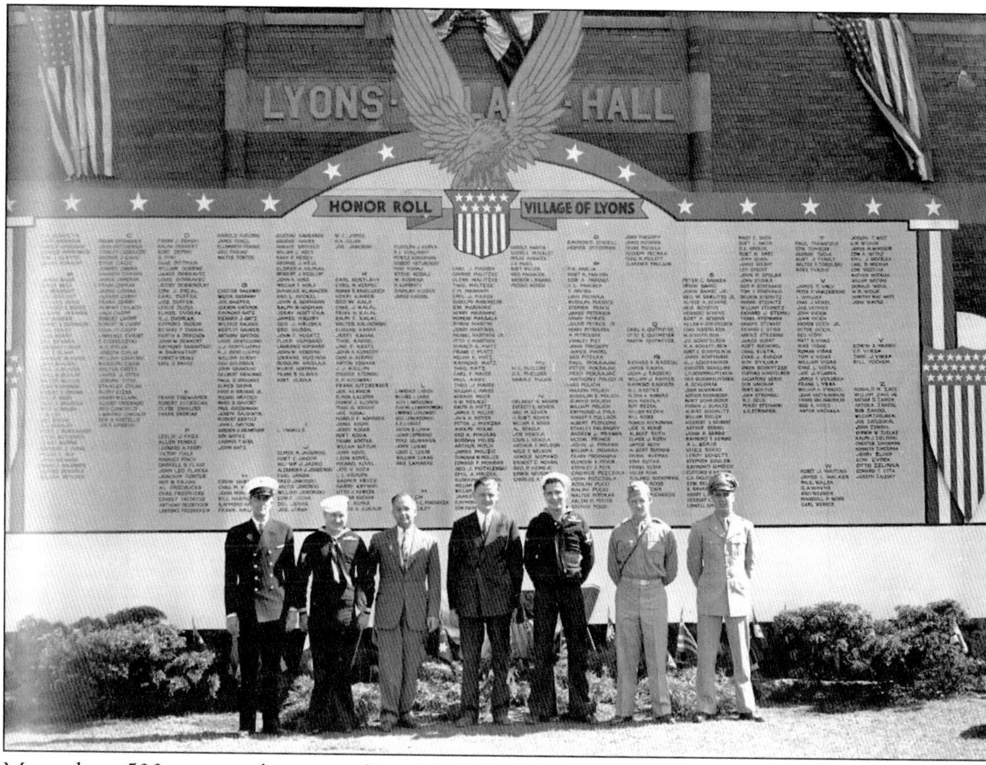

More than 500 men and women from Lyons—a tenth of its population at the time—served during World War II. A group of unidentified armed forces members stand in front of a sign listing a Memorial Day commemoration in 1944.

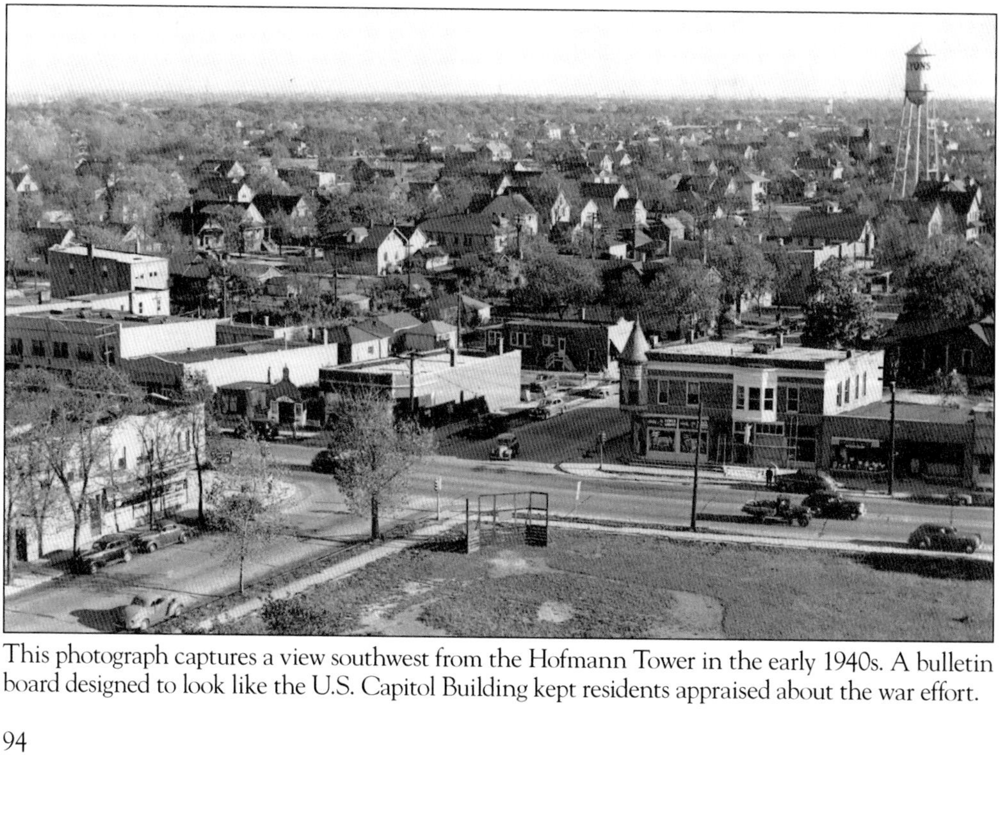

This photograph captures a view southwest from the Hofmann Tower in the early 1940s. A bulletin board designed to look like the U.S. Capitol Building kept residents appraised about the war effort.

Four

Crisis, Controversy, and Change

Like many suburban American communities after World War II, Lyons had a population explosion thanks to a growing economy; the number of residents more than doubled between 1940 and 1960, from 4,882 to 9,913. The children of the baby boom accounted for much of that growth, of course, and numerous facilities sprung up to accommodate them, including the village's Tee Pee Club and Fairyland Park. The latter was founded by Richard Miller in 1938; it was taken over by his son, Allen, and Allen's wife, Georgia, in 1955, and grew to feature bumper cars, a merry-go-round, a Ferris wheel, and a picnic grove. At its peak it attracted 75,000 visitors a season. It closed in 1977.

Starting in the 1960s, Lyons also began attracting adult businesses—strip clubs began populating the stretch of Ogden Avenue that ran through town, and by the 1970s the seedy area—with its brightly-lit signs promoting "Girls Girls Girls" and "Miss Nude America"—began to be known as a site for barely-concealed prostitution activity. In the early 1980s, federal agents began investigating; raids began in 1984, and by the end of the decade the clubs were all but erased from the map.

Many local officials fell under scrutiny for their roles regarding the clubs; in 1990, two Lyons officers, Donald Kroft and William Teeter, plead guilty to receiving sexual favors in return for overlooking the prostitution activity at one club, My Uncle's Place. Mayor Smith drew attention as well as federal agents built their case—he had long been criticized for serving as liquor commissioner while also selling dram shop insurance to the clubs—although his death in 1989 halted an investigation of his activities. Smith's willingness to accommodate the businesses stung many Lyons residents, who publicly voiced their concerns about the town's reputation. "My friends would always say to me, 'How are things in Smutville?'" one resident told the *Chicago Tribune* in 1992, explaining why he wanted Smith's name erased from a local baseball field.

In the late 1980s and early 1990s, Lyons settled back into a predominantly residential town that concentrated on attracting new businesses and improving its schools; in 2004 District 103 superintendent Dr. Ray Lauk successfully convinced residents to approve a 50 percent property tax increase to benefit schools.

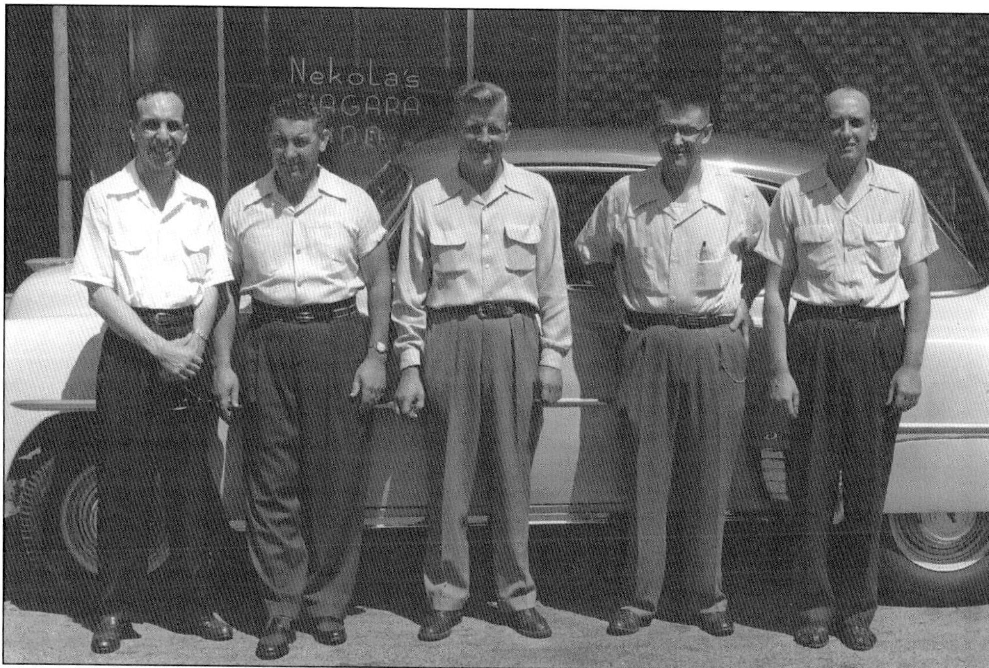

William G. Smith, center, stands along with a group of friends in the 1950s in front of Nekola's Niagara Inn at 3919 Joliet Avenue. John Hofmann, at far left, was Smith's predecessor as mayor, running the town from 1953 to 1961.

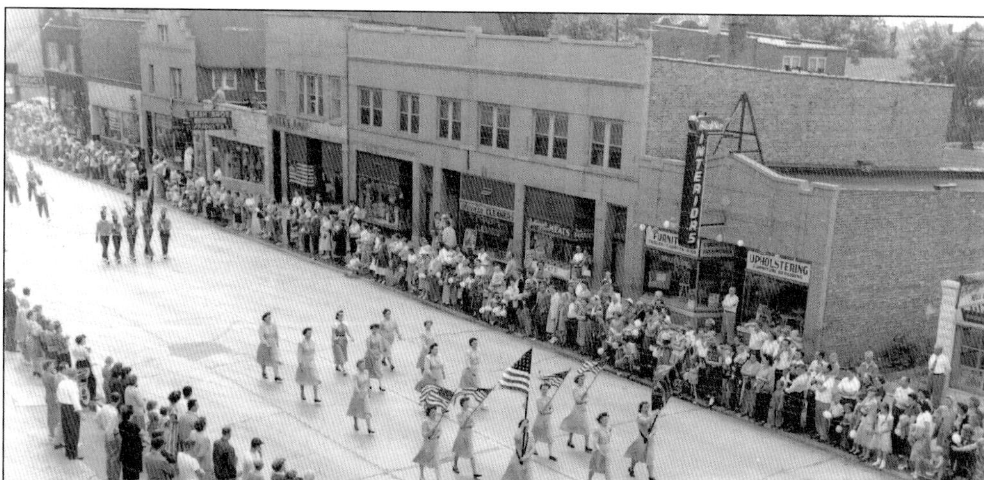

Pictured here is the Fourth of July parade in Lyons in 1951.

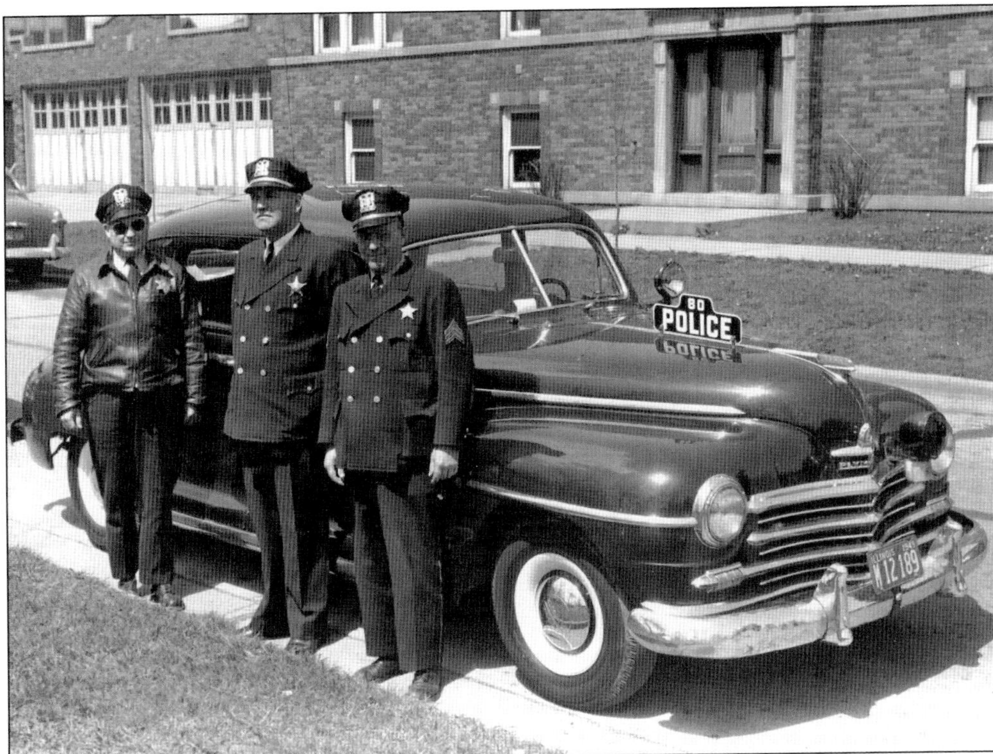

Three Lyons policemen are seen in 1948; officer Les Dusik (left), Chief Ralph White (center), and Sgt. Herman Marose.

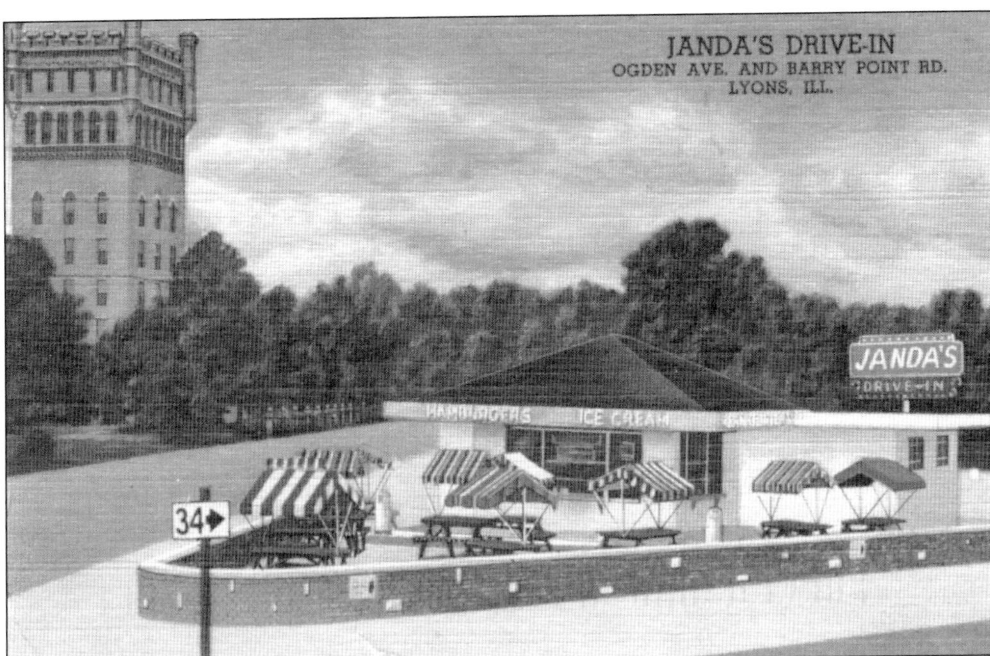

Janda's Drive-In opened on the triangle property in 1949, and operated into the 1950s; the reverse of this postcard proclaimed that Janda's offered "the best food by a dam site."

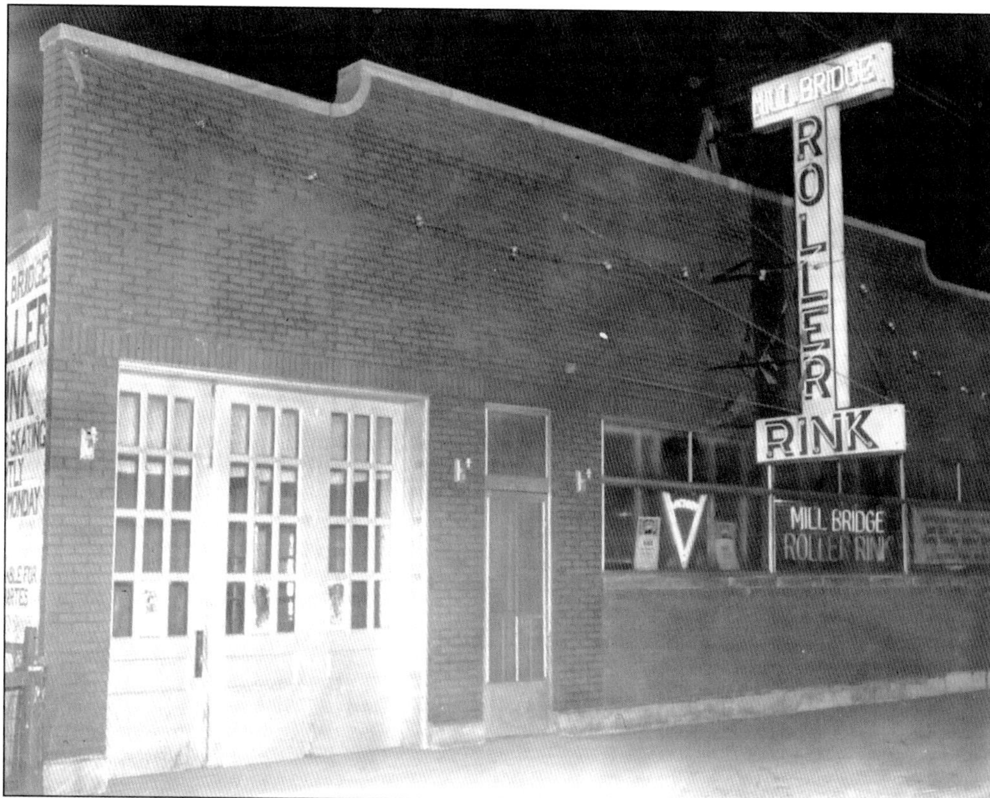

The Mill Bridge Roller Rink, at 8027 West Ogden, was opened in 1925 by Joachim "Jokes" Fonter, who ran the place until it closed in 1992. Fonter died in 1997. This photograph dates to World War II. The rink burned down on May 9, 1993; the small neon sign currently resides in the Hofmann Tower, where the Lyons Historical Commission keeps a museum.

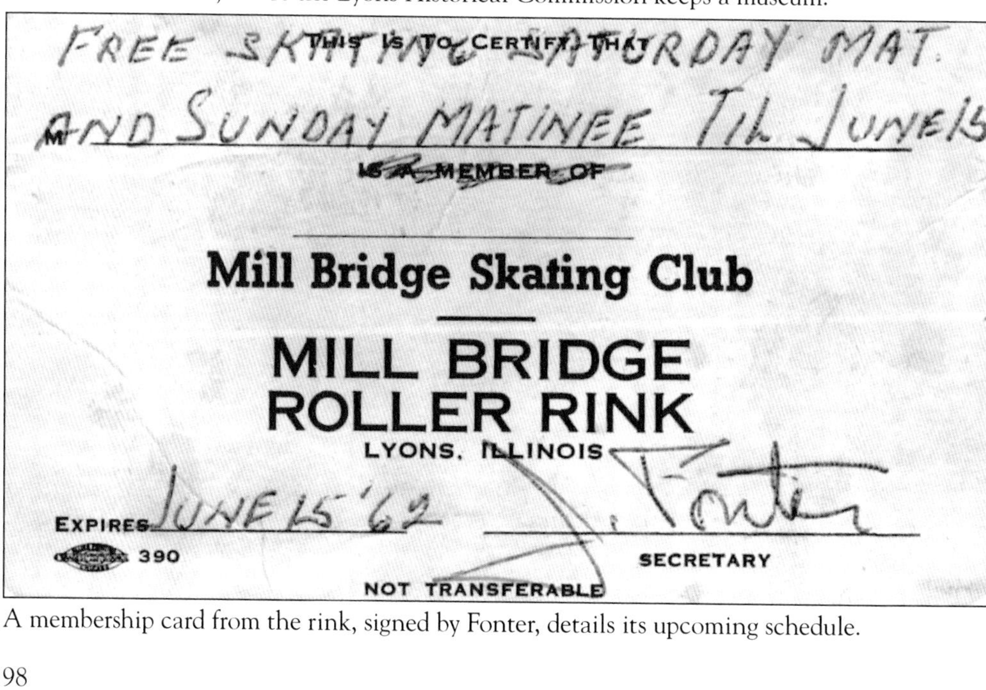

A membership card from the rink, signed by Fonter, details its upcoming schedule.

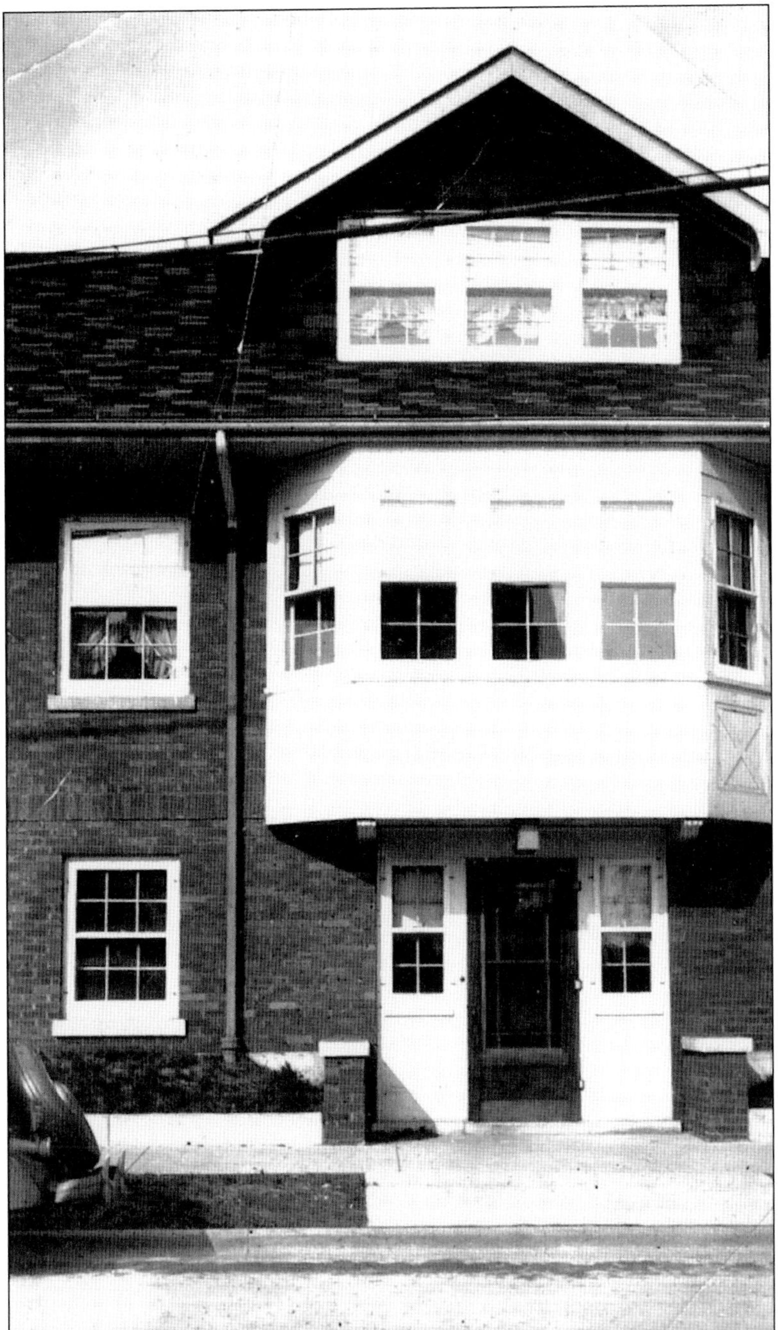

From the 1920s through the 1950s, Dr. William Davies served many Lyons residents out of his offices on the corner of Salisbury Street and Joliet Avenue. Organized health care in Lyons began in 1918 with the opening of an infant-care clinic on Ogden Avenue, which served residents from surrounding communities as well. In the 1920s, dental service was added. In 1957, the village renovated the garage next to village hall to make it the headquarters for the Lyons Health Center, which opened in 1958, handling physicals for school children, administering tuberculosis tests, and other duties. (In 1960, for example, it treated 52 animal bites.)

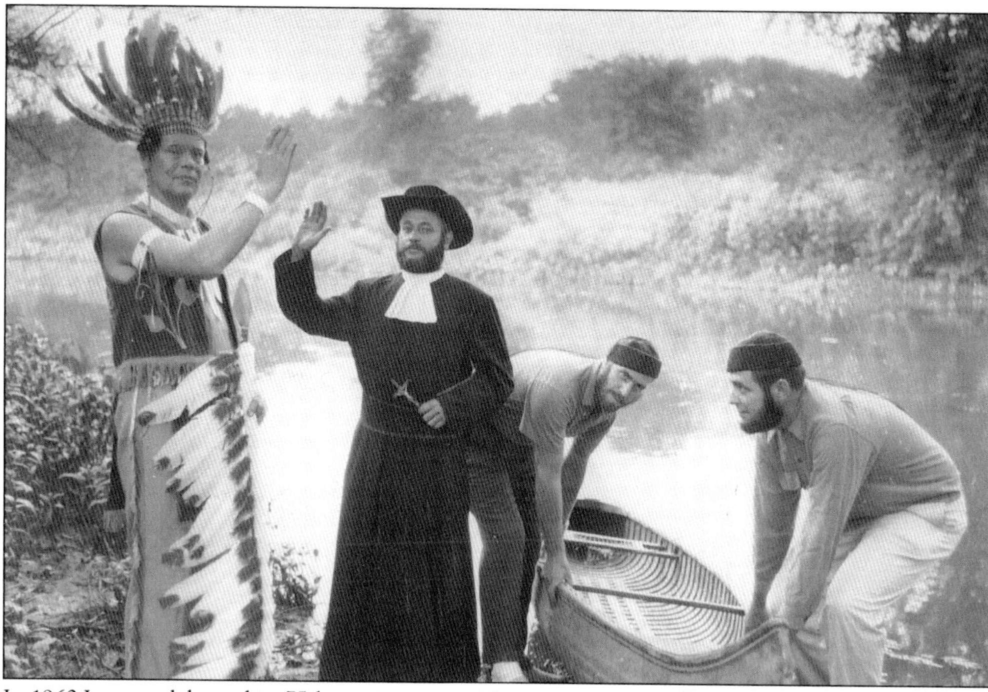

In 1963 Lyons celebrated its 75th anniversary with a reenactment of Marguette and Joliet's journey in town. Shown here from left to right are Roger Tagtimier as a Native American guide, Robert Tyrolt as Marquette, and John Reh and John Zendol as two voyagers traveling alongside.

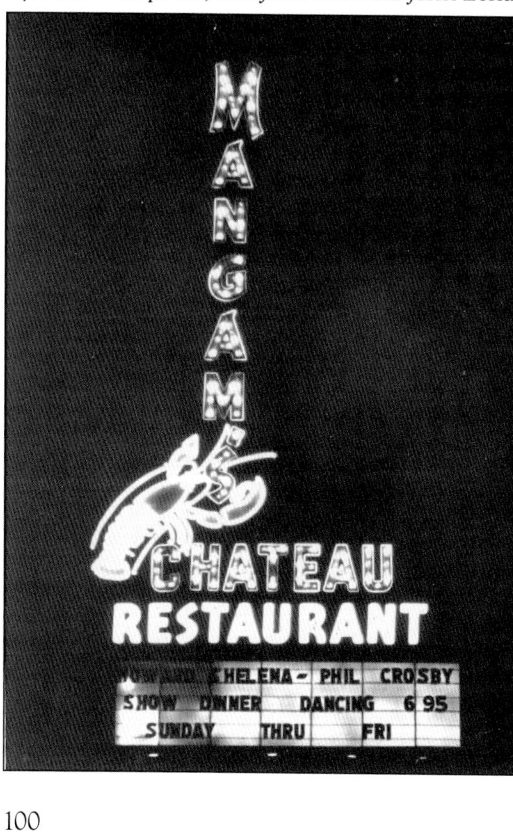

The gleaming neon sign and the Casino Room of Mangam's Chateau was as close as the suburbs got to Vegas-style entertainment. Comedian Joe Conti was a regular performer at Mangam's during the 1950s, as did fan dancer Sally Rand, who made her most famous performance at Chicago's 1933 World's Fair but worked into her 60s. Carol Lawrence, born Carol Maria Laraia in nearby Melrose Park, sang and danced at the club early in her career.

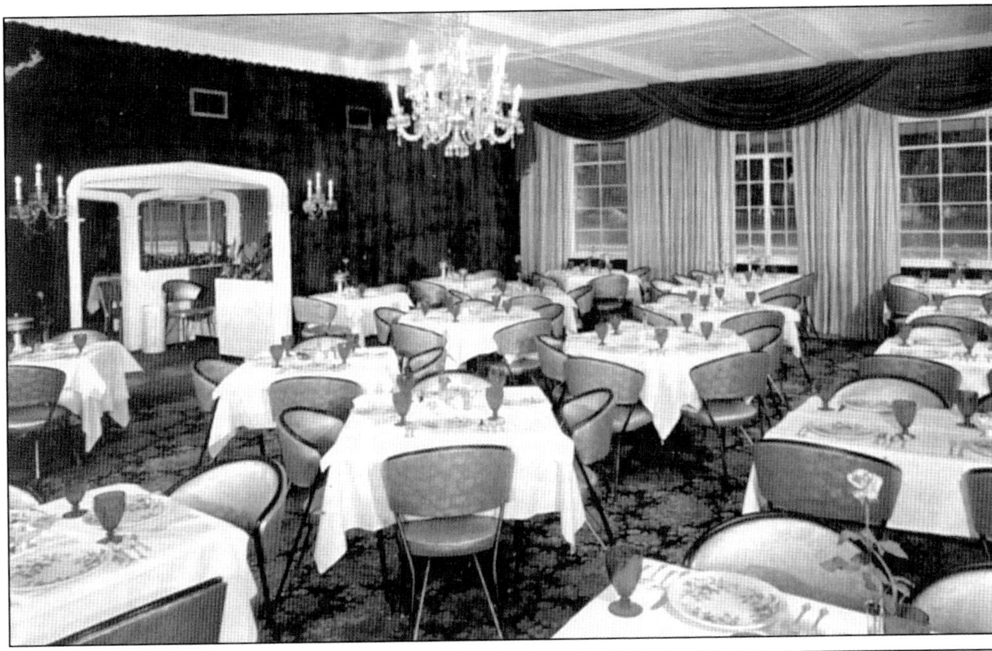

A postcard from the 1950s shows the Crystal Room at Magnam's Chateau, along with an invoice for customers' tabs.

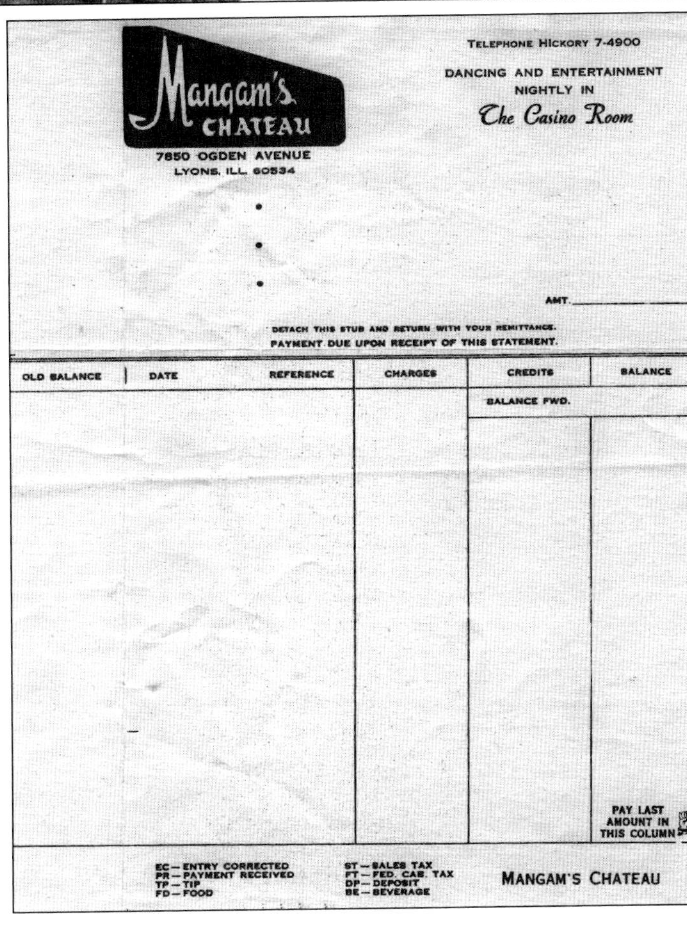

Mangam's CHATEAU

7850 OGDEN AVENUE
LYONS, ILL. 60534

TELEPHONE HICKORY 7-4900

DANCING AND ENTERTAINMENT NIGHTLY IN
The Casino Room

AMT. ____________

DETACH THIS STUB AND RETURN WITH YOUR REMITTANCE.
PAYMENT DUE UPON RECEIPT OF THIS STATEMENT.

OLD BALANCE	DATE	REFERENCE	CHARGES	CREDITS	BALANCE
				BALANCE FWD.	
					PAY LAST AMOUNT IN THIS COLUMN

EC — ENTRY CORRECTED
PR — PAYMENT RECEIVED
TP — TIP
FD — FOOD

ST — SALES TAX
FT — FED. CAB. TAX
DP — DEPOSIT
BE — BEVERAGE

MANGAM'S CHATEAU

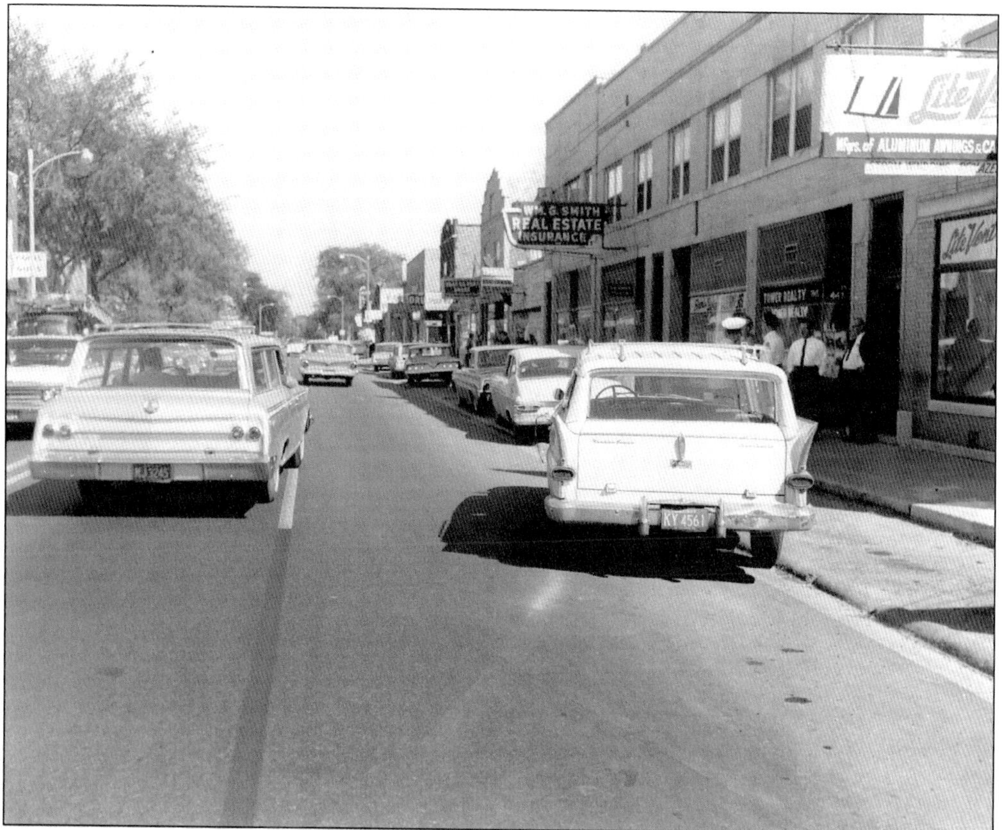

A view of Ogden Avenue looking east in 1962, a year after William G. Smith was elected mayor, is seen here. The sign for his real-estate insurance office can be seen up the street.

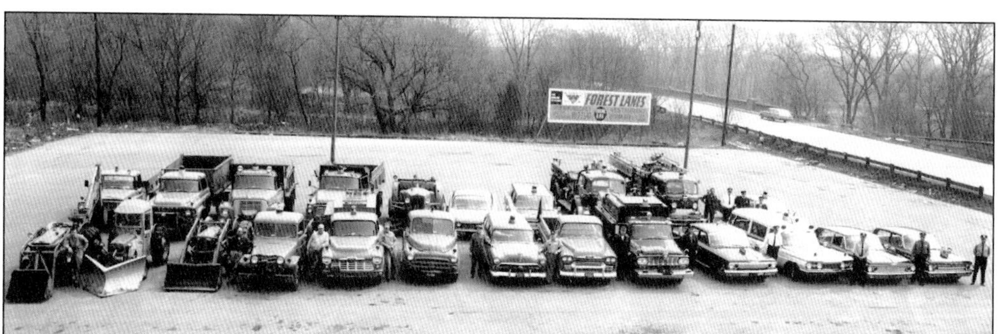

This picture from 1963 shows a display of Lyons public-service vehicles in the parking lot of AMF Bowling's Forest Lanes on Forty-seventh Street, just west of the Des Plaines River. The bridge crossing the river can be seen at rear right.

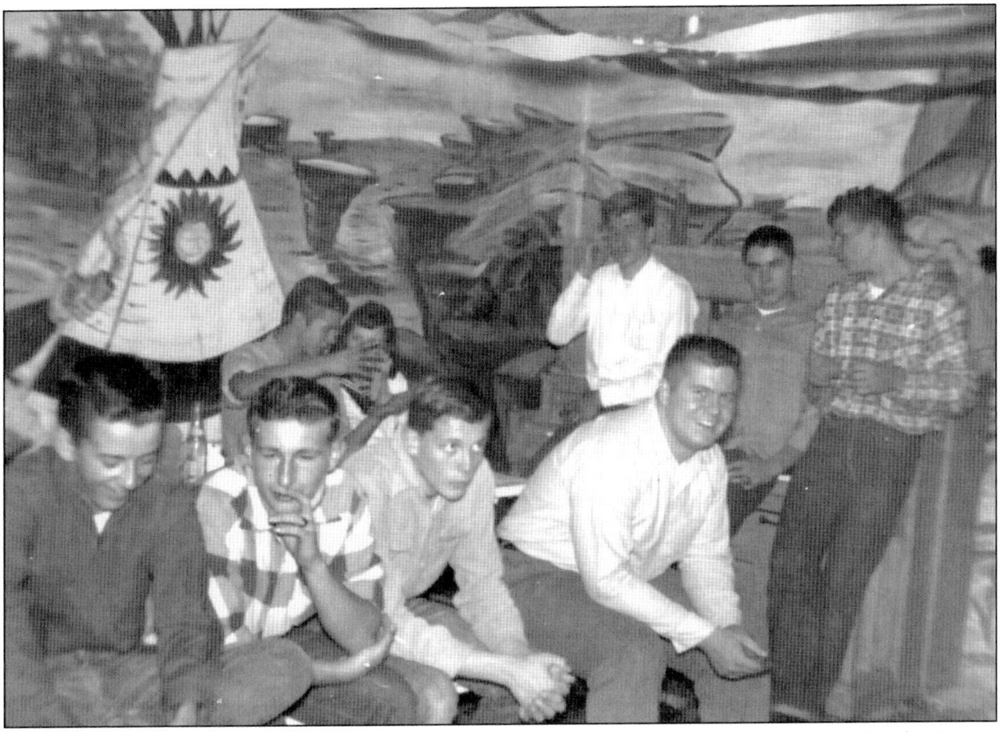

Concerns about juvenile delinquency prompted many towns to establish places like the Lyons Youth Center, nicknamed the Tee Pee Club for its Native American–themed murals. It was opened in 1953 in the village hall's basement. This photograph dates to 1954. Sitting on the far right and smiling for the camera is Herb Goldback; Richie Besjak is seated second from right.

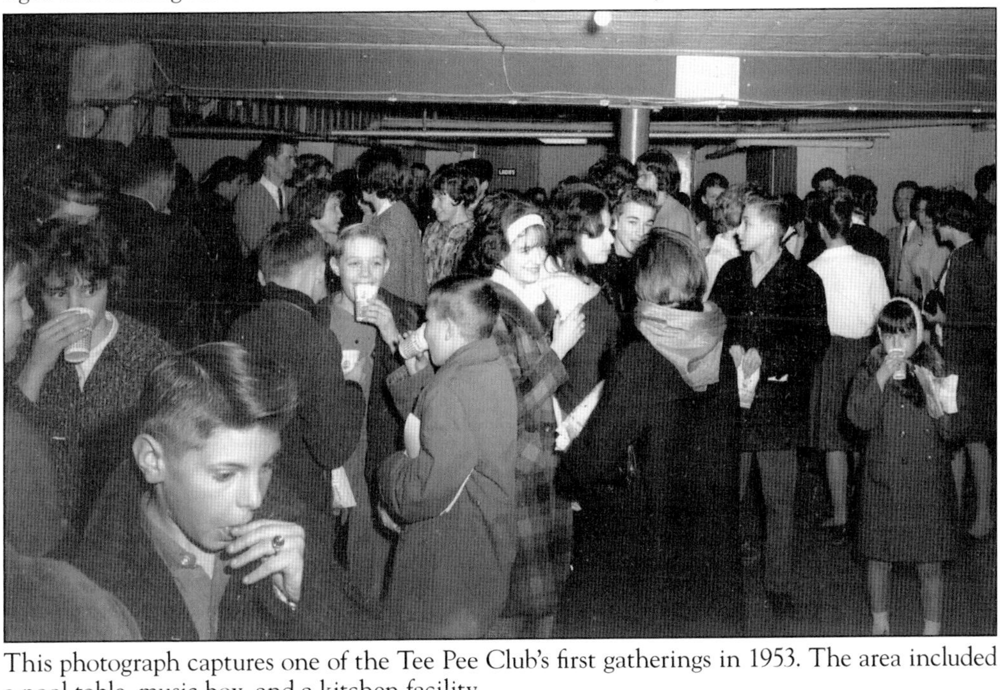

This photograph captures one of the Tee Pee Club's first gatherings in 1953. The area included a pool table, music box, and a kitchen facility.

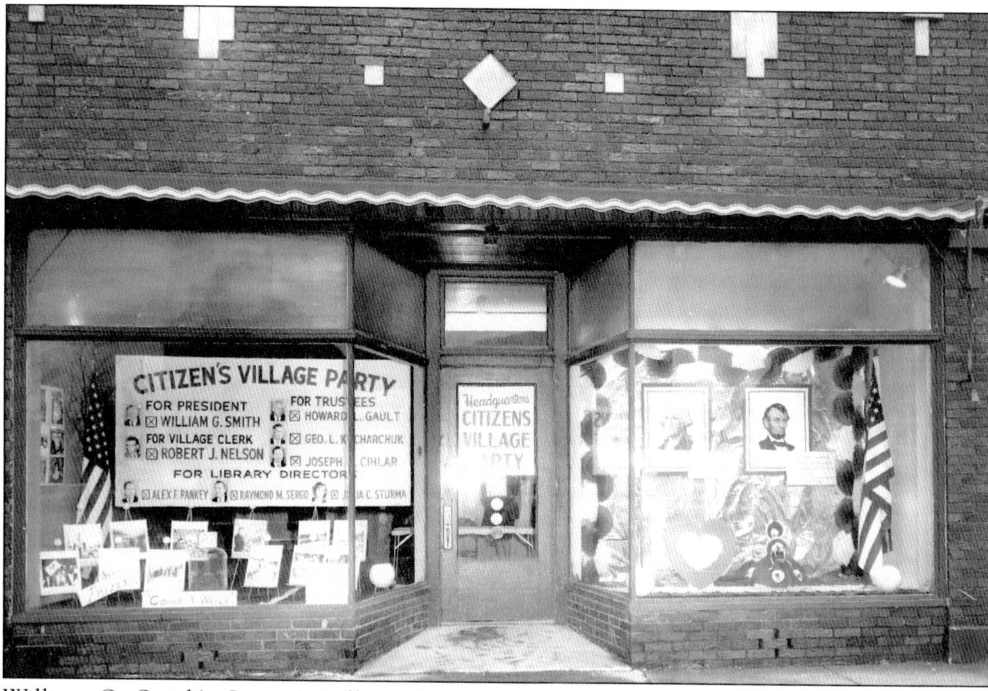

William G. Smith's Citizen's Village Party was headquartered in the same location as his insurance and realty offices at 7941 West Ogden Avenue. Smith was elected mayor in 1961 on a low-tax platform.

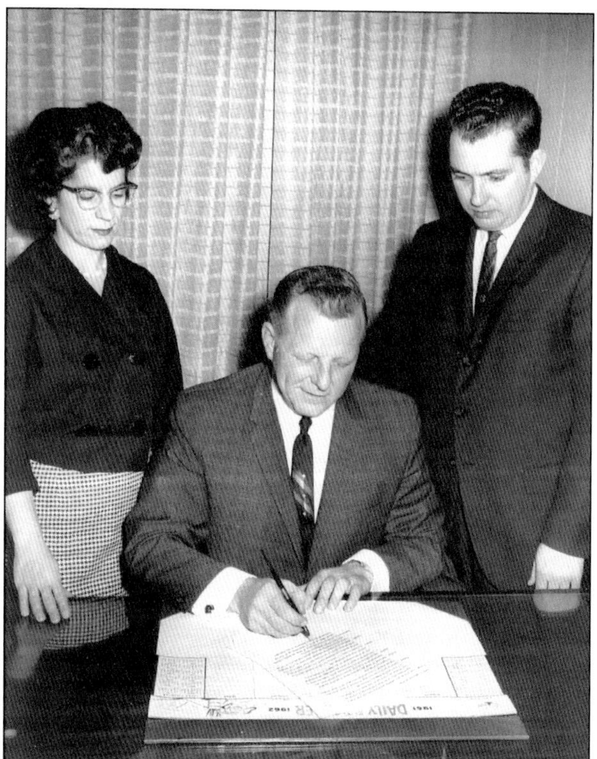

Mayor Smith is shown here during his first year in office. He is flanked by two village officials, Mary Kalfas and Elwood Graunke. Smith himself served as a trustee for five years before he became mayor.

In 1963, Lyons celebrated the 75th anniversary of its incorporation with a monthlong series of celebrations, including a reenactment of Marquette and Joliet's travels. Mayor Smith is shown here with a young jubilee king and queen.

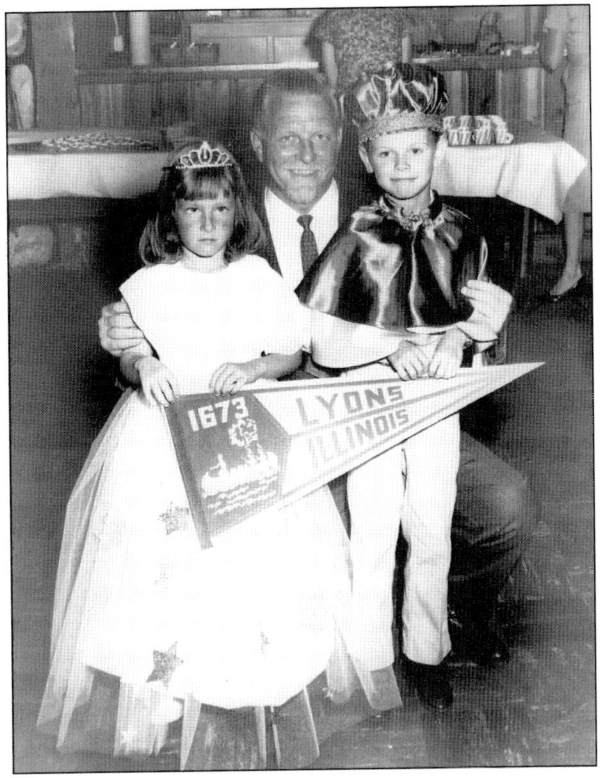

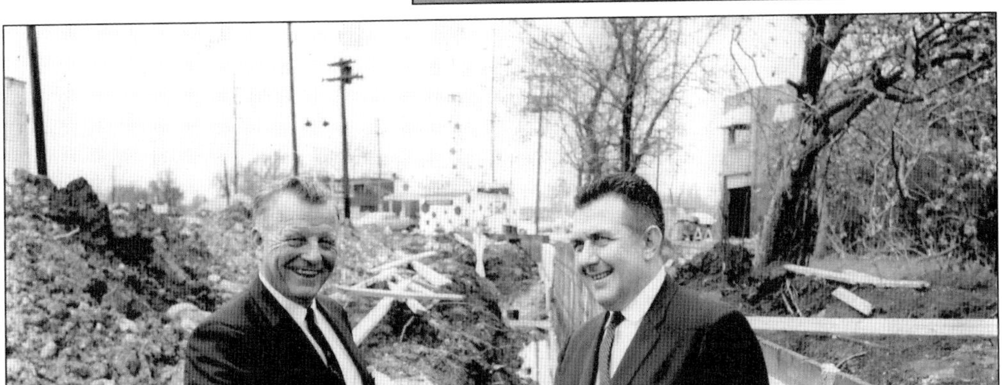

This photograph from the mid-1960s shows Mayor Smith at left shaking hands with Rick Binder of Jarvis Engineering, an area construction company, at the triangle property at Ogden Avenue and Plainfield Road. In the background is the Lighthouse, a custard shop.

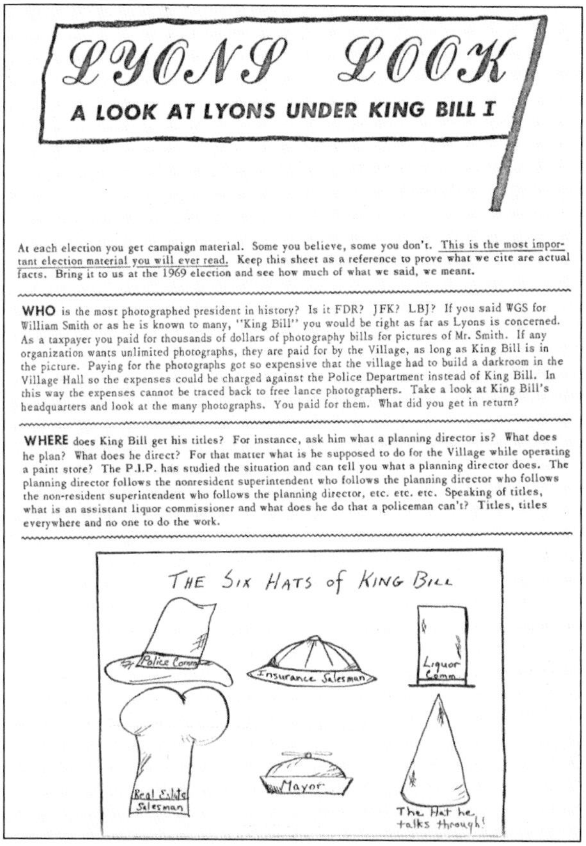

LYONS LOOK

A LOOK AT LYONS UNDER KING BILL I

At each election you get campaign material. Some you believe, some you don't. This is the most important election material you will ever read. Keep this sheet as a reference to prove what we cite are actual facts. Bring it to us at the 1969 election and see how much of what we said, we meant.

WHO is the most photographed president in history? Is it FDR? JFK? LBJ? If you said WGS for William Smith or as he is known to many, "King Bill" you would be right as far as Lyons is concerned. As a taxpayer you paid for thousands of dollars of photography bills for pictures of Mr. Smith. If any organization wants unlimited photographs, they are paid for by the Village, as long as King Bill is in the picture. Paying for the photographs got so expensive that the village had to build a darkroom in the Village Hall so the expenses could be charged against the Police Department instead of King Bill. In this way the expenses cannot be traced back to free lance photographers. Take a look at King Bill's headquarters and look at the many photographs. You paid for them. What did you get in return?

WHERE does King Bill get his titles? For instance, ask him what a planning director is? What does he plan? What does he direct? For that matter what is he supposed to do for the Village while operating a paint store? The P.I.P. has studied the situation and can tell you what a planning director does. The planning director follows the nonresident superintendent who follows the planning director who follows the non-resident superintendent who follows the planning director, etc. etc. etc. Speaking of titles, what is an assistant liquor commissioner and what does he do that a policeman can't? Titles, titles everywhere and no one to do the work.

Mayor Smith was often criticized for the amount of control he wielded over Lyons business and politics. This political flyer from 1969 dubbed Smith "King Bill I" and critiqued the multiple "hats" he wore in town: real estate salesman, insurance salesman, mayor, police commissioner, and liquor commissioner. The sixth hat is "the hat he talks through."

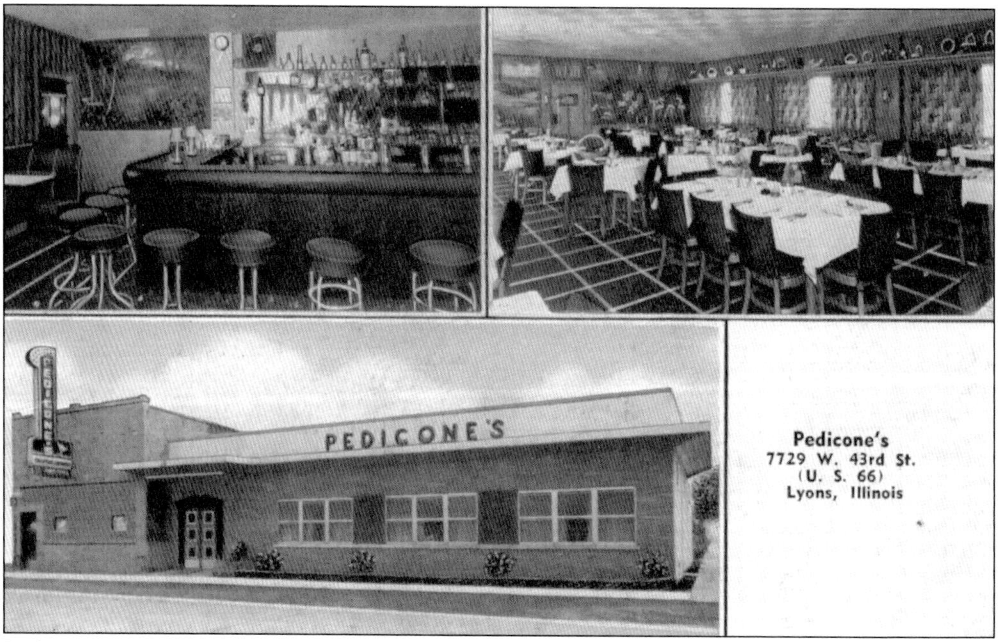

Pedicone's restaurant was located on Joliet Road, a strip of Route 66 that ran through Lyons. It closed after a fire on New Year's Day, 1963.

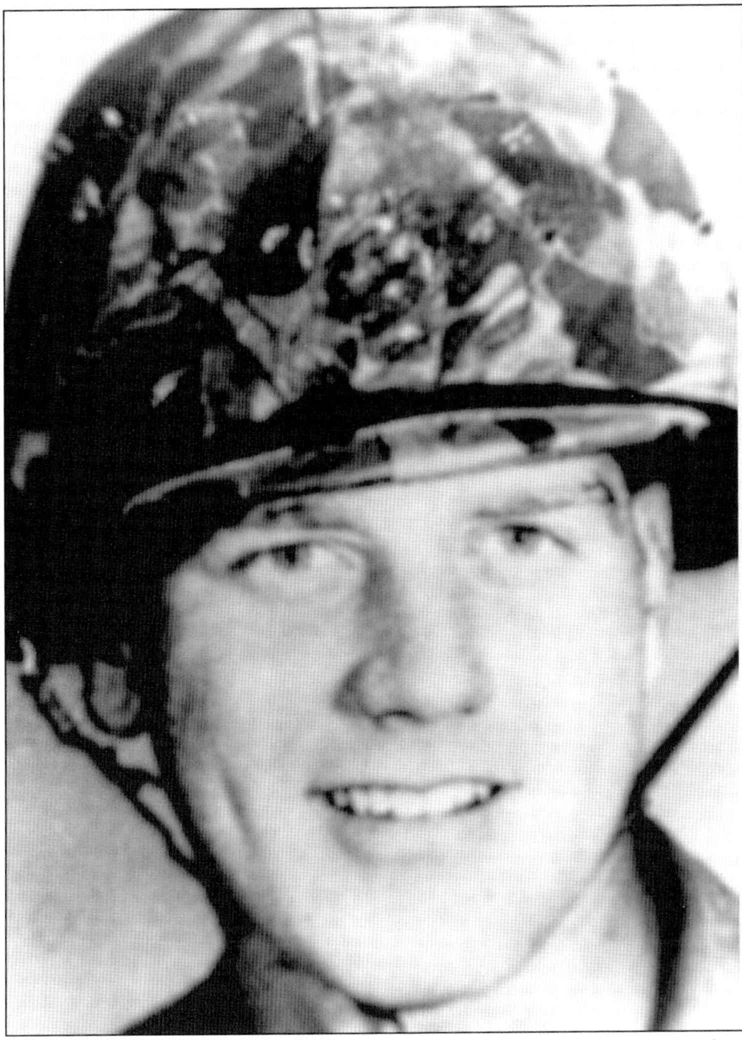

RENAME LYONS SCHOOL TODAY AFTER SLAIN GI

Won Medal of Honor for Action in Viet

The Elm Elementary school in Lyons will be renamed today in honor of Sgt. James W. Robinson Jr., who was posthumously awarded the nation's highest military honor.

Sgt. Robinson was killed in action in Viet Nam April 11. On July 12 Robinson's parents were given the Congressional medal of honor that had been awarded to him. He was the 16th service man in the Viet Nam war to win the medal.

Mother to Get Flag

The renaming ceremony will begin at 1:30 p. m. in the school, 4550 Elm st., Lyons, with the 5th army band and

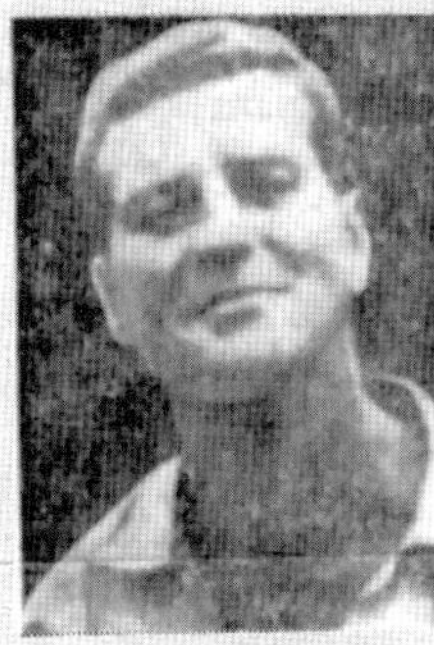

Sgt. James Robinson Jr.

Sgt. James W. Robinson Jr., a Lyons resident, served in the U.S. Army during the Vietnam War, and was killed in battle on April 11, 1966. Born in Westmont, Robinson attended Washington School, Morton West High School, and Morton College. He was posthumously awarded the Congressional Medal of Honor. The citation for the medal notes, in part: "Seeing a medic hit while administering aid to a wounded sergeant in front of his position and aware that now the 2 wounded men were at the mercy of the enemy, he charged through a withering hail of fire and dragged his comrades to safety, where he rendered first aid and saved their lives." Elm School was renamed in his honor later that year. A high school in Fairfax, Virginia, bears his name as well.

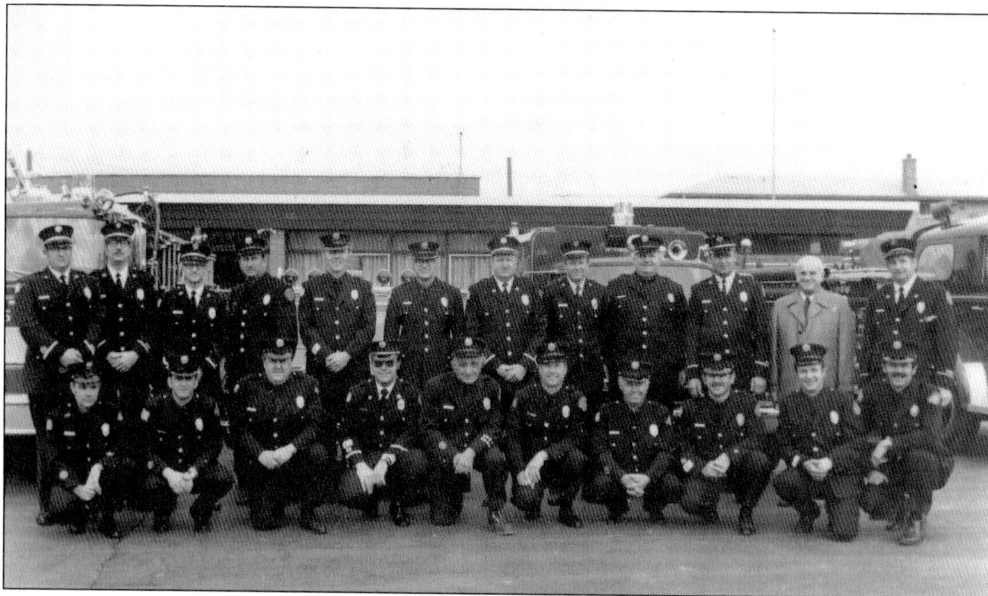

The Lyons Fire Department is seen here in March 1973. From left to right are (first row) Donald Bergman, Robert Sullivan, Arthur Grosse, Kenneth Kucera, Andy Serio, Joseph Pacentine, Charles Sustr, Ronald Komarek, Raymond Pietrzak, and John Pankow; (second row) Charles Scheffel, Donald Pincuspy, Raymond Rembles, Frank Konopka, Edward Przeklaza, Eugene Jezek, Burton Steig, James Ritz, Richard Bezjak, Richard Wuest, fire commissioner Howard Gault, and Chief James Spolar.

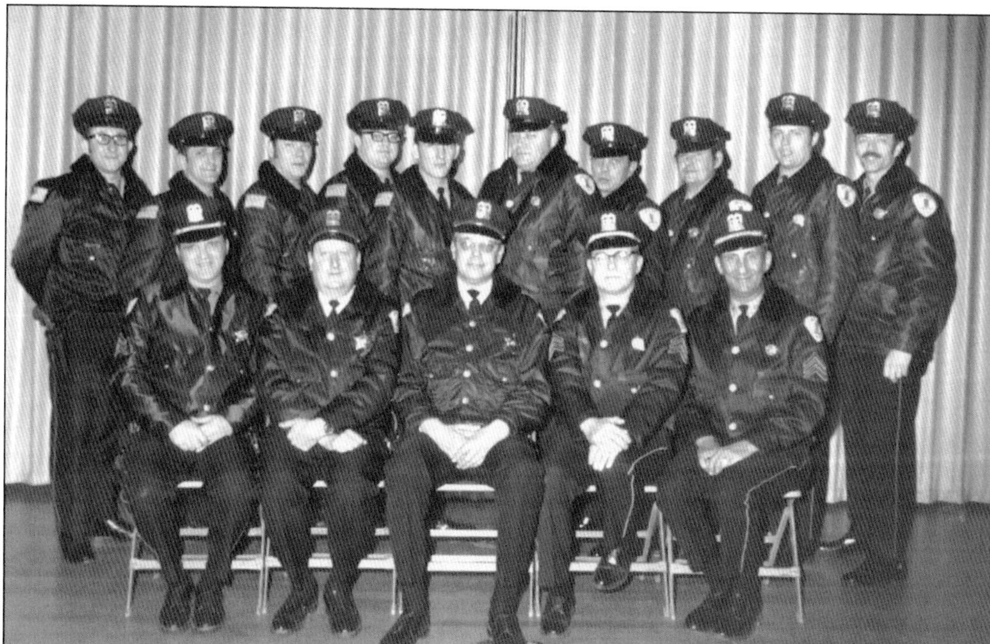

The Lyons Police Department is pictured in 1973. From left to right are (first row) Sgt. Donald Kroft, Lt. Burton Stieg, Chief James Svoboda, Sgt. Robert Brownell, and Sgt. Frank Krall; (second row) officers James Couch, Robert Sullivan, William Teeter, John Flanagan, Richard Husarik, Robert Eddy, William Kruzich, James Cleveland, Stanley Augustyniak, and John Pankow.

This photograph from 1976 shows the site of Joe's Club at 8173 Ogden Avenue. In 1925, Sophie Kusper Kowalczyk bought the mansion from the Schultz family and ran it as a restaurant, "modernistic cocktail lounge," and, some say, a brothel. An adjoining restaurant opened in 1948. Kowalczyk died in 1965. The site is now an apartment complex.

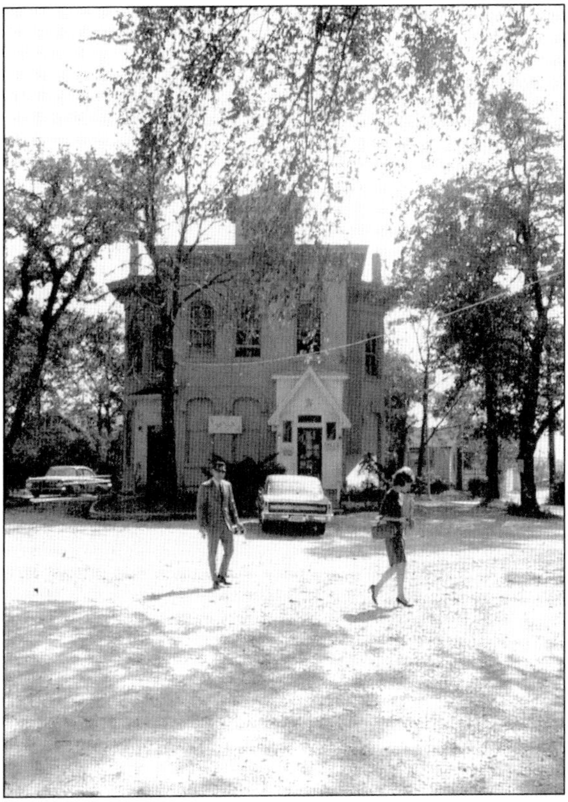

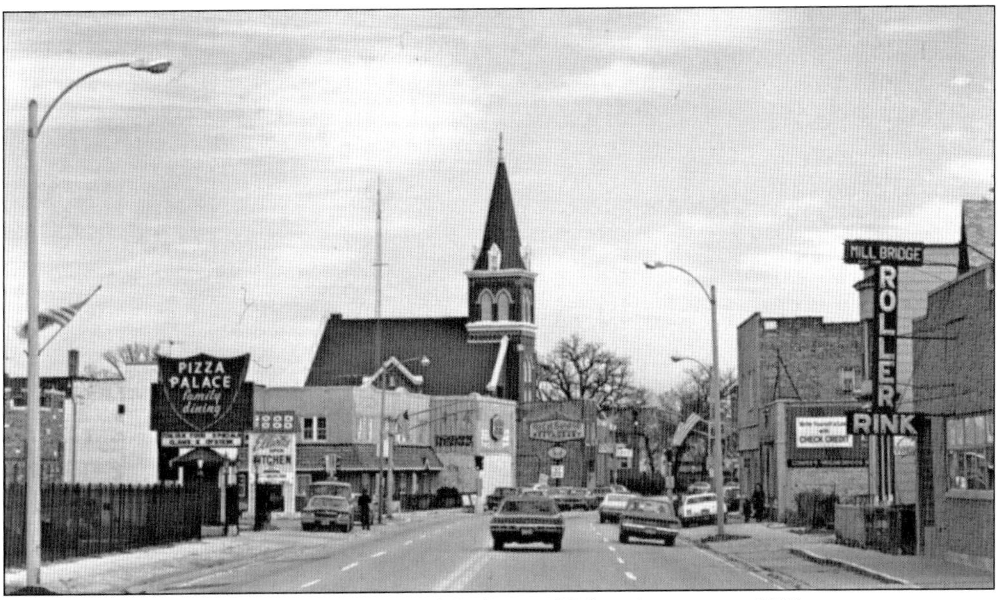

This postcard captures the intersection of Ogden and Joliet Avenues in 1976.

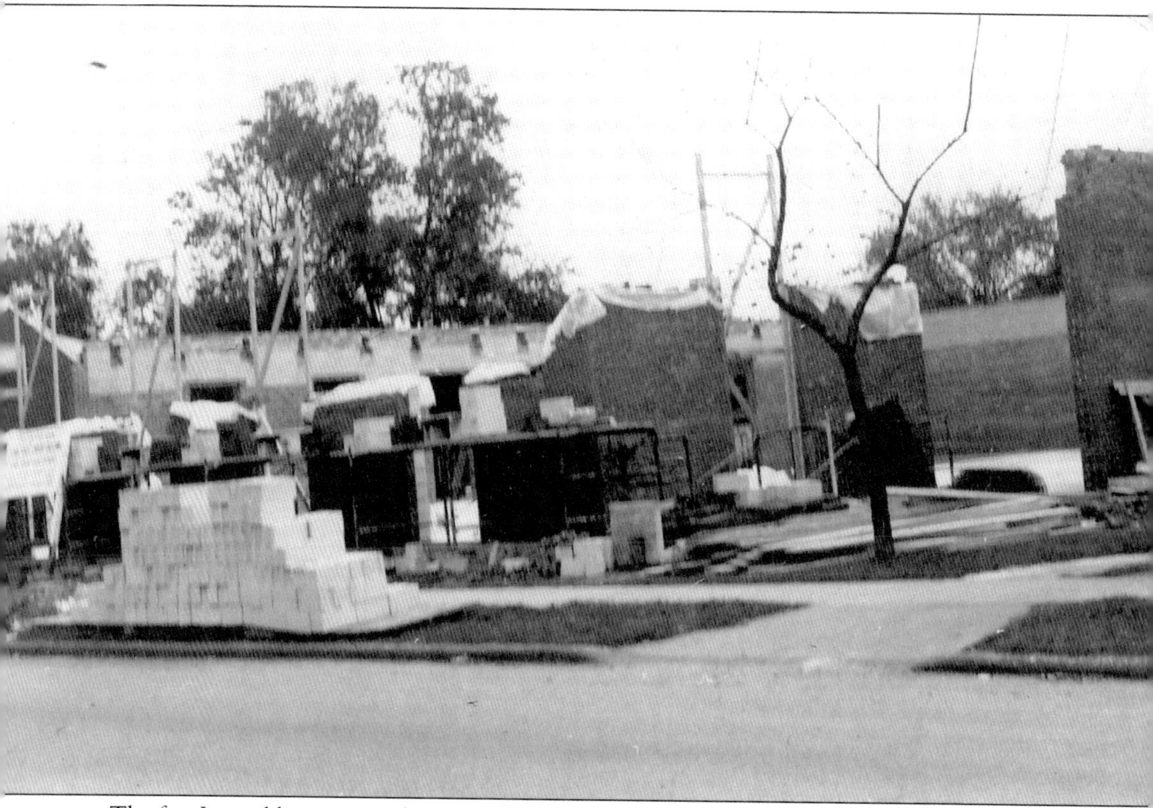

The first Lyons library opened in 1936 in the home of Ruth Ingalls Mitch, and moved to the village hall two years later. In 1941, it moved into a storefront space on 4112 Joliet Avenue, in what later became the American Legion building. By the early 1960s, the Lyons Public Library had begun to outgrow its converted storefront space. In 1964, a referendum passed to build a new library, which opened on August 22, 1966. This photograph shows the library under construction.

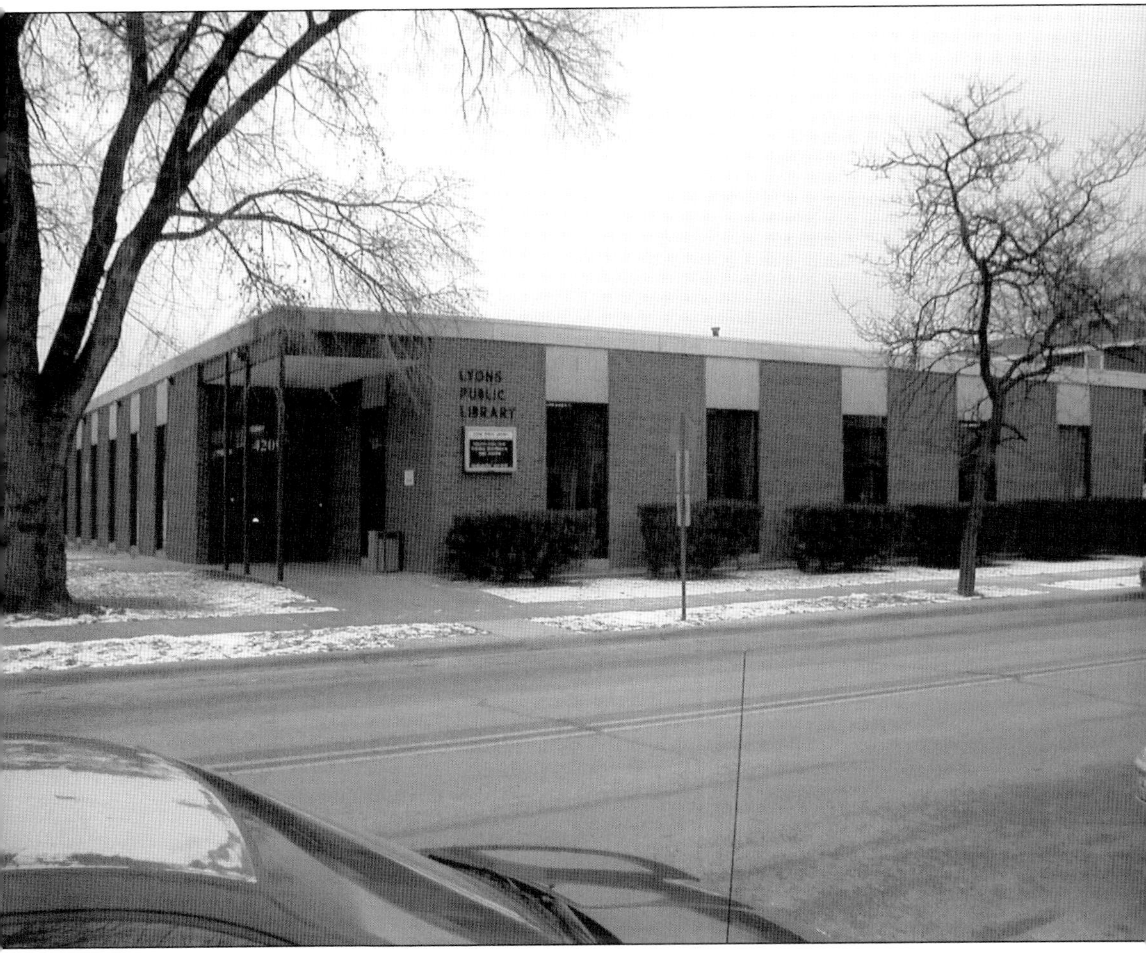

This is the Lyons Public Library as it appears today.

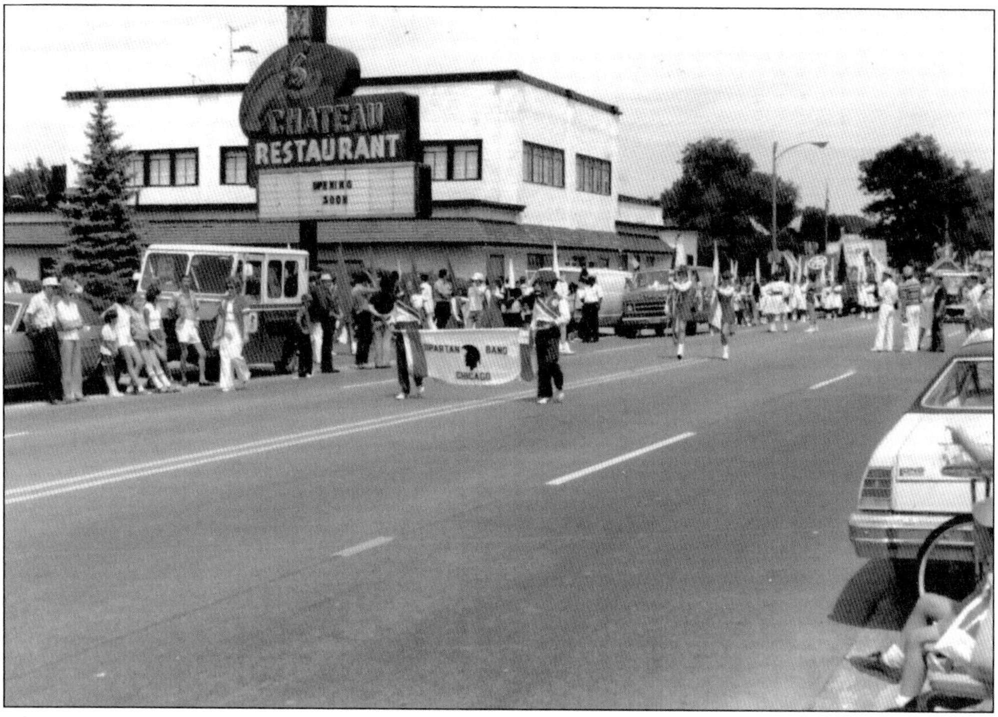

This photograph from the 1976 Fourth of July parade shows Mangam's Chateau shortly before reopening after a renovation.

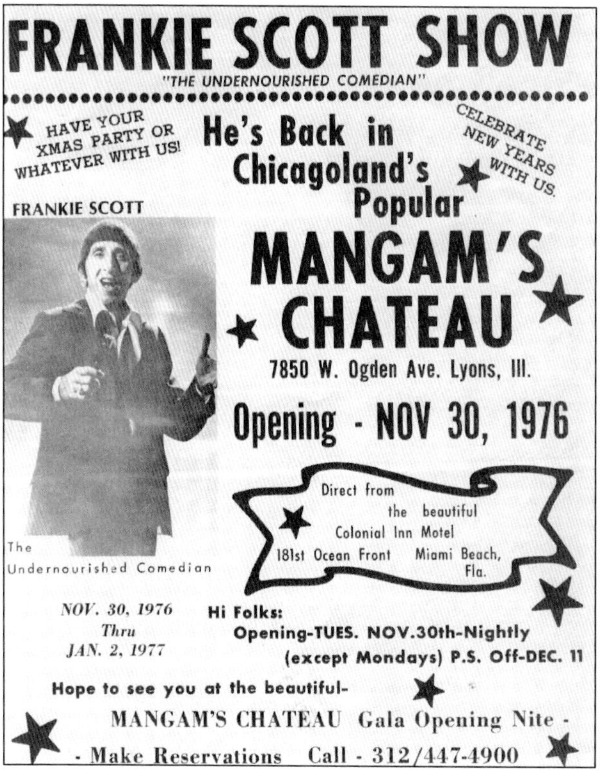

Chicago-area club comic Frank Abruscato, also known as Frankie Scott, who died in 1995, helped kick off the reopening of Mangam's Chateau.

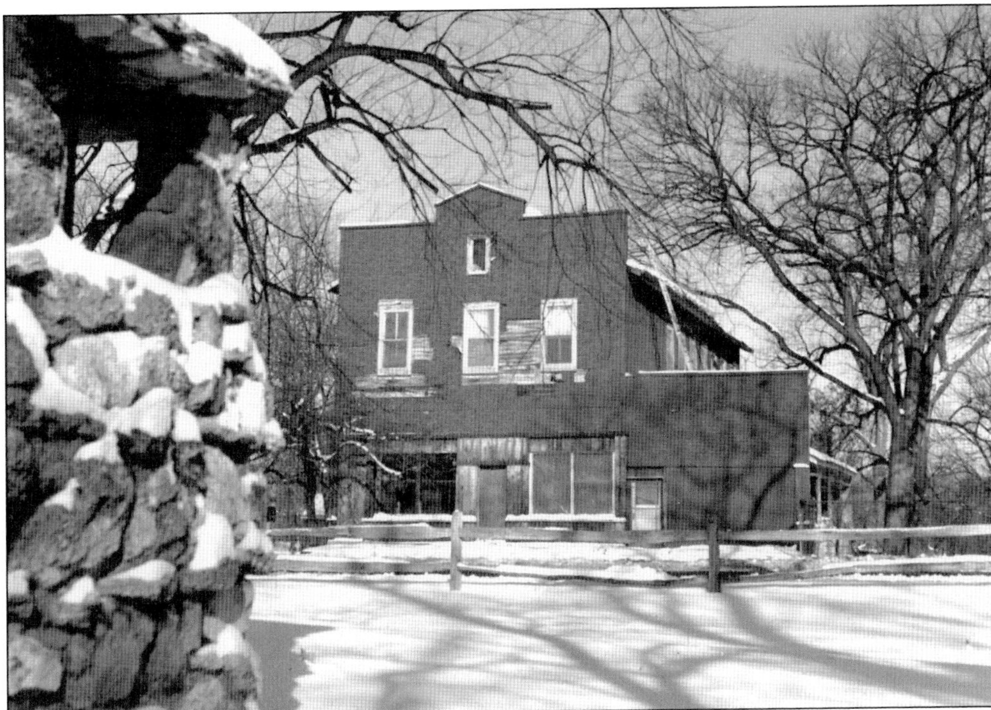

Neher's Tavern is seen here, shortly before it was demolished in 1977. A painting of Mueller's brewery hung on its wall before it was transferred to the Lyons Village Hall.

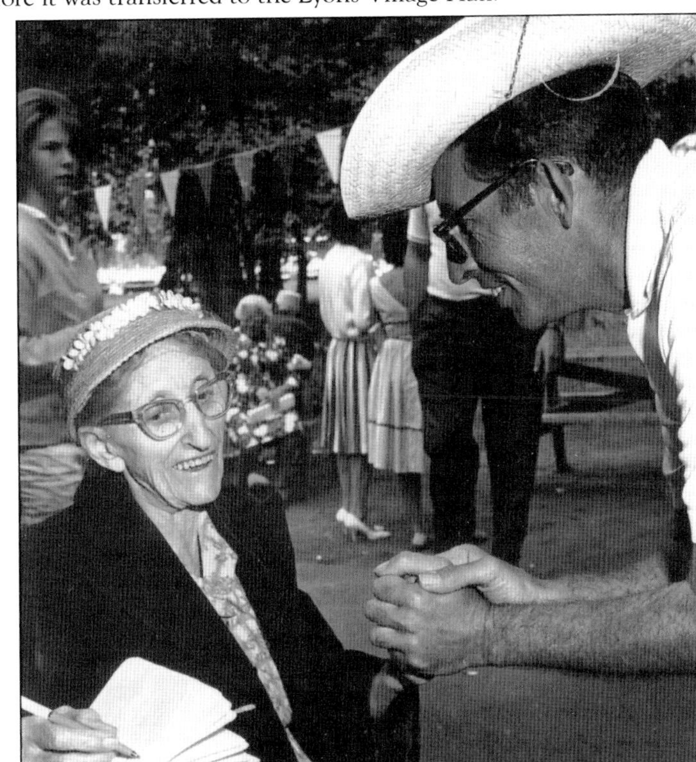

Kate Leonhardt, who cofounded the Lyons Health Center, is shown here in this photograph taken during the 1963 jubilee. She died the following year.

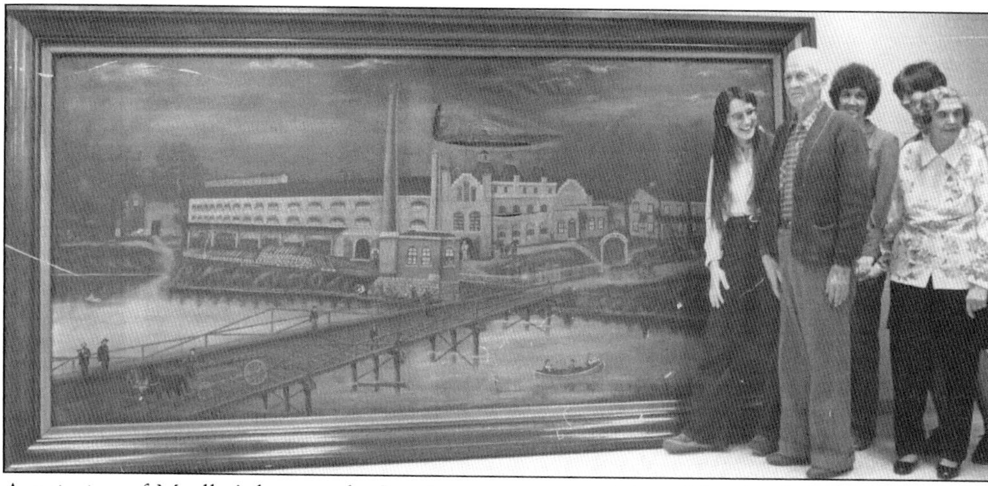

A painting of Mueller's brewery by Joe Antos was commissioned by Frank Neher Jr. in 1898; the rip in the canvas near the smokestack happened when Neher took the painting down to wallpaper the tavern. Wally and Margaret Neher, along with other members of the Neher family, shown here, gathered in 1977 to commemorate the donation of the Neher's painting to the Lyons Village Hall.

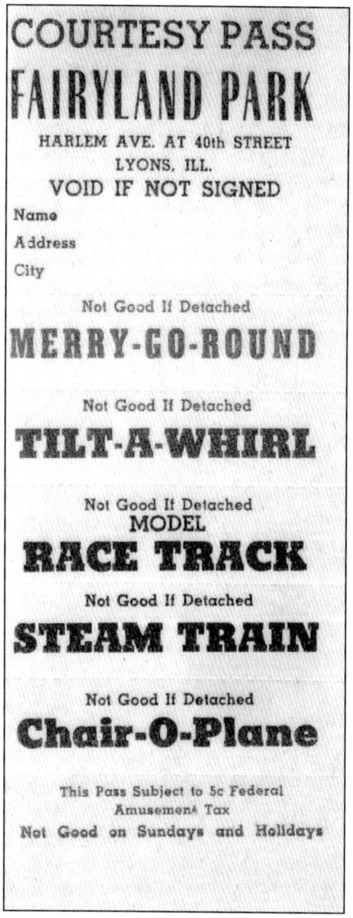

COURTESY PASS

FAIRYLAND PARK

HARLEM AVE. AT 40th STREET

LYONS, ILL.

VOID IF NOT SIGNED

Name

Address

City

Not Good If Detached

MERRY-GO-ROUND

Not Good If Detached

TILT-A-WHIRL

Not Good If Detached

MODEL

RACE TRACK

Not Good If Detached

STEAM TRAIN

Not Good If Detached

Chair-O-Plane

This Pass Subject to 5c Federal Amusement Tax

Not Good on Sundays and Holidays

A Fairyland pass lists the various attractions at the park; the steam train was moved to Kiddieland in Melrose Park when Fairyland closed in 1978, 50 years after it opened. Its 11-car Ferris wheel went to Georgia, and its merry-go-round to Barrington, Illinois.

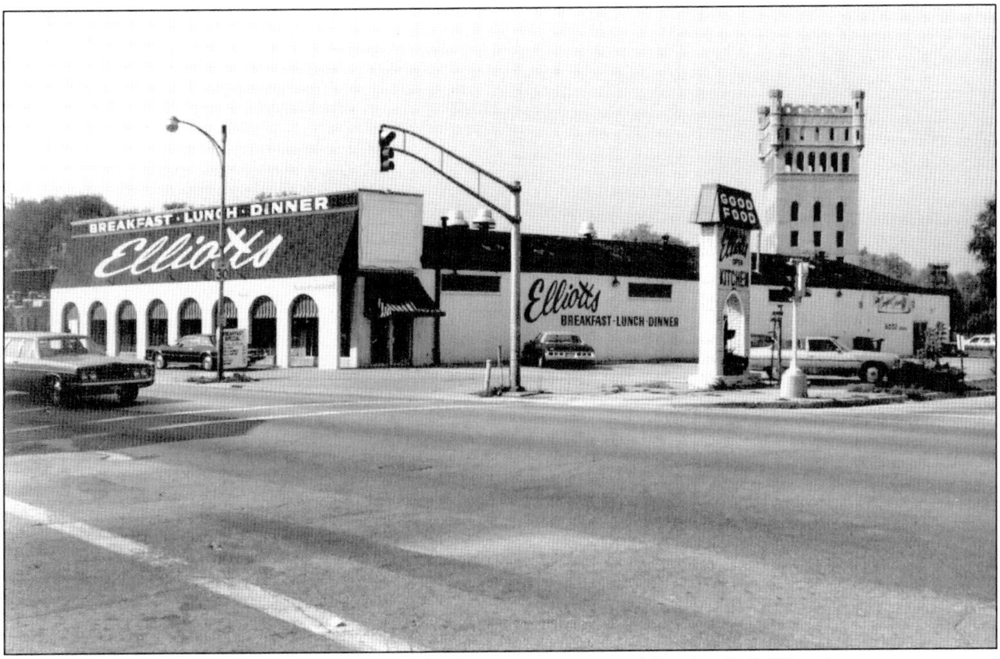

The site at 8000 West Ogden Avenue, which is now occupied by the P. J. Klem's restaurant, was a Kroger's grocery store in the 1960s. In the mid-1970s, it became Elliots, a barbecue joint first located on Garfield Boulevard in Chicago.

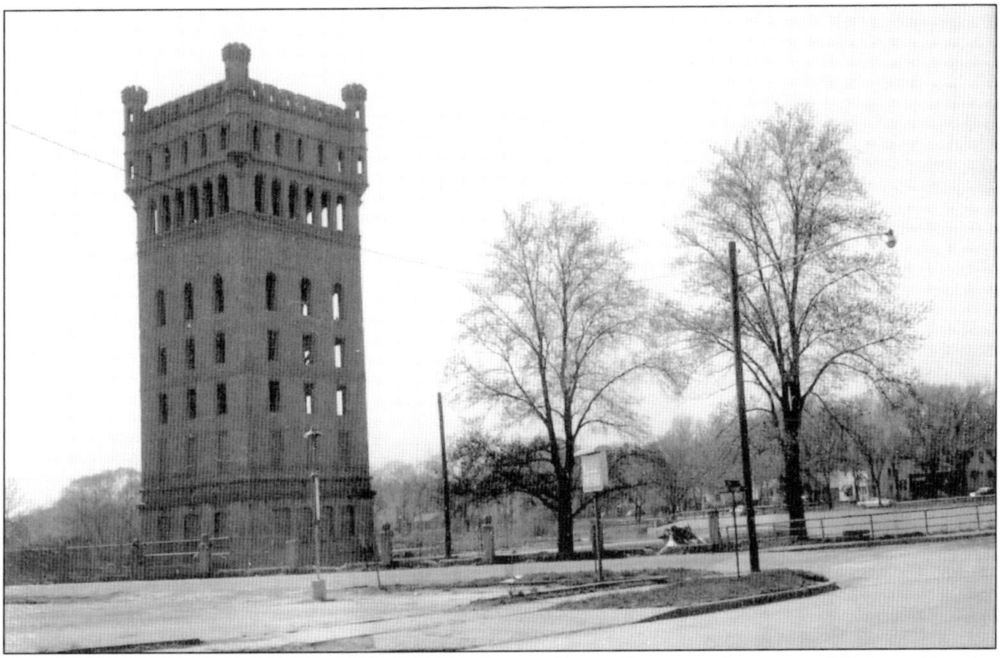

Hofmann's heirs sold the tower to the Cook County Forest Preserve district in 1946, and by the mid-1960s, the Hofmann Tower had fallen into disrepair. For safety's sake, the windows on the upper floors were removed and the ones on the first floor bricked in. Efforts to restore the tower would not begin in earnest until the late 1970s; in 1978 the tower was placed on the National Register of Historic Places.

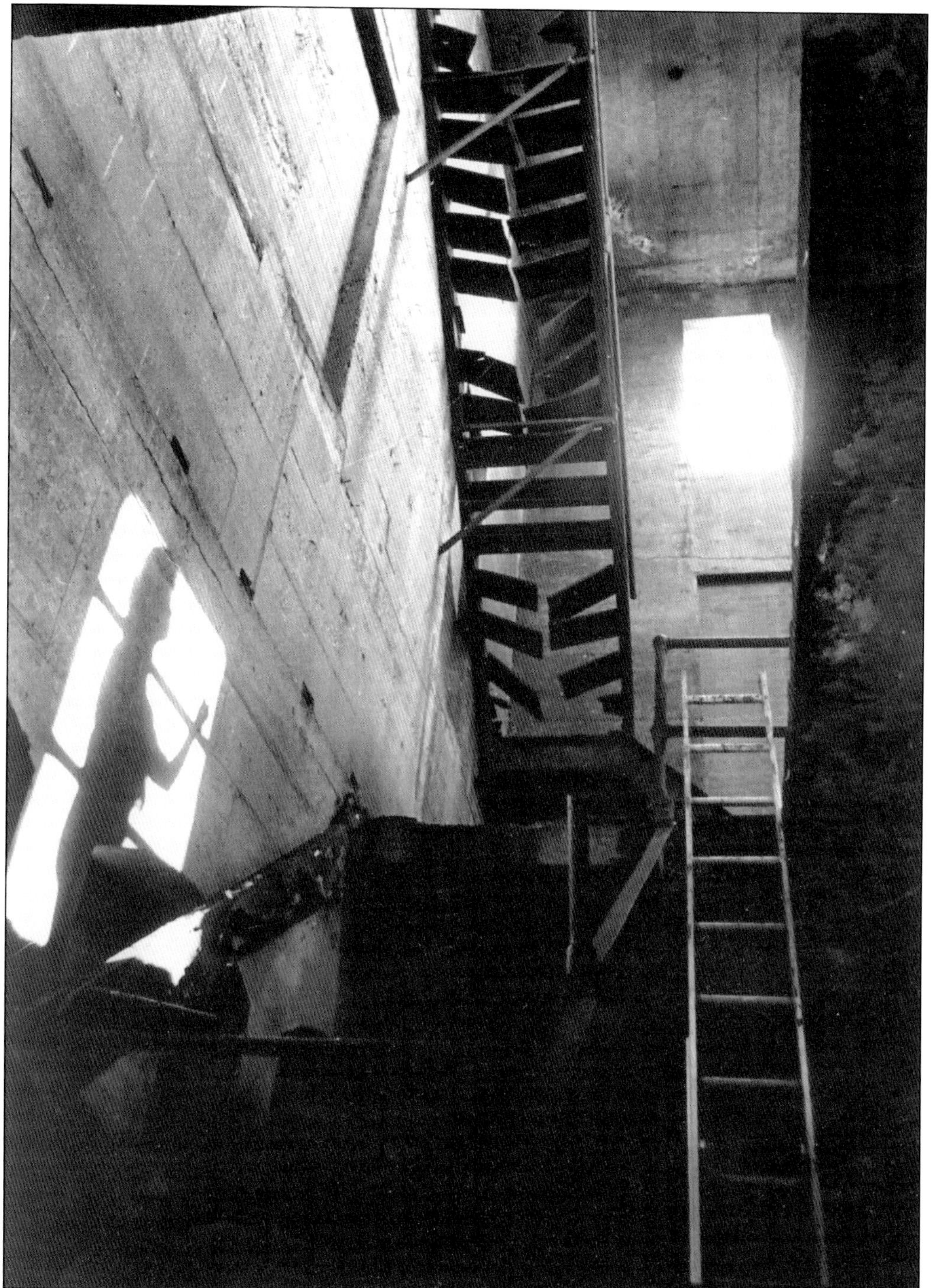

Before efforts to renovate the Hofmann Tower began in the 1980s, the interior stairwells were severely damaged. Grants from individuals and the Lyons Township paid for closing the windows from the elements (and pigeons). In 1984, the building was turned over to the State of Illinois, which paid for a new roof, reinforced floors, steel stairs, and exterior lighting. A museum operated by the Lyons Historical Commission is now open inside the tower during the summer.

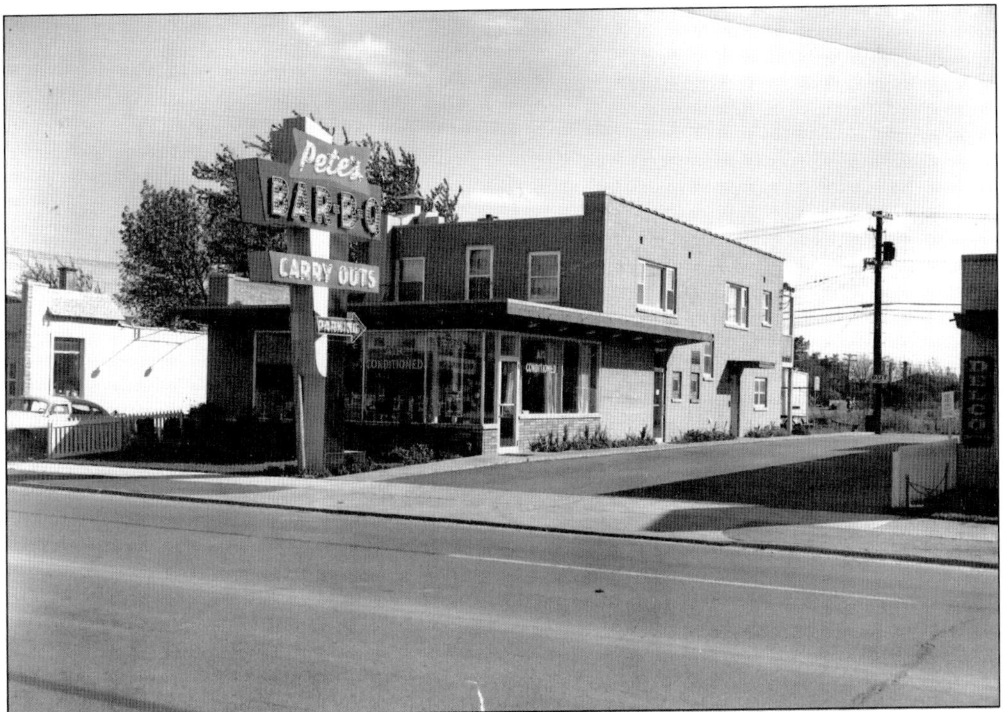

In the 1970s, Pete's Barbecue moved to the west end of town, at 8605 Ogden Avenue.

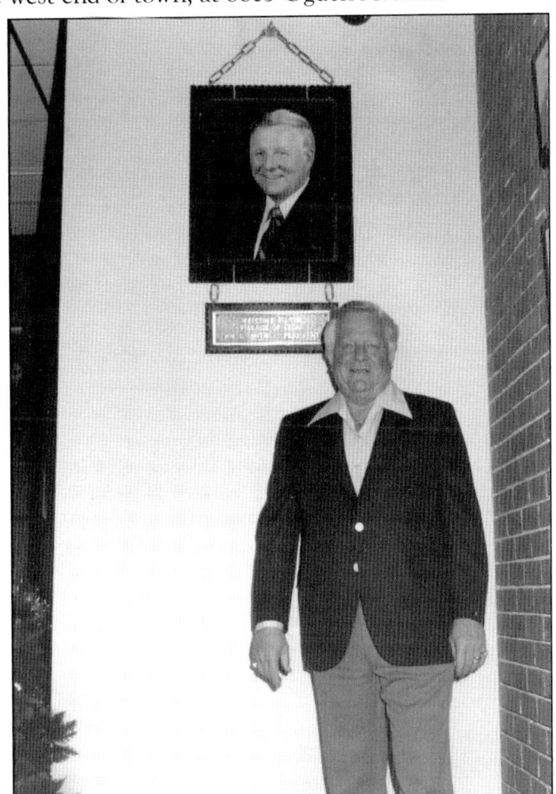

Mayor Smith stands by a portrait of himself at Lyons Village Hall in 1981. He resigned in February 1989, shortly after suffering a heart attack. He died April 29, 1989.

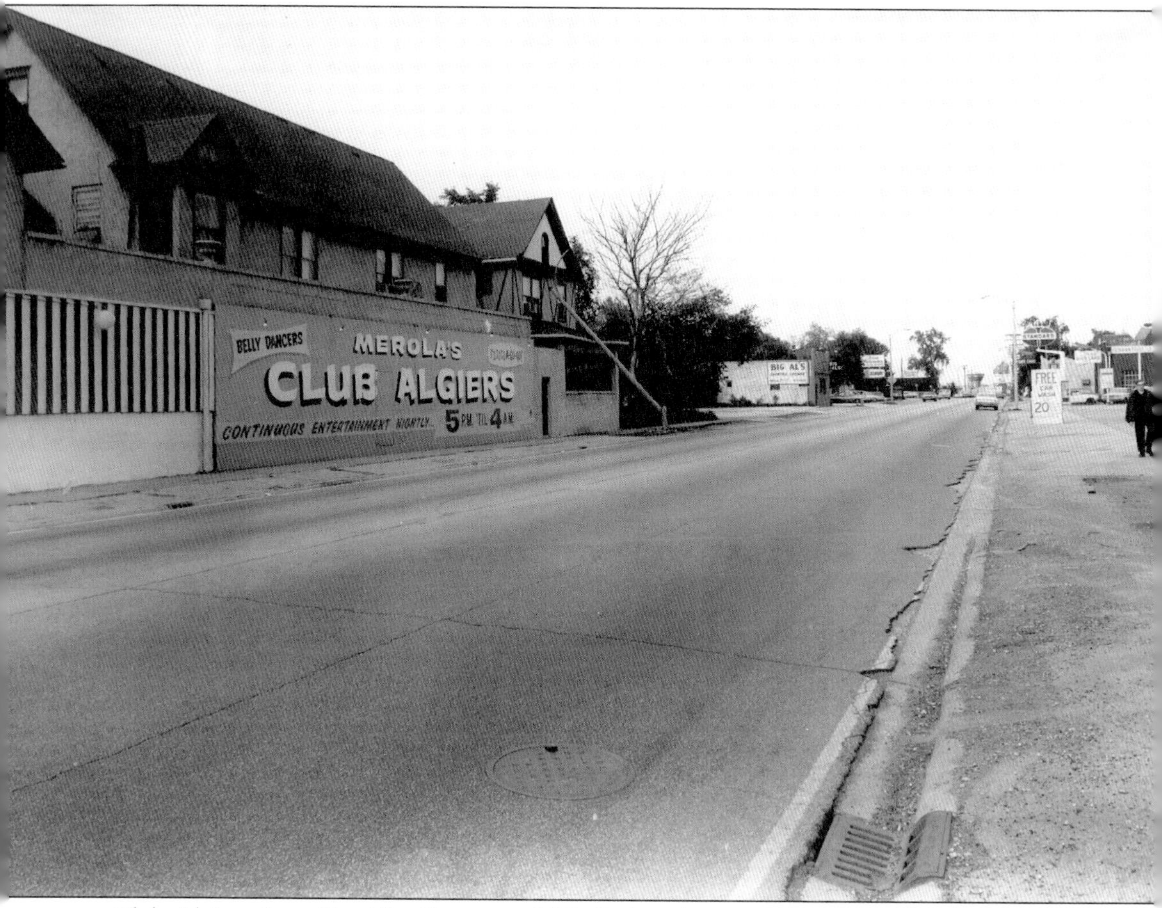

Club Algiers, later Picadilly Circus, at 8039 Ogden Avenue, was one of the main targets of Operation Safebet, a federal vice investigation in Chicago's west suburbs in the 1980s. In 1988, owner Guy Merola and his father, John, were indicted on charges of operating a prostitution service from 1981 to 1987.

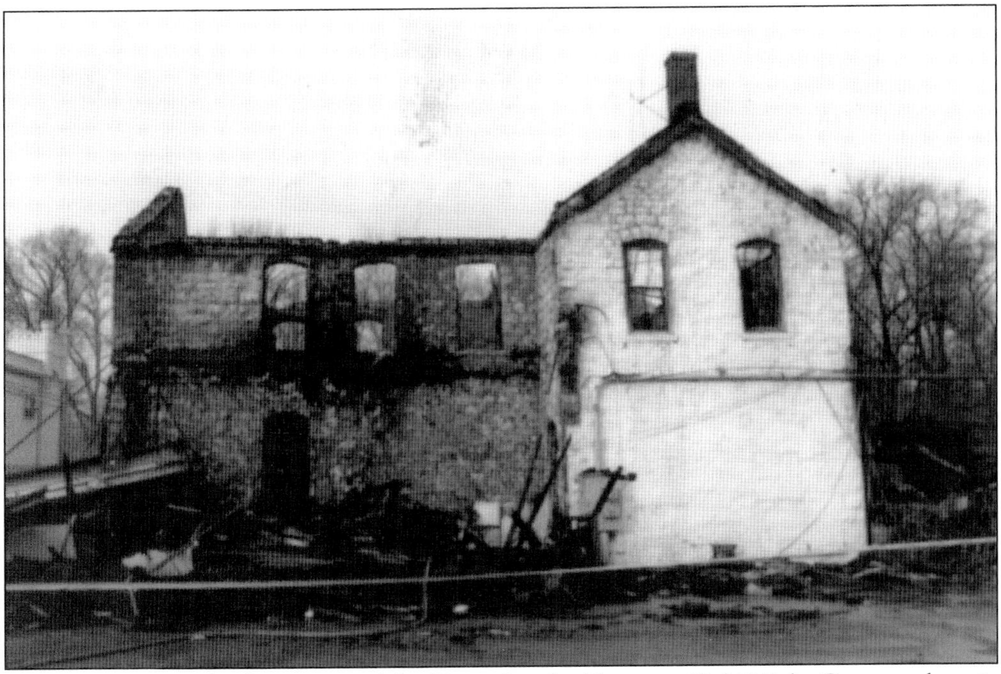

By the late 1970s, the former site of the Tower Inn had become Girls' Night Out, a male strip club. It burned down on January 25, 1981.

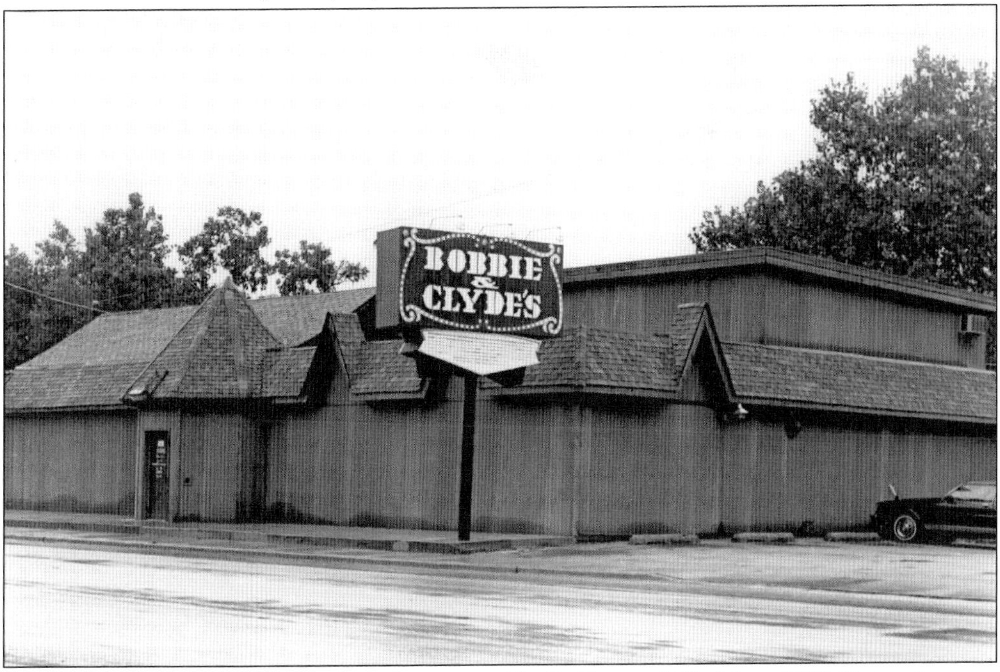

By the mid-1980s Lyons was home to 39 taverns like Bobbie and Clyde's, at 8210 Ogden Avenue, which were permitted to stay open until 4:00 a.m. Under increasing pressure from residents, in 1985, the village board enacted an ordinance forcing bars to close at 2:00 a.m. That same year, Judith B. Petrucci, an outspoken critic of the taverns and strip clubs, lost the mayoral election to Smith by 36 votes.

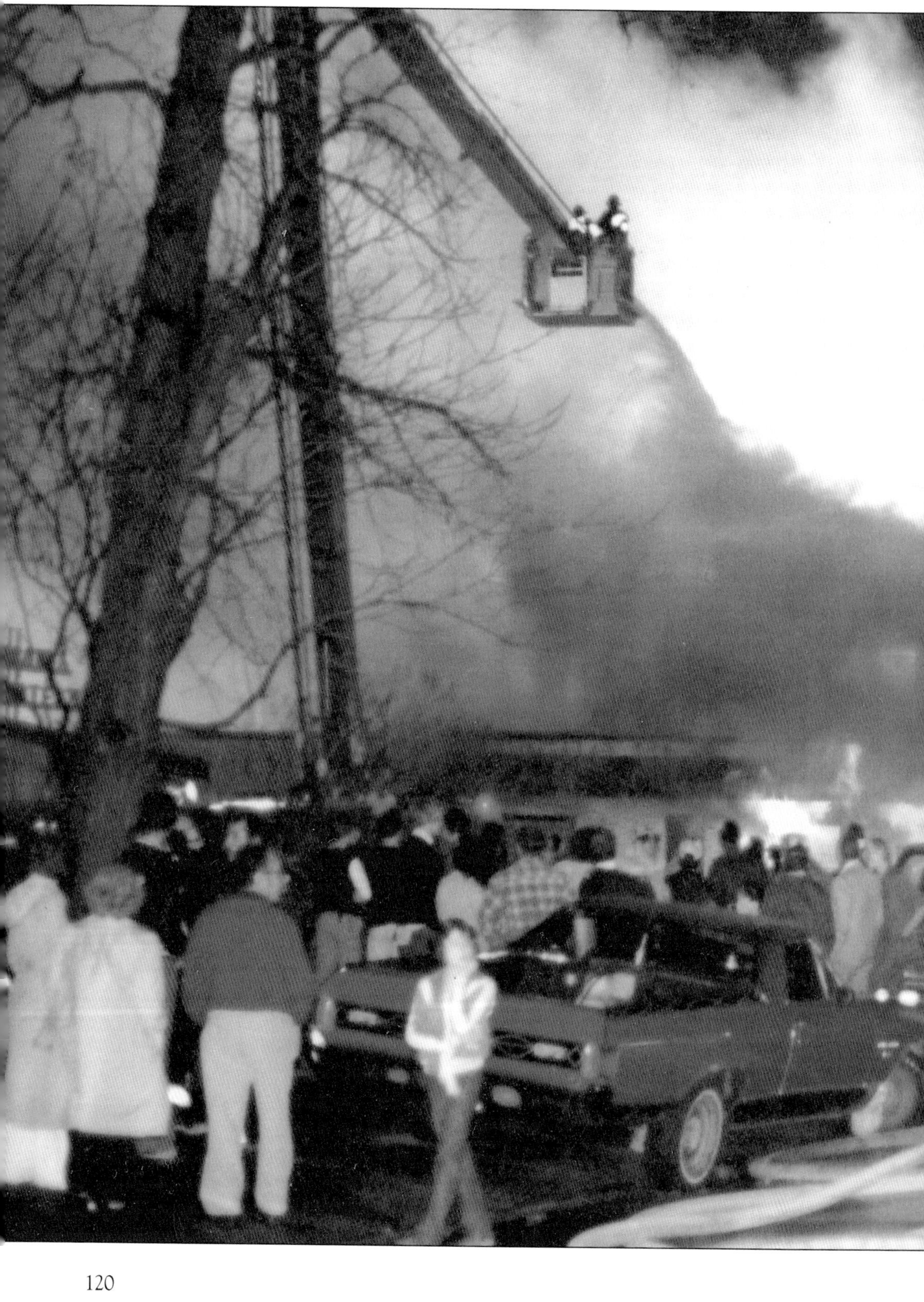

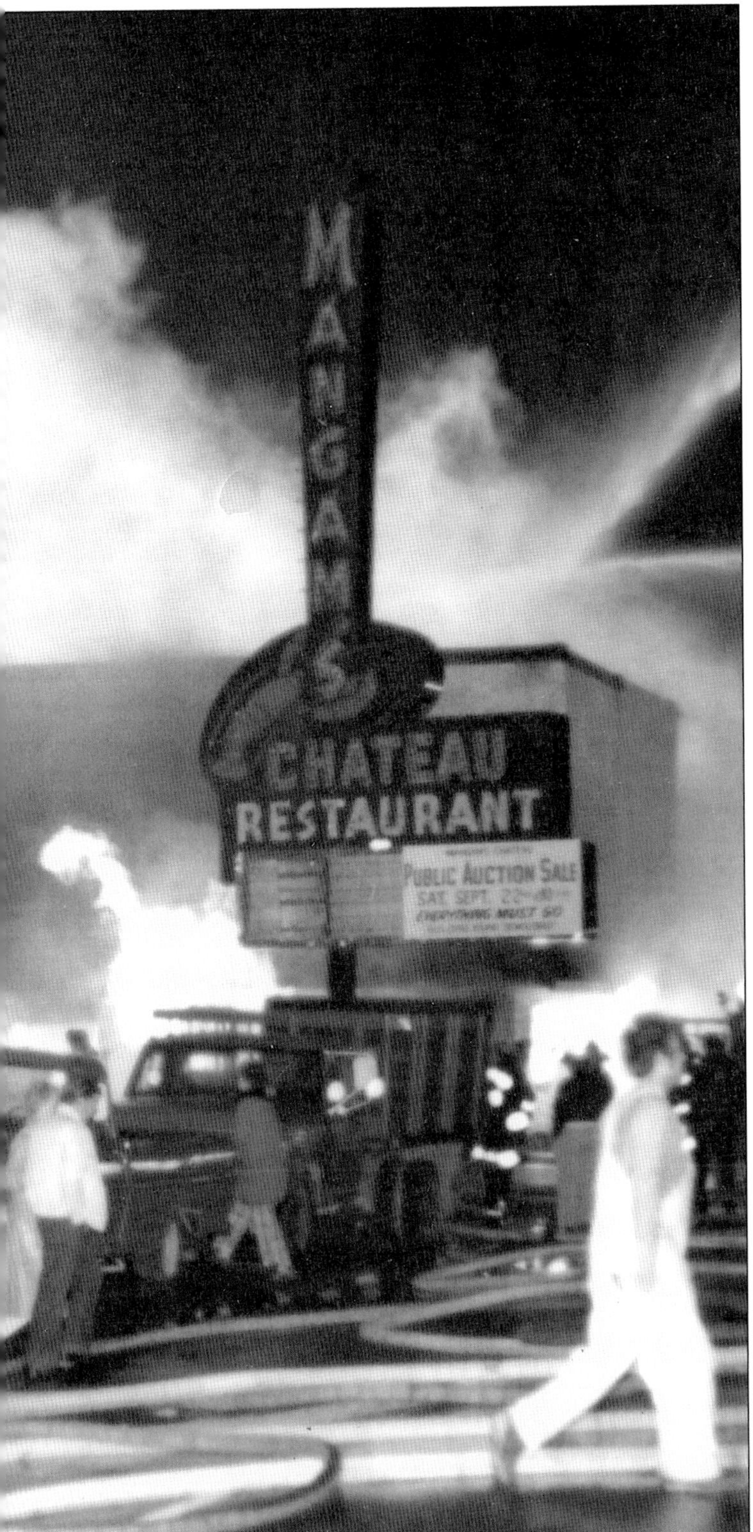

Mangam's Chateau had been closed for two years and was slated to be demolished when it burned down on Halloween 1979. Investigators studied the site of the blaze for evidence of arson, but the cause of the fire was never officially determined. In a memorial in the Lyons *Sun* newspaper, Lorraine Hardt wrote: "I remember those Mangam mirrors. How we used to pause and primp in front of those baroque beauties seemingly everywhere. We'd be trying on glittering costume jewelry, perhaps, from the tempting rings-'n-things selection in the little shop in the lobby across from the garden-terrace bar with its tinkling piano. By the welcoming (in season, of course) warm fireplace. Near the tank with the (ugh) live lobsters for your choosing, if you dared."

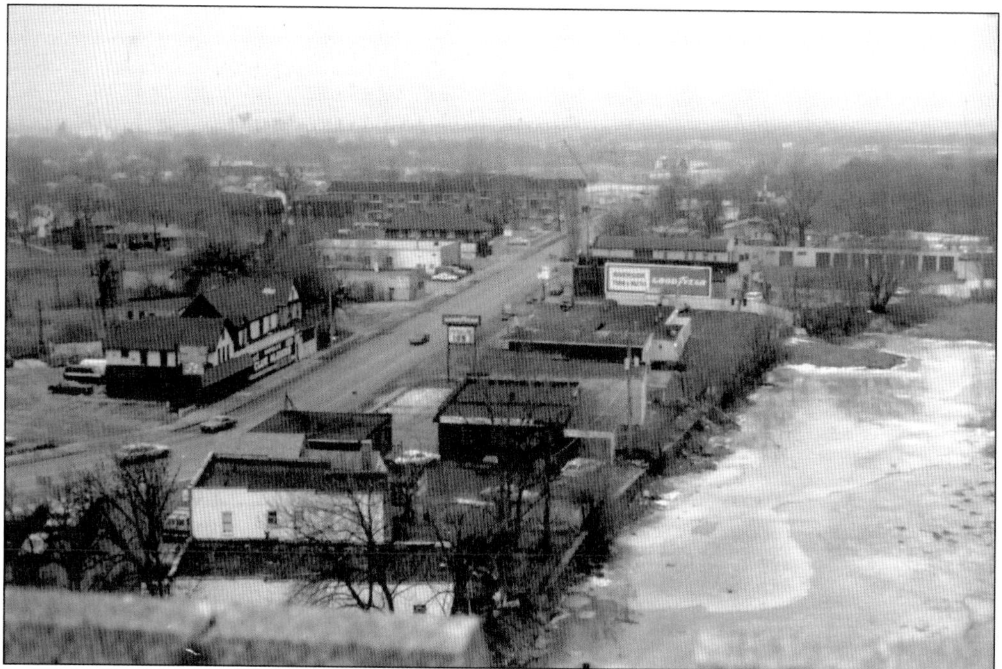

This aerial view from the Hofmann Tower taken in the 1970s offers views of the Des Plaines River as well as Merola's Club Algiers (left). The apartments at the rear of the photograph are located at the former site of the Schultz mansion, later Sophie's.

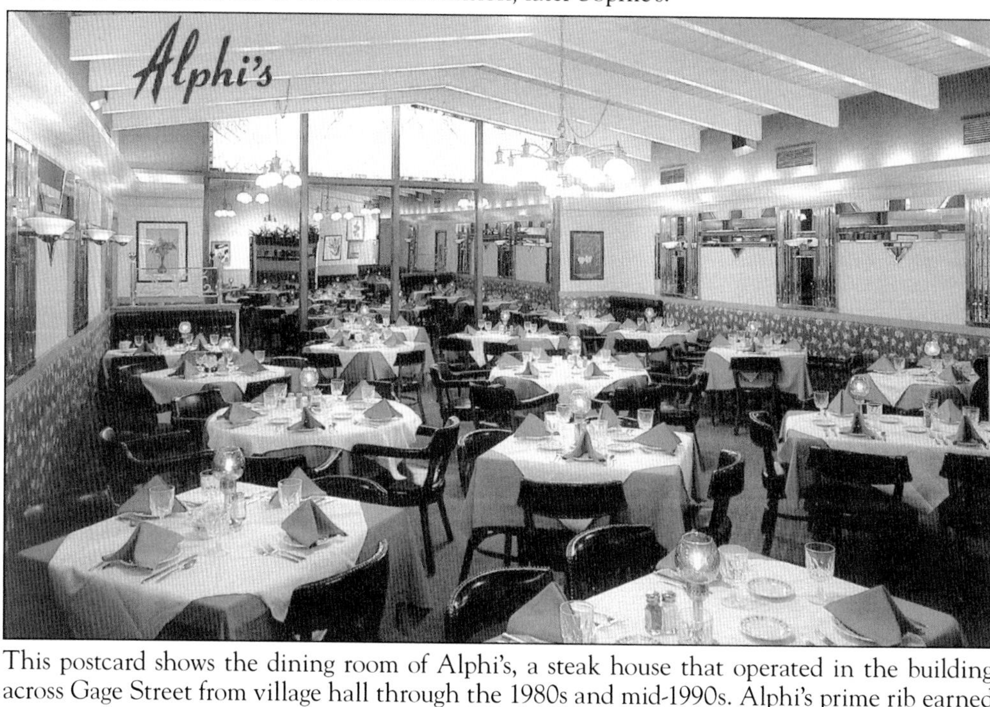

This postcard shows the dining room of Alphi's, a steak house that operated in the building across Gage Street from village hall through the 1980s and mid-1990s. Alphi's prime rib earned raves from *Sun-Times* readers numerous times. "The trencherman's cut is way over two pounds, with not one but two bones in the cut," one resident wrote. "Fast all day before trying to finish this one."

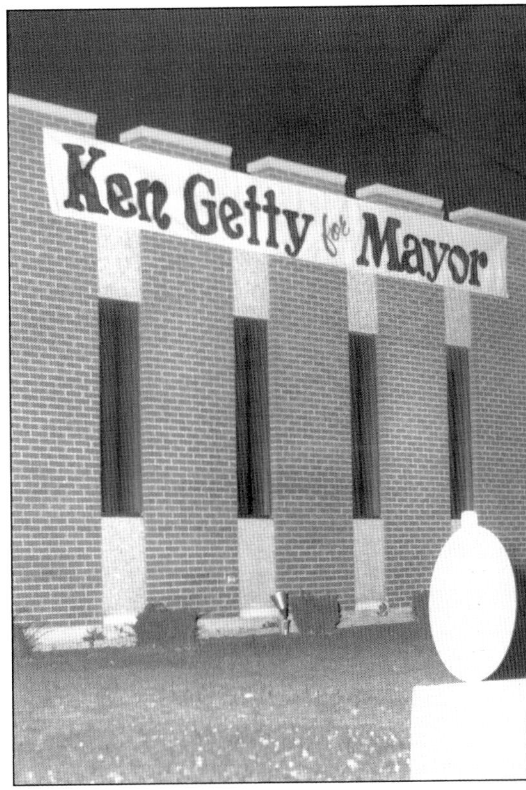

In 1985, Kenneth Getty ran for mayor on a platform criticizing both William Smith's control of the town and Judith B. Petrucci's lack of experience. His Village Party of Lyons pulled a prank after a meeting at the village hall, putting up this banner in front of the building from which Smith ran Lyons. Getty became mayor in 1996, but was indicted on 21 felony counts involving bid-rigging the following year. A jury found him guilty in 1998; he served five years in three federal prisons.

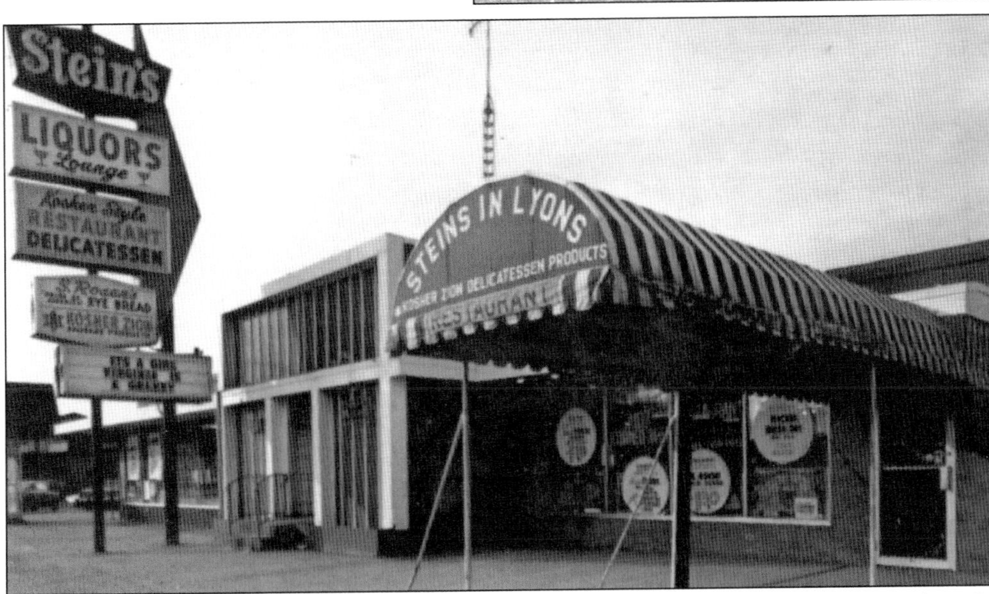

Stein's in Lyons, at 8560 West Ogden Avenue, was one of the most popular New York–style, kosher-style delis in the Chicago area for more than three decades, selling up to 2,000 pounds of corned beef a week. The 185-seat restaurant served, among other things, the Fresser's Delight: a pound of corned beef and salami on rye bread, with fries and slaw ($10.95). Leonard Stein opened the restaurant with his wife, Annette, and his brother-in-law in the early 1960s and continued operating it until his death in 1992. His son, Martin, ran Stein's until it closed the late 1990s.

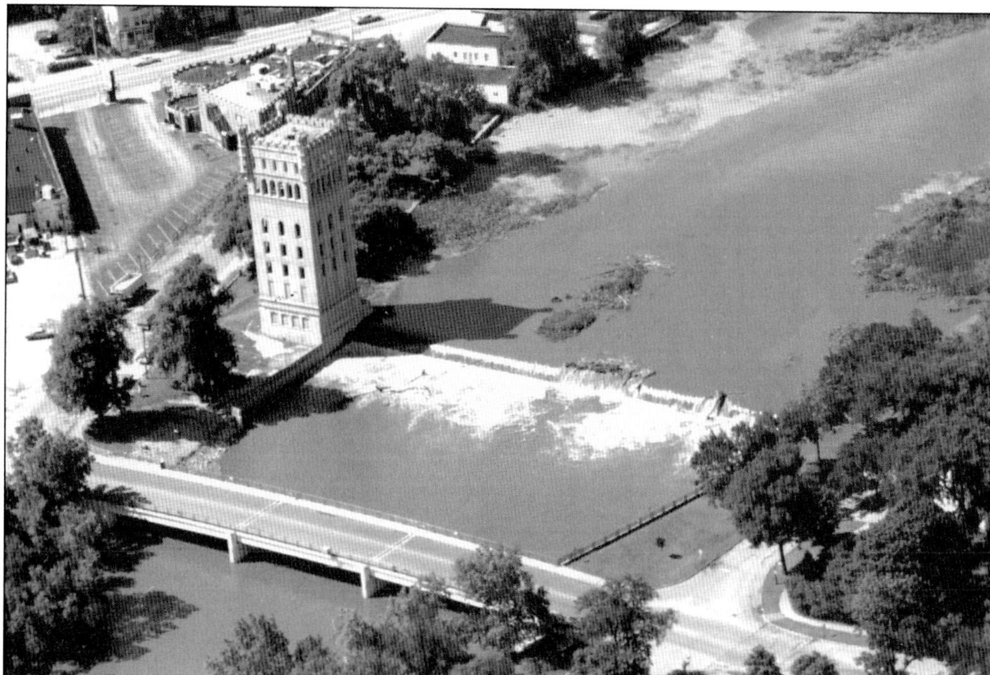

This aerial shot, taken in the 1980s, captures the building (just above the tower), that held the Pizza Palace and, upstairs, the Comedy Womb, a local spot for up-and-coming comedians. Emo Philips and Judy Tenuta, who grew up in the area, were two of the best-known comedians working there.

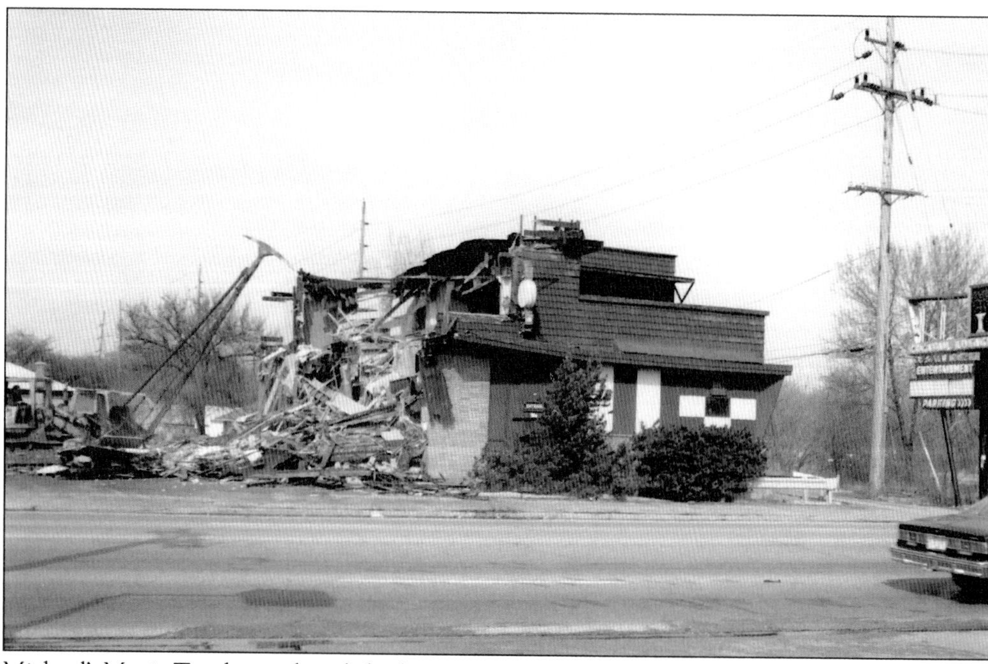

Michael's Magic Touch was demolished in 1989. Five men, including owner Michael Russo, were sentenced to prison terms the previous September for their involvement in a prostitution ring out of the club.

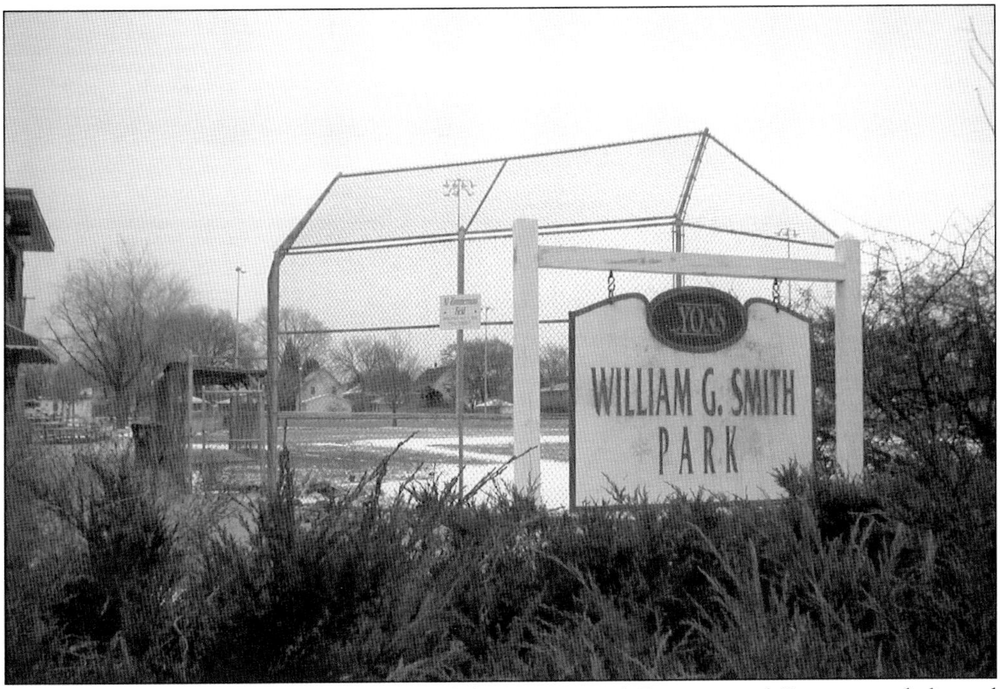

The baseball field on the corner of Lawndale Avenue and Forty-second Street was dedicated to Mayor Smith in April 1988, a year before his death. In the late 1970s, Smith negotiated a $1-per-year lease of the site from the Materials Service Corporation, which owned the site. In 1992, a local resident petitioned for a referendum to have the park take "some other name" due to the criticisms of Smith's administration, but the effort failed.

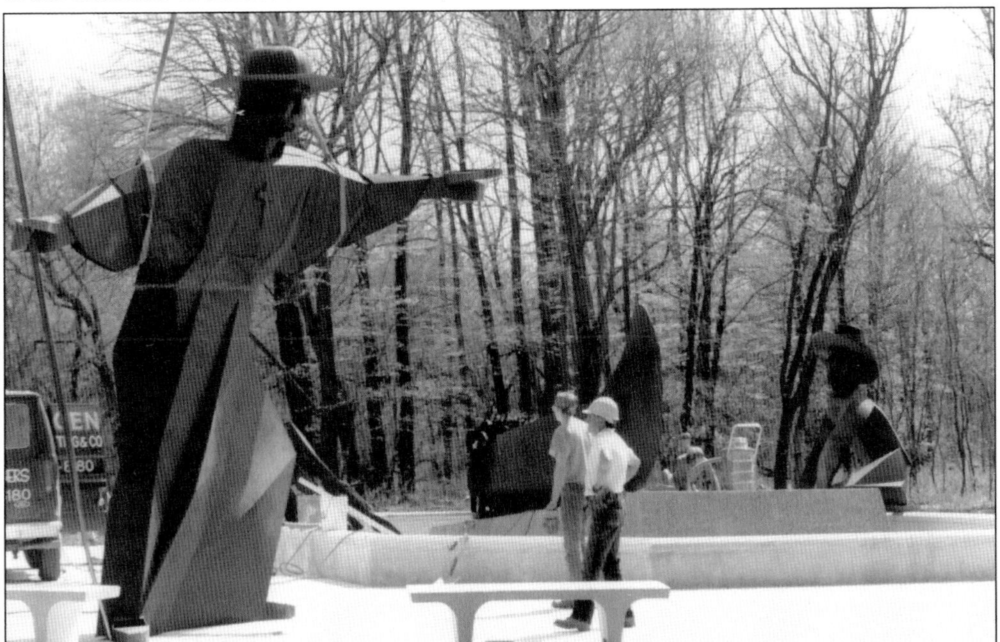

This image shows Ferdinand Rebeccini's statue, *The Waterway West*, at the Chicago Portage National Historic Site.

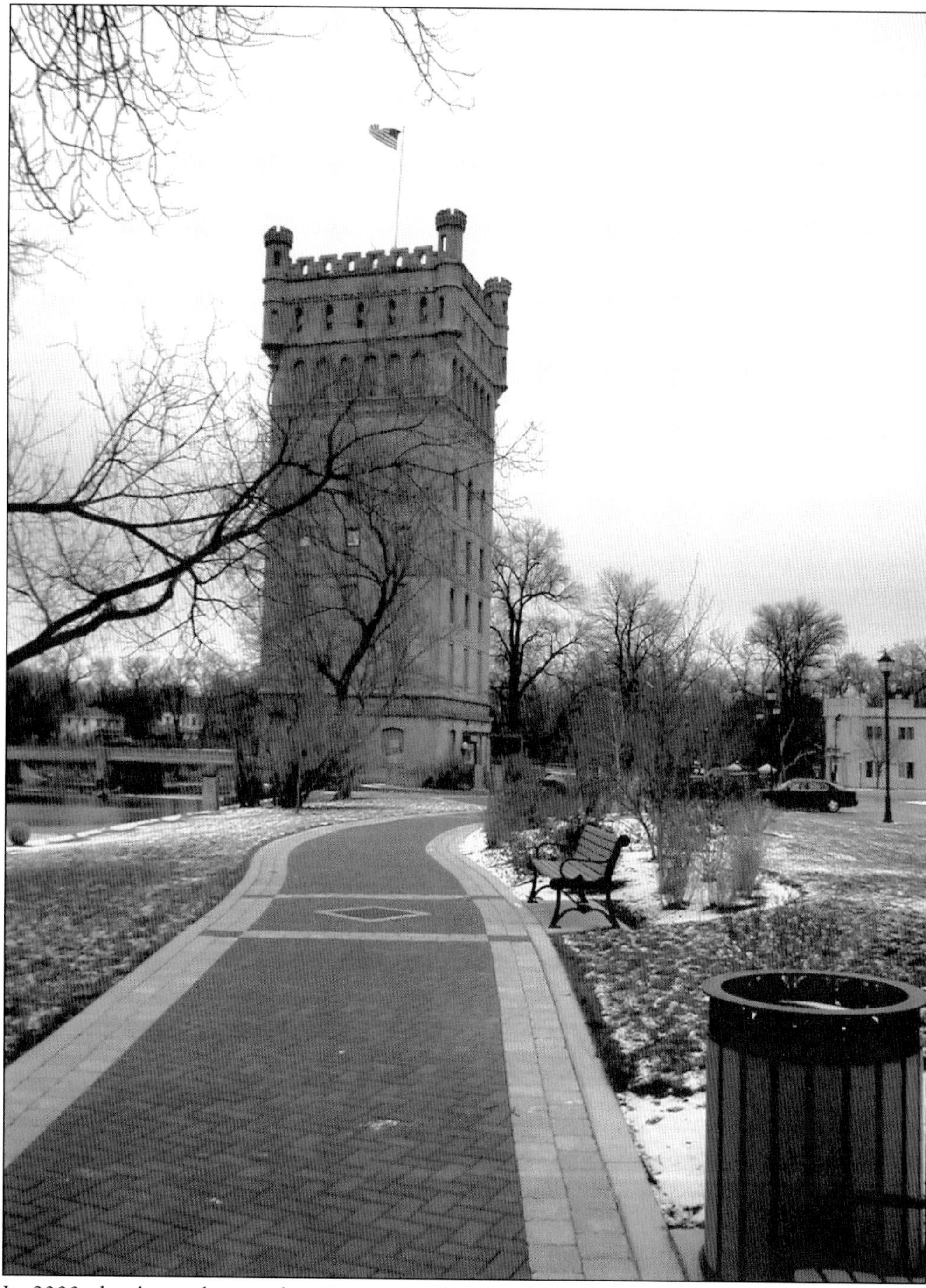

In 2000, developers began planning to use the site alongside the Des Plaines River near the tower for a condominium development. Construction of a river walk, which wends from the Barry Point Bridge to Ogden Avenue, was finished in 2005.

BIBLIOGRAPHY

Andreas, A. T. *History of Cook County, Illinois, From the Earliest Period to the Present.* Chicago, 1884.

Benedetti, Rose Marie. *A Village on the River 1888–1988: A History of Lyons, Illinois in Celebration of the Centennial of Its Incorporation.* Lyons, IL: Lyons Centennial Commission, 1988.

Benedetti, Rose Marie, and Virginia C. Bulat. *Portage, Pioneers, and Pubs: A History of Lyons, Illinois.* Lyons, IL: Angel Guardian Orphanage Press, 1963.

Bilek, Edward T., Jr. "Mueller's Brewery." Lyons, IL.

Danckers, Ulrich, and Jane Meredith. *Early Chicago: A Compedium of the Early History of Chicago to the Year 1835 When the Indians Left.* Chicago: Early Chicago, Inc., 2000.

Deuchler, Douglas. *Berwyn.* Charleston, SC: Arcadia Publishing, 2005.

Eichacker, John C. *Twin Towers.* Lyons, IL, 1976.

Grossman, James R., Ann Durkin Keating, and Janice L. Reiff, eds. *The Encyclopedia of Chicago.* Chicago: University of Chicago Press, 2004.

Mitchell, Harley Bradford. *Historical Fragments of Early Chicagoland.* Chicago, 1928.

Wm. E. Rose and Associates, Inc. "Design Study: The Chicago Portage and Laughton Trading Post Area, 'The Waterway West.'" Hinsdale, IL, 1975.

Vierling, Philip E. *A Self-Guided Loop Hiking Trail to the Chicago Portage National Historic Site.* Chicago, 1973.